CHANCELLOR'S CLUB
CHAPEL HILL
MAY '99

# A Paul Green Reader

A CHAPEL HILL BOOK

# A
# PAUL
# GREEN
# Reader

EDITED WITH AN INTRODUCTION BY

## Laurence G. Avery

The University of North Carolina Press

Chapel Hill and London

Excerpt from *The Lost Colony* © The Roanoke Island Historical Association
and The Paul Green Foundation. Reproduced by permission.

All other pieces by Paul Green are individually copyrighted by
The Paul Green Foundation and are reproduced here by permission.

The paper in this book meets the guidelines for permanence and durability
of the Committee on Production Guidelines for Book Longevity of the Council on
Library Resources.

Library of Congress Cataloging-in-Publication Data
Green, Paul, 1894–1981.
[Selections. 1998]
A Paul Green reader / edited with an introduction by Laurence G. Avery.
p.   cm. — (Chapel Hill book)
Includes bibliographical references (p.).
ISBN 0-8078-2386-4 (cloth: alk. paper). — ISBN 0-8078-4708-9 (pbk.: alk. paper)
1. Southern States — Literary collections. I. Avery, Laurence G. II. Title. III. Series.
PS3513.R452 A6
812'.52 — dc21      97-40365
CIP

02  01  00  99  98      5  4  3  2  1

Publication of this volume was aided by a generous grant from
The Paul Green Foundation.

# Contents

# Introduction

Paul Green once received a letter from a person compiling a book called *Favorite Cocktails of Famous Men*. Describing the book as "a collection of the drink preferences of distinguished men in Art, Music, Science, the Theatre and other prominent areas of endeavor," the compiler asked if Green would "be kind enough to contribute a recipe for a cocktail or other drink innovation which you favor." Normally such a fawning request would have received no more than a glance from Green, but this time, on impulse or perhaps inspiration, he replied. His letter, a little masterpiece of good-humored dismissal, reveals much about Green. "Yassuh," the reply began, "in my ignorance it looks like I will be left out of your book." He went on:

> Then maybe I deserve to be, for I am totally ignorant of the wherefores, the whethers and the whys of cocktails. I say this truthfully even though I was born and have been raised in the land of the mint juleps. The greatest drink innovation I can think of—and it's not really an innovation but my favorite—is a jug of cold water out of the spring below my house. Here the Indians drank and the deer and the furtive night possum long, long ago. I get a good animal kinship from drinking there likewise. And I reach a hand to civilization by using a jug.[1]

For all its whimsicality, this letter is a value-laden statement suggesting a sane vision of life. Green rejects the world of urban sophistication associated with cocktails and coffee-table books in favor of the natural world with its rhythms, customs, and inhabitants, and in so doing implies his characteristic preference for the natural and lasting over the artificial and passing. The letter, just right in self-characterization, tone, and cadence for its purpose of congenial dismissal, also shows a writer in control of his craft. To take but one example, notice how nicely the imagery functions, with mint julep (itself humorously appropriate as the distinctive but jaded southern cocktail) upstaged by the cold spring water and its cluster of Indians, deer, and possum.

Green's plays and stories reflect the same moral atmosphere and artistic

---

1. Laurence G. Avery, ed., *A Southern Life: Letters of Paul Green, 1916–1981* (Chapel Hill: University of North Carolina Press, 1994), p. 480.

control as his letter, prompting the spirit and exercising the mind in ways that are at once demanding and fulfilling. My purpose in this book is to bring together some of Green's finest work for the pleasure of new generations of readers.

Green's writing career went into full swing when he returned to college following military service in France during World War I. Even without his writing his lifetime accomplishments are remarkable. Born on 17 March 1894 on his family's farm in Harnett County, North Carolina, he spent his first twenty-one years in that rural community along the Cape Fear River in the southeastern part of the state. In 1916 he enrolled at the state university in Chapel Hill and the next summer enlisted for a two-year stint in the army, the second year of which found him in France for the final months of the war and the first several months following the armistice. Returning to school in Chapel Hill in the fall of 1919, he graduated in 1921, remained for a year of graduate work in philosophy, married Elizabeth Lay, then with her went to Cornell University for a second year of study. In the summer of 1923 Paul and Elizabeth came back to Chapel Hill, where they lived the rest of their lives, and Paul joined the university faculty as a member of the philosophy department.

In 1928 Green received a Guggenheim fellowship to study theater in Europe. With his family (he and Elizabeth had two children by then; eventually they would have four) he spent sixteen months first in Berlin, then in London. In Chapel Hill during the 1920s he had begun to speak out for the rights of black people in America; during the 1930s he devoted more time to social causes such as prison reform, aid for textile workers in southern mills, and the abolition of capital punishment. In the 1930s he also began taking periodic leaves from the university to write film scripts in Hollywood, and during the war years of the early forties he gave much time to this occasionally fulfilling, always remunerative occupation. Back in North Carolina after the war, his energy hardly flagged. He was an influential supporter of school desegregation during the turmoil following the 1954 Supreme Court ruling in *Brown v. Board of Education*. In the 1960s he was an early and outspoken opponent of the Vietnam War. Through the seventies and into the eighties he argued vigorously for disarmament and against the arms race between the "nuclear superpowers," frequently taking on his fellow North Carolinian, Senator Jesse Helms. When he died on 4 May 1981, at the age of eighty-seven, it was clear that his life had made a difference in the building of the New South and had contributed in important ways to North Carolina's growing reputation as the most progressive of southern states.

But Green's real lifework was writing. While still a student in the early twenties, he began publishing stories in magazines and saw several of his short plays produced in Chapel Hill and across the country, some to great acclaim. A Pulitzer Prize for *In Abraham's Bosom* in 1927 brought him to the attention of a much larger public. During the 1930s the Group Theater produced two of his finest plays: in 1931 the Group inaugurated its ambitious Broadway career with *The House of Connelly*, a powerful look at the decay and regeneration of a southern family, and in 1936 the Group produced the antiwar musical drama *Johnny Johnson*, for which Kurt Weill composed his first score after fleeing Hitler's Germany. A moving theatrical work with a charming score, *Johnny Johnson* is frequently revived in Europe as well as America. In 1937 Green also wrote and oversaw the production of the first of his outdoor historical plays, *The Lost Colony*, staged on Roanoke Island off the coast of North Carolina. And in 1940–41 he dramatized Richard Wright's epoch-making novel, *Native Son*, for a production directed by Orson Welles. After the war he devoted much time to his outdoor historical plays, which were performed throughout the country. All told, seventeen of these had been produced by the time of his death. His other published full-length plays, written for indoor professional production, number eleven. In addition he published three volumes of short plays, two novels, five volumes of short stories, and five volumes of essays in his lifetime. The huge collection of folklore that he began in the 1920s and continued throughout his life was posthumously published in two volumes as *Paul Green's Wordbook: An Alphabet of Reminiscence*.

The central project in Green's writing life was the creation of Little Bethel Country. Like Thomas Hardy's Wessex a little earlier and William Faulkner's Yoknapatawpha later, Little Bethel Country is the imaginatively reconstructed territory of its creator's seminal experience. Green included a hand-drawn map of Little Bethel Country at the beginning of one of his short-story volumes, *Salvation on a String*. The map depicts the valley of the Cape Fear River with its major tributaries, a river system flowing southeastward from central North Carolina to the coast. Notations on the map identify places and events from colonial to modern times, most of the notations clustering in the rural area of Green's youth and young manhood, between Fayetteville in the southeast and Chapel Hill in the northwest. Little Bethel Country is based closely on the people, history, and geography of that region. All of Green's novels and short stories are set there, as are virtually all of his plays except for the outdoor historical dramas, which are set in the regions of their historical subjects but inhabit the same moral universe as the rest of his work. Even *Johnny Johnson*, much of which transpires in France during World War I, opens in a Little Bethel community and takes its leading characters from the people Green knew best.

The name Green chose for his imagined country is suggestive of his upbringing and, indirectly, of his outlook as well. "Bethel" in Hebrew means "house of God" and derives from the story of Jacob's ladder in *Genesis* 28, in which Jacob, fleeing his home, dreams that God gives him and his descendants the territory in which he now finds himself—or renews the promise first made to Jacob's grandfather, Abraham. In the dream Jacob sees a ladder between earth and heaven with angels moving down it and back up. God appears to Jacob and declares:

> "I am the Lord, the God of Abraham your father and the God of Isaac; the land on which you lie I will give to you and to your descendants." . . . Then Jacob awoke from his sleep and said, "Surely the Lord is in this place; and I did not know it." And he was afraid, and said, "How awesome is this place! This is none other than the house of God, and this is the gate of heaven." So Jacob rose early in the morning, and he took the stone which he had put under his head and set it up for a pillar and poured oil on the top of it. He called the name of that place Bethel (28: 13–19; RSV).

Clearly the shape of this story derives from its developing reverence toward a place, with Jacob's indifference toward the spot where he lay his head gradually changing to awed enlightenment. If we think of this new attitude, this conviction that Bethel was the site of a supremely important experience worthy of memorialization, then we are well along toward understanding Green's attitude toward his own home territory, which led him to adopt the Hebrew name for it. And like Jacob's stone, Green's plays and stories serve as a memorial—in Green's case, to the human experience, some of it tragic, some of it comical, in *his* promised land.

There is however a small irony in Green's use of a word meaning "house of God" for the name of his imagined territory. As the usage suggests, he grew up with daily exposure to the Bible and at times was himself preoccupied with Bible study. His plays and stories abound with biblical allusions, paraphrases of biblical language, and religious events ranging from country revivals to deep struggles of the soul. Although his upbringing made him thoroughly at home with the Bible, however, by the 1920s, when he began creating Little Bethel Country, he had developed the humanistic outlook that would stay with him throughout life. Anything godlike or holy resided in human beings themselves, he felt. People, who had the potential for great evil, also had the potential for good and were responsible for their behavior. Environmental and hereditary factors might set the parameters within which people could act, and coincidence contributed as well to the outcome of a life. But for all that, individuals had a will and were accountable for their actions. "Do we count in the scheme of things?" he once queried a correspondent. "I maintain we all do, whatever color, calling or kind we may be. Question—do we count for good? We should, we must."[2] For their part, he believed, religious people misused the idea of God more often than not, ascribing things to God's will as a way of avoiding human responsibility for human affairs gone awry and invoking God as a cover for their own greed, lust, or ambition. So for Green the phrase "house of God" had a meaning probably quite different from its meaning for an Old Testament patriarch. It was the human experience of Little Bethel Country, including Green's own, that made it holy ground.

Like *Salvation on a String* with its localized map, *Wide Fields*, another short-story volume, includes as an appendix a list of "Little Bethel People." Green's fictional world was forever developing in his mind, and *Wide Fields*, earliest of the short-story volumes (it was preceded by two volumes of short plays), is far from complete in its roster. Still, the list includes eighty-one names, most of them accompanied by a brief character sketch. As the stories, plays, and novels came along over the years, they depicted a wide diversity of human experience in the rural and small-town South during the early decades of the century. African Americans (then, of course, the usual term was "Negroes") are the focal characters in a number of works. The Lumbee Indians of the region and wandering bands of gypsies also appear. A few people, white and black, are well-off—bankers, large landowners, some preachers. Most, though, are not—people working small farms, hired field hands young and old, tenant farmers, mill workers, convicts, traveling salesmen, and, in the towns, shopkeepers, teachers, and day laborers, with assorted drifters and ne'er-do-wells mixed in. In the essay "Drama and the Weather" Green makes clear the rationale behind his concern for these people. In a passage obviously written by the person who preferred a jug of spring water to any cocktail, he describes "the people who . . . matter most to me." They are "those who live as it were with their feet in the earth and their heads bare to the storms, the lightning and the gale—those who labor with their hands, wrestling from cryptic nature her goods and stores of sustenance—these develop a wisdom of living which seems to me more real and beautiful than those who develop their values and ambitions from rubbing shoulders in a crowded city."[3]

The Negro plays and stories, which Green began writing in the 1920s, are among the early attempts in our literature to take seriously the experiences of black men and women and children. During the era when Ralph Ellison was developing the insights that led him to write *Invisible Man*, which takes invisi-

<hr />

2. Ibid., p. 556.

3. "Drama and the Weather," in *Drama and the Weather: Some Notes and Papers on Life and the Theatre* (New York: Samuel French, 1958), pp. 49–50.

bility as the central image for black experience in America, Green was able to put aside the stereotypes of character and the racial and class prejudices that, according to Ellison, blocked or clouded the vision of so many of their contemporaries. The black characters in Green's work are highly individualized and intensely imagined, but they also share with one another the experience of living as a minority in a dominant society that denies their humanity in overt and subtle ways. Indeed, a defining trait is the way each character responds to the dehumanizing pressures of life in a segregated society. In a preface to an early collection of one-act plays, *Lonesome Road: Six Plays for the Negro Theatre*, Green recalls the history of a large portion of black people in the South. It is a story of continuous exploitation and defiance of exploitation from the days of slavery on into the era of segregation. Black workers always bore "the brunt of the brutal dirty work," Green notes, and usually died ill-rewarded for their labor, unrecognized for their contributions. "Through a few winter rains perhaps a falling head-board strove futilely to tell that [the Negro field hand] had been, and then the plow passed over him and a hill of corn or cotton flourished from his breast. Such is his story before imagined justice." A brief, elegant rationale for the book concludes the preface: "In the following pages a first effort is made to say something of what these people . . . have suffered and thought and done. For it seems apparent now that such things are worthy of record."[4]

Several plays and stories in this anthology feature black characters, but the ones with black focal characters are the play *In Abraham's Bosom* and the short story "Fine Wagon." *In Abraham's Bosom* attracted a great deal of attention when it was produced on Broadway in 1926–27 and won the Pulitzer Prize for drama that season, and it has continued as a viable stage piece through the years. In the spring of 1994 its powerful opening scene was woven into a documentary about Green and staged in Chapel Hill as part of the centennial celebration of his birth. Set around the turn of the century, the play focuses on a man with a Moses-like vision of leading his people out of the bondage of poverty and ignorance through education. Concerning the races, Abraham McCranie declares, "God Almighty knows they ain't no difference at the bottom. Color hadn't ought to count. It's the man, it's the man that lasts." So black people as well as white are entitled to a life of opportunity, and education is the key. "We want our children and our grandchildren to march on toward full lives and noble characters," he proclaims, rehearsing a speech he

4. "Author's Note," in *Lonesome Road: Six Plays for the Negro Theatre* (New York: Robert McBride, 1926), pp. xix–xx.

never has an opportunity to deliver, "and that has got to come, I say, by education. We have no other way" (scene 5).

No one would expect a person with Abe's views to have an easy time of it in the rural South of the early twentieth century. The play has powerful examples, drawn from life, of the workings of racism in the minds of both blacks and whites as well as in the relationships between them. But the play is a moving tragedy, not a sociological tract, and there are a number of reasons for its outcome in addition to racism, some having to do with Abe's own mental and psychological makeup, some stemming from his relations with other black people in the community. But if Abe fails to put his dream into effect, it is still a noble dream that has attracted more and more adherents as the century has progressed.

Although a tragedy, *In Abraham's Bosom* is a hopeful work, in the sense that Václav Havel has depicted hope, as "a state of mind, not a state of the world":

> Either we have hope within us or we don't; it is a dimension of the soul, and it's not essentially dependent on some particular observation of the world or estimate of the situation. . . . Hope, in this deep and powerful sense, is not the same as joy that things are going well . . . but, rather, an ability to work for something because it is good. . . . The more unpropitious the situation in which we demonstrate hope, the deeper that hope is. Hope . . . is not the conviction that something will turn out well, but the certainty that something makes sense, regardless of how it turns out.[5]

This statement, won at the cost of imprisonment by the playwright who became the first president of the Czech Republic, is fortifying for any time and all good efforts. For Abe McCranie, mired in a racist environment, the situation could hardly have been "more unpropitious," yet his dream is "good" and "makes sense," and his life continues to "demonstrate hope" to the end.

The short story "Fine Wagon" is set in a college town like Chapel Hill and focuses on a boy who goes with his father to haul wood at a professor's house. The story traces the boy's coming-of-age, or loss of childhood innocence, in the classic manner by taking him through an experience that deepens his understanding of life and the world around him. The power of the story derives from the fact that his life is the life of a black child and the world

5. Václav Havel, *Disturbing the Peace*, trans. Paul Wilson (New York: Alfred A. Knopf, 1990), p. 181.

around him is the world of the segregated South. Once read, the story haunts the mind.

Green had a sense of humor as well as a social conscience, and his affinity for fun displays itself in some of the works about black experience, such as "The No 'Count Boy" and "The Man Who Died at Twelve O'Clock." Unfortunately, limited space prevents their inclusion here. Green's humorous temperament comes through in a number of other stories in the *Paul Green Reader*, however. Three of the included stories have a comic form—that is, a pattern of events in which the problems of the sympathetic characters are closer to solution at the end than they were at the beginning. These include "Salvation on a String," "Saturday Night," and "The Cornshucking." While the comic form does not necessarily imply humor (you could read all the way through some great comedies, such as Dante's *Divine Comedy*, and never crack a smile—except in the enjoyment of excellence), common usage nevertheless suggests a natural connection between the two, and humor is certainly present in a variety of shapes and flavors in Green's comic stories and plays.

When Green was a child, storytelling was part of the routine on the farm, as the family passed an evening on the porch after a day in the fields or socialized with neighbors on Saturday night. Echoes of oral storytellers' cadences and devices are present throughout Green's work. Several of the stories, "Salvation on a String" among them, open with an equivalent of the storyteller's "once upon a time," a formulaic beginning sometimes extended over a paragraph or two and intended to orient readers to the story before them. The voice of a narrator is also present in the stories, an equivalent of the voice and gestures of a physically present storyteller, and while the voice is not intrusive, it performs its job of managing the story efficiently. "Salvation on a String" supplies an example when, near the climax, the narrator seems to suspend the story momentarily by calling attention to a character named Ike but in reality is merely setting up the climax.

"Salvation on a String" is a tall tale, a kind of story originating in the oral tradition of the southern and western frontiers and featuring the blatant humor of exaggerated, even fantastic incidents mixed in with realistic detail and delivered with deadpan solemnity. "Salvation on a String" focuses on a Little Bethel strongman and brawler, a Paul Bunyan-like fellow in physical prowess, who devours half a bushel of cornbread and eleven hog jowls for a snack and comes striding home one day with a cow under one arm and her calf under the other. The story is about the community's effort to convert this strongman from his loud and rough ways and save his soul, and it reaches a climax with the kind of striking visual image—where the "string" of the title comes in— characteristic of tall tales.

But not all of the stories are boisterous and extravagant. "Saturday Night" is quiet in tone and deals gently with its subject. The piece evokes those week-end neighborhood gatherings in a Little Bethel farming community where someone makes ice cream and people swap stories and play music and per-haps do a little courting. By definition it is a pleasant time, but the pleasure acquires a poignant richness from its restorative nature, and the story clearly lays down as a subsurface the hard work, hard questions, and hard knocks that weigh down the characters most of the time. For readers the humor of the piece derives from the pleasure of recognition as the characters and their situation develop before our eyes. The sense emerging from the story is a heartening optimism about decencies and impulses in daily life.

"The Cornshucking," one of the few pieces among Green's works with a noticeable autobiographical element, focuses on a farm boy in the grip of first love and his growing resolve to become a writer. The beauty of the story lies in the way it catches the nuances of the boy's feelings and modulates the reader's response through a tone of gentle humorous irony. A nice example describes the boy's first throes of creativity. On a Sunday afternoon he sits "in the woods on a log with a stub of pencil and a sheet of paper, pouring out his soul in poetry." Then we are treated to a verse of his poem:

If the high mountains and the deep sea
Loosed their power and wrath on me,
'Twould not be like the pain I feel.
Bring me your balm, love, my heart heal.

In his enthusiasm the boy cannot help feeling "there were fifteen verses as good as that," a remark inspiring in readers a deliciously divided reaction. The phrase "as good as that" allows us to enjoy the boy's pride of authorship, while also letting us think what we will about the strained and stilted writing he has so far accomplished. Or perhaps the response is not so much a divided one as it is a fusion of feelings into a sympathetic but not sentimental appreciation of adolescence. In any case the subtle, empathic irony of this piece complements the gentle humor of some stories and the blatant tall-tale humor of others to suggest the wide range of humor present in Green's work.

I referred above to the trials of the work-week and, indeed, of mortality lurking like a subsurface in the referential framework of "Saturday Night." Most plays and stories elevate this subsurface and use it as the main stage of action, but a few works, because they are unusually resonant with life, do this in ways that are especially memorable. Perhaps I should not include "Bernie and the Britches" in this portentous-sounding group. Essentially it is only an anecdote, and a wryly humorous one, elaborated to its bittersweet conclusion.

But on the one hand, in our lives it is hard to escape the experience of ironies — disappointments that turn out to be fine if totally unforeseen opportunities, relationships that reverse themselves in ways that are bewildering when they occur but in retrospect are perfectly plausible — and on the other hand, it is equally hard to think of another short work that catches the ironic dimension of existence with quite the satisfying piquancy of "Bernie and the Britches."

"The Ghost in the Tree" and *Hymn to the Rising Sun* differ radically in their modes of attack; the first, a short story, works quietly by implication, while the second, a short play, hits like a sledgehammer. Despite their differences of method, however, the two clearly belong in a group of works powerful in their own right and broad in their implications for the world we live in and endure. "The Ghost in the Tree" makes literal use of the storytelling framework, as a group of men on a stalled 'possum hunt sit around a fire in the woods and swap yarns one night, the chief yarn being the story of the ghost in a nearby tree. But with a crescendo effect the overall story shifts focus twice, expanding the tragedy of a family into the tragedy of a race and then into a tragedy of the whole South. Although its organization is unusual, each new level of awareness subsumes the previous level, and at the end, after the surprises, the story has the feel of inevitability characteristic of deeply imagined art.

With the exception of some of the outdoor historical plays and perhaps *Johnny Johnson*, *Hymn to the Rising Sun* is the most frequently performed of Green's plays. Written during the summer of 1935 and reflecting Green's outrage over the abuse of prisoners in the state's chain gangs, the piece has had a sustained stage life, clearly demonstrating that the outrage of the human being and citizen was under the control of the artist completely. In fact, *Hymn to the Rising Sun* has always transcended the historical case that prompted it. The play makes scant reference to the inciting abuses (see headnote to the play) and, for all its attention to the suffering of convicts, focuses on the captain of the chain gang. Captain Huff, the most vivid creation of the play, is a monster, chilling in his believability. He embodies both the rationale of enlightened social justice (that the penal system should strive to rehabilitate criminals for responsible citizenship) and the sadistic brutality actually present in the prison system of the state. His words and actions together expose a great failure of American democracy, the failure represented by the gulf between society's civilizing ideals and the brutalizing reality of life in the lower depths, where, in the words of Oscar Wilde, "some grow mad, and all grow bad" ("The Ballad of Reading Gaol"). As soon as the play was published, Green sent copies to all members of the state legislature, superior court judges, and editors of major newspapers in North Carolina, and from the Depression era to the present, the play has been performed steadily in all parts of the country.

While it has stimulated no reforms directly as far as I know, we can feel sure *Hymn to the Rising Sun* has played its part in the slow process of humanizing society by its influence over the years on the sensibilities of readers and viewers. It was his admiration for *Hymn to the Rising Sun* that led novelist Richard Wright to collaborate with Green on the dramatization of Wright's *Native Son*.

Of the plays and stories in the *Paul Green Reader*, only *The Lost Colony* remains to be mentioned. The first of Green's outdoor historical plays, it has gained historical significance of its own as the work largely responsible for reshaping a genre. In Europe historical pageantry has a lively tradition going back at least to the Middle Ages, and in America the late nineteenth and early twentieth centuries saw a number of large and spectacular staged events that ministered to civic pride in one way or another. Pageants were not plays, however, but chronicles, with events following one another as historical chronology, not dramatic necessity, dictated. They had no characters in a dramatic sense but only representations of prominent figures who, if they said anything at all, were likely to step forward one at a time and give speeches like this: "I am George Washington. I led the Continental Army in our glorious War of Independence from the British crown, then accepted the verdict of my fellow countrymen and became the first President of these United States of America." Beyond the important social aim of helping to formulate and keep alive a sense of the past, little about pageants has remained of interest to students of culture or theater. Although it makes direct use of historical material, *The Lost Colony*, by contrast, is unmistakably a play. It is a well-formed dramatic work with points of interest appropriate to a drama, and its success has encouraged a movement over the last half-century in which hundreds of historical plays have sprung up under the stars all over the country, with new ones appearing every year.

*The Lost Colony* was written in 1937 for production on Roanoke Island, off the coast of North Carolina, and it has played there every summer since, except for three years during World War II. The play commemorates the first attempt, in the 1580s, to plant an English colony in what was then called the New World, a colony now thought of as lost because after a few months on Roanoke Island its people vanished completely from recorded history. With regard to historical building material, therefore, Green was not quite empty-handed, but almost, and he used the situation as an opportunity to write a play with well-developed characters who carry forward a plot made coherent and significant by its theme. Thematically *The Lost Colony* complements *Hymn to the Rising Sun* and *In Abraham's Bosom*. While those two plays call attention to failures of American society to live up to its best principles, *The Lost Colony* dramatizes the establishment of one of those principles. In colonial and early republican days, when the memory of stratified European societies was still fresh, the principle was called "equality of condition." Alexis de Tocqueville's *Democracy in America* provides an example. Dealing first and last with all the complications and contradictions in American society, even slavery, *Democracy in America*'s opening pages announce Tocqueville's basic observation about the new nation as a whole. When he began his study with a visit to the United States in 1831, "nothing struck [him] more forcibly," Tocqueville says, "than the general equality of condition among the people. . . . The more I advanced in the study of American society, the more I perceived that this equality of condition is the fundamental fact from which all others seem to be derived and the central point at which all my observations constantly terminated."[6] Today we refer to this principle in various ways that reflect our own preoccupations: as equality of opportunity, for instance, or as equality before the law, or simply as equality.

Founded on belief in the intrinsic importance of individuals, equality is fundamental to a democratic way of life. With *The Lost Colony* Green hoped to rekindle a feeling for equality, a feeling for its social importance, in contemporary audiences. The play works to that end by showing how frontier conditions in America broke down European class distinctions between serf, peasant, yeoman, and nobleman (and social distinctions between men and women, too, for that matter) and placed all citizens on a level playing field in the game of life. Like any fine play, however, *The Lost Colony* is more than a thematic statement. It is in fact a complex theater piece that incorporates music, dance, song, special lighting effects, narration, and an acting style commensurate with the script, both of which are based on large gestures. All of these presentational elements are appropriate and useful in a play intended for performance before a large audience outdoors, but they may pose a challenge for the imagination of readers. Another challenge is to remember, and adjust for the fact, that reading is a private experience, whereas plays are written for the collective experience of the theater.

Over the years countless readers and viewers have responded enthusiastically to Green's stories and plays. After rereading a number of the early stories, Clifford Odets called them "not only beautiful, but as fresh and touching and authentic as they were when written." Odets, a friend and coworker from the days of the Group Theatre in the 1930s, was not just being nice. At the time of his remark Odets was producing a season of television plays for NBC and had turned to Green's work for an adaptation, so a lot of money, as well as his pro-

6. Alexis de Tocqueville, *Democracy in America*, trans. Phillips Bradley, 2 vols. (New York: Vintage Books, 1945), 1:3.

fessional reputation, rested on his judgment that the work was beautiful and fresh, touching and authentic.[7]

Seamus Heaney, in speaking of "memorable readings," described the kind of experience Odets and others have had in the presence of Green's work. Talking about the poems he chose to discuss in a series of lectures, Heaney said there was little common ground among the works except that all of them, because of their initial impact on him, had stayed in his mind over the years with great pleasure. He describes the impact as that "exhilarating moment which lies at the heart of any memorable reading, the undisappointed joy of finding that everything holds up and answers the desire that it awakens." Heaney's experience can occur in response to any kind of art. The "undisappointed joy" comes, as he goes on to suggest, when the work converges with the sense of life derived from our own experience (when "everything holds up") and the artist has found the appropriate form for the work and realized it successfully (when everything "answers the desire that it awakens").[8]

I will take a cue from Heaney. In making selections for this volume I have attempted to convey the range of Green's talent and provide a fair representation of his work. But in fact the Green corpus offers a plenitude of material, and no play or story is included here that has not provided me with the kind of memorable experience that comes from an encounter with a wise and well-formed work of the imagination.

To help place the stories and plays in the context of Green's life, and also to call attention to a life that was in its own right remarkable for its range of good and useful achievements, I have added several of Green's letters and essays and an excerpt from the *Wordbook*. The first of the letters, to Ward Morehouse, recounts an experience that served as background for *In Abraham's Bosom*. The remaining letters show Green's involvement in capital punishment cases and reveal the crucial role, the "life-instead-of-death" role, he was sometimes able to play. These letters will bring to mind "The Ghost in the Tree" and "Fine Wagon" as well as *Hymn to the Rising Sun*. The first two essays, "Drama and the Weather" and "The University in a Nuclear Age," grew out of the core activities of Green's life: writing and teaching. The former outlines the rationale for his own fiction and drama and makes clear his allegiances in the Western tradition of speculation about the arts. The latter gives his views on the centrality of the arts and humanities in a liberal education and is as timely now as

7. Avery, *A Southern Life*, p. 622 (n. 8). Odets's sudden death forestalled the television series.

8. Seamus Heaney, *The Redress of Poetry* (New York: Farrar, Straus and Giroux, 1995), pp. 8–9.

it was when written. The essay-letter to Holly Hanford provides an energetic account of the history of North Carolina and reveals as much about Green's own temperament as it does about the development of his home state. *Paul Green's Wordbook* is probably unique; at least I know of nothing else like it. Commonly referred to as folklore, it contains much folk material (sayings, remedies, practices, etc.) but also many other things (hymns, stories, and quotations from the Bible and world literature, to name a few). Essentially it is a compendium, alphabetically arranged, of everything that came to Green's mind over a sixty-year period associated with his home territory. The *Wordbook* is thus the largest and most inclusive depiction of Little Bethel Country that Green devised, and to represent it I include a short selection of entries under the letter *R*.

Throughout the anthology I have included headnotes when I thought background information might be helpful, and near the end of the book I have provided textual notes on the pieces, identifying the source of each text and adding other information as the textual situation warranted. The *Paul Green Reader* concludes with a list of Green's book publications.

# I
# Plays

# In Abraham's Bosom
## *The Tragedy of a Southern Negro*

CHARACTERS

BUD GASKINS, LIJE HUNNEYCUTT, and PUNY AVERY
*turpentine hands and fieldworkers for Colonel McCranie*

ABRAHAM McCRANIE *ambitious Negro field hand and worker*

COLONEL McCRANIE *southern gentleman, once the owner of slaves*

LONNIE McCRANIE *his son*

GOLDIE McALLISTER *Abraham's sweetheart, later his wife*

MUH MACK *Abraham's aunt*

EDDIE WILLIAMS, NEILLY McNEILL, and LANIE HORTON
*students in Abe's school*

DOUGLASS McCRANIE *son of Abraham and Goldie*

VOICES

TIME: *the latter part of the nineteenth century and first part of the twentieth*
PLACE: *somewhere in the southern part of the United States*


SCENE 1

[*A turpentine woods somewhere in the southeastern part of the United States on a summer's day many years ago — near a spring at the foot of a hill. The immediate foreground is open and clear save for a spongy growth of grass and sickly ground creepers. In the rear a wide-spreading tangle of reeds, briers, and alder bushes shuts around the spring in a semicircle. At the right front the great body of a pine, gashed and barked by the turpentine farmer's ax, lifts straight from the earth. To the left a log lies rotting in the embrace of wild ivy. Maples, bays, dogwoods, and other small trees overrun by tenacious vines raise their leafy tops to shade the spot. Through interstices in the undergrowth one can see the pine for-*

17

*est stretching away until the eye is lost in a colonnade of trees. The newly scraped blazes on the pines show through the brush like the downward-spreading beards of old men, suggestive of the ancient gnomes of the woods, mysterious and forever watchful.*

*At the left front, four tin dinner pails hang on a limby bush. The sound of axes against the trees, accompanied by the rhythmically guttural "Han-n-h! Han-n-n-h!" of the cutters, comes from the distance. One of the laborers is heard breaking into a high mournful song.*]

> Oh, my feets were wet — with the sunrise dew,
> The morning star — were a witness too.
> 'Way, 'way up in the Rock of Ages,
> Up in God's bosom gwine be my pillow.

[*Presently there is a loud halloo near at hand, and another voice yodels and cries, "Dinnertime — m — m — e! Get your peas, everybody!" Voices are heard nearer, a loud burst of laughter, and then three full-blooded Negroes shuffle in carrying long thin-bladed axes, which they lean against the pine at the right. They are dressed in nondescript working clothes, ragged and covered with the glaze of raw turpentine. As they move up to the spring they take off their battered hats, fan themselves, and wipe the streaming sweat from their brows. Two of them are well built and burly — Lije, stout and past middle age with some pretension to a thin scraggly mustache, Bud, tall and muscled — and Puny, wiry, nervous, and bandy-legged. They punctuate their conversation with great breathings of cool air.*]

BUD: Tell 'bout the fiery furnace — [*jerking his thumb backward*] musta meant these old turpentime woods.

LIJE: Yeh, yeh, and us the Hebrew chillun frying in the flame — while the sweat do roll.

PUNY: That old Saddy night corn liquor frying in you. Hee-hee.

BUD: [*roughly*] Talk, talk, little man!

[*They stand fanning themselves. Puny gets down on his belly at the spring.*]

PUNY: Mouth about to crack — can drink this spring dry.

LIJE: [*slouching his heavy body toward the pool*] Hunh, me too. That ax take water same like a sawmill.

[*He gets down flat and drinks with the other. The water can be heard gluking over the cataracts of their Adam's apples. The younger Negro opens his torn and sleeveless undershirt and stands raking the sweat with curved hand from his powerful chest.*]

BUD: [*after a moment*] Heigh, Puny, you'n Lije pull your guts out'n that mudhole and let the engineer take a drink.

[*With a sudden thought of devilment he steps quickly forward and cracks their heads together. Puny starts and falls face foremost in the spring. Lije, slow and stolid, saves himself, crawls slowly up on his haunches, and sits smiling good-naturedly, smacking his lips and sucking the water from the slender tails of his mustache.*]

LIJE: [*cleaning his muddy hands with a bunch of leaves*] Nunh-unh, not this time, my boy.

PUNY: [*scrambling to his feet, strangling and sputtering*] Dang your soul, why you push me, Bud Gaskins?

BUD: [*a threatening note slipping into his laugh*] Here, here, don't you cuss at me, bo'.

PUNY: Whyn't you impose on somebody your size? Better try Lije there.

[*Bud gets down and begins drinking.*]

LIJE: [*drawling*] Don't care if he do. Ducking cool you off.

PUNY: [*helplessly*] Always picking at me. Wisht, wisht —

BUD: Here I is lying down. Come on do what you wisht. [*Puny makes no reply but turns off, wiping his face on his shirt sleeve and staring morosely at the ground. Bud gets to his feet.*] Yah, reckon you sail on me and I jam your head in that spring like a fence post and drownd you.

PUNY: [*his anger smoldering*] Talk is cheap, hosscake, cheap! [*Suddenly afraid of his boldness in replying, he turns and looks at Bud in a weak pleading defiance.*]

BUD: [*making a frightening movement toward him*] Mess with me a-jowing and I knock your teeth through your skull.

LIJE: Here, Bud, you let Puny alone. [*He moves over to his bucket, gets it, and sits down on the log at the left.*]

BUD: [*turning for his bucket with a movement of disgust*] Sure I ain't gwine hurt him — poor pitiful bowlegs.

[*Puny clenches his hands as if stung to the quick, and then beaten and forlorn reaches for his bucket, the weak member of the herd. He throws off his overall jacket, revealing himself stripped to the waist, and sits down at the body of the pine tree.*]

LIJE: [*laying out his food and singing*]
'Way, 'way up in the Rock of Ages,
In God's bosom gwine be my pillow.

[*He loosens his belt, pulls out his shirt tails, undoes his shirt, and pats his belly.*] Lord, Bud, you sure led us a race this morning on them there boxes. Must have sweat a peck or more.

BUD: [*taking his bucket and sitting on the ground near the center*] Race? Hunh, wait till four o'clock this evening, you gwine call for the calf rope, sure enough. [*tickled at the tribute to his powers*] And poor Puny, the heat monkey have rid him to death.

PUNY: Ain't no monkey rid me, I tell you. Little but loud. Put us in the cotton patch, and I can kill you off the way a king snake do a lizard.

BUD: Picking cotton! That woman and chillun's job. No regular man mess with that. [*waving his hand at the woods behind him*] Turpentiming's the stuff.

[*They fall to eating heartily, peas, side meat, molasses poured in the top of the bucket lid from a bottle, bread, and collards. The ax of a fourth hand is heard still thudding in the forest.*]

LIJE: [*jerking his bread-filled hand behind him*] Whyn't Abe come on? Time he eating.

BUD: Let him rair. Won't hurt hisself a-cutting. Getting to be the no-'countest hand I ever see.

LIJE: Used to could cut boxes like a house afire.

PUNY: And hack! Lord, that man could hack.

LIJE: The champeen of the woods and the swamps.

PUNY: Better'n Bud, better'n all. Knowed him to dip eight barrels many day.

BUD: Can't help what has been. Ain't worth my old hat now. Colonel Mack say so too. And I heard Mr. Lonnie talking rough to him over at the weaving house day before yesterday about his getting trifling here lately.

PUNY: Been getting no 'count since two year ago. The time when the white folks hang that Charlie Simpson on a telegram pole—him they said attacked a white 'oman, and they shoot him full of holes, ayh!

BUD: They did. And that Abe got his neck stretched, hadn't been for the Colonel. Fool went down there in the night and cut that man down and bury him hisself.

PUNY: Yeh, and Mr. Lonnie was for getting the law on Abe. Ain't no love 'twixt them two.

LIJE: [*looking around him*] 'Twon't do to mess with white folks and they riled up.

BUD: You said it, brother.

PUNY: [*looking around him also*] Won't do. Keep to your work, that's all.

BUD: Yeh, work, work for 'em. Get your money and your meat, push on through, ask no questions, no sass, keep to your work.

LIJE: Yeh, keep the mouth shut, let white man do the talking. Safe then.

BUD: Safe! You done said. No telegram poles, no shooting, no fire burning.

PUNY: Safe is best.

[*They lapse into silence under the touch of worry, something undefinable, something not to be thought upon. They swallow their food heavily. Presently Lije stops and looks to the ground.*]

LIJE: Abe ain't safe.

BUD: Eyh?

LIJE: [*gesturing vaguely behind him*] Abe talk too much.

PUNY: [*nodding*] Can't help it, I bet.

BUD: Can too. Didn't talk much before that boy was hung. Worked hard then and say nothing.

LIJE: Sump'n on his mind. Sump'n deep, worry him, trouble—

BUD: Trouble about the colored folks. Want to rise 'em up with education— fact!

PUNY: Hunh, rise 'em up to get a rope around they neck. The colored's place is down at the bottom. Get buried in his own graveyard, Abe don't mind out.

BUD: Right on the bottom with their hands and legs, muscle power, backbone, down with the rocks and the shovels and the digging. White man on top.

LIJE: You's talking gospel.

PUNY: Abe say he gwine climb. I heard him tell the Colonel that.

BUD: 'Fore God! What Colonel say?

PUNY: He ain't say nothing, just look at him.

LIJE: Abe is bad mixed up all down inside.

BUD: White and black make bad mixtry.

LIJE: Do that. [*thumping on his chest*] Black down here. [*thumping his head*] White mens up here. Heart say do one thing, head say another. Bad, bad.

PUNY: The white blood in him coming to the top. That make him want to climb up and be something. The black gwine hold him down, though. Part of him take after the Colonel, part after his dead mammy, division and misery inside.

LIJE: Ssh!

PUNY: [*starting and looking around*] Colonel Mack the daddy, everybody knows. Like as two peas, see the favor.

BUD: [*bitingly*] Talk too much! Little bird carry news to the Colonel and he fall on you and scrush you. Ain't black, ain't white, what ails him. Them damn books he got to studying last year or two. Can't go to the woods without 'em. Look up there on his bucket, for cripes sake. [*He points to the remaining tin bucket in the bush. A small book is lying on the top under the handle. He snorts.*] 'Rifmatic, I bet. Give a darky a book and just as well shoot him. All the white folks tell you that.

PUNY: [*pouring molasses on his bread*] He smart enough, though, in his head. That buddy got sense.

LIJE: Has that. Getting so he can cipher right up with the Colonel.

PUNY: [*looking at Bud*] Bet some day Colonel Mack put him woods boss over us.

BUD: Ain't no black man gwine boss me, old son. Split his head with my ax.

LIJE: [*leaning back and emitting a halloo*] Heighp, you Abe! Dinner! Gwine cut all day?

BUD: Give him the full title and he'll hear you.

LIJE: [*grinning*] Aberham, Aberham McCranie!

PUNY: Yeh, you Aberham Lincoln, you better get your grub!

[*An answering shout comes out of the forest.*]

BUD: Trying to cut past time — maybe us'll think he's smart.

PUNY: Don't care what you think, Bud, getting so he look down on you and the rest of us.

BUD: Damn your runty soul, what you know about it? Ain't no darky living can look down on me and get by with it. Do, and I make him smell of that. [*He clenches his heavy fist and raises it to heaven.*]

PUNY: Jesus! That Abe take you up in one hand and frail your behind to a blister.

LIJE: What make you two blackguard so much?

BUD: [*to Puny*] Keep on, keep on, little man. Some these days you gwine come missing. [*He crams a handful of corn bread into his mouth.*]

LIJE: [*drawling*] Try a little fist and skull and work the bile out'n your systems. [*looking off and singing*]

Dark was the night and cold the ground —

BUD: [*spitting in scorn*] Ain't gwine bruise my fistes on his old skull. Don't 'spect to notice him no more. [*He falls to eating in huge mouthfuls.*] But he better quit throwing that Abe in my face, I tells him that.

PUNY: Don't see why that make you mad.

BUD: It do though. I don't like him and his uppity ways, I don't.

PUNY: Hunh, and you was one of the first to brag on him for going on short rations so the Colonel buy him books and learn him to teach school.

BUD: Short rations. Ain't no short rations, and that Goldie gal bringing him pies and stuff every day. Be here with a bucket in a few minutes, I betcha. Fool love the very ground he squat on! And he look down on her 'cause her ignorant. And teach school! Been hearing that schoolteaching business the whole year. He ain't gwine teach no school. Colored folks won't send to him, they won't. They don't want no schooling.

PUNY: Mought. Abe told me this morning that the Colonel gwine fix it with the commissioners or something in town today. I know what the matter with you, Bud. Hee-hee.

BUD: What?

PUNY: [*hesitating*] Abe come riding by in two-horse coach. Us'll be bowing and a-scraping. Us'll pull off our hats and be "Howdy, Mister Aberham." [*Bud turns and looks at him with infinite scorn, saying nothing.*] And Bud? [*Bud makes no answer.*] Bud?

BUD: What?

PUNY: That Goldie business what worrying you, hee-hee. She love Abe and—

BUD: [*bounding up and kicking Puny's bucket and food into the bushes*] Damn your lousy soul, I'm a mind to stomp you in the dirt! [*He towers over the terrified Puny, who lies flat on his back whimpering.*]

PUNY: Don't hit me, Bud. For God's sake! I just joking.

LIJE: Go at it, fight it out. [*singing to his inner self as he watches them*]
    The bones in the grave cried Calvary
    The night King Jesus died.

BUD: [*kicking dirt at Puny and going back to his bucket*] Done told him now. Ain't gwine say no more! Next time be my fist rammed down his throat, and turn him wrong side outwards.

[*Abe comes in at the right, carrying his ax. He is a young Negro, with a touch of the mulatto in him, of twenty-five or six, tall and powerfully built and dressed much like the others in cap and turpentine-glazed clothes. He puts his ax by the pine at the right, pulls off his cap and fans himself, while he pinches his sweaty shirt loose from his skin. His shaggy head, forehead, and jaw are marked with will and intelligence. But a smoldering flash in his eye that now and then shows itself suggests a passionate and dangerous person when aroused. From the change in the actions of the others when he enters it is evident that they respect and even fear him.*]

ABE: What's the trouble between you and Puny, Bud?

BUD: [*sullenly*] Ain't no trouble.

PUNY: [*crawling around on the ground and collecting his spilled food*] Ain't nothing, Abe, I just spilled my rations.

[*Abe gets his book down and seats himself in the shade at the left. He begins working problems, using a stub of a pencil and a sheet of crumpled paper.*]

LIJE: Puny, I got some bread left you can have. [*He pulls a mouth harp from his pocket and begins to blow softly.*]

PUNY: [*straightening out his masked bucket and closing it*] I don't want nothing else, Lije. Et all I can hold. [*after a moment*] Put your bucket up for you.

[*He gets Lije's bucket and hangs it along with his own in the limby bush. Bud eats in silence, puts up his bucket, gets a drink from the spring, and resumes his seat, hanging his head between his knees. Puny goes to the spring and drinks.*]

BUD: [*pouring snuff into his lip*] Don't fall in and get drownded, Puny.

PUNY: Want some water, Lije? [*He goes to the log, curls himself up in the shade beside it and prepares to sleep.*]

LIJE: [*stirring lazily*] Believe I does. [*He goes to the spring and drinks, returns to the pine tree and sits down.*]

PUNY: Ain't you gwine eat no dinner, Abe?

[*Abe makes no reply.*]

LIJE: Call him again. [*touching his head with his finger*] Deep, deep up there.

PUNY: Heigh, Abe, better eat your grub.

ABE: [*starting*] You call me?

PUNY: You so deep studying didn't hear me. Better eat your dinner. Get full of ants setting up there.

ABE: I'm going to eat later.

BUD: Yeh, when Goldie come.

ABE: Hunh!

BUD: You heared me.

ABE: Don't let me hear no more.

BUD: Hunh!

ABE: You heard me. [*Puny snickers from his log with audible delight. Lije waits a moment and then lies down. Bud reaches out and tears a bush from the ground and casts it angrily from him.*] I'll eat my dinner when it pleases me, you gentlemen allowing. [*There is a touch of anger in his voice which he apparently regrets on second thought, for he goes on more kindly.*] Goldie said she's going to fetch me something to eat today. I got to work this problem. Been at it two days now. Can't get it out'n my head. Ain't been able to sleep for two nights. [*Bud sits staring and spitting straight before him. Presently Lije begins to snore, then Puny follows. Abe goes on with his figuring. Bud turns over on the ground and goes to sleep. Abe becomes more and more absorbed in the problem he is working. He mutters to himself.*] Answer say fifteen. Can't make it come out fifteen, can't, seem like, to save me. Man must have answer wrong. Six go into fourteen, three, no, two times and — two over. [*His voice dies away as he becomes lost in his work. Presently his face begins to light up. He figures faster. Suddenly he slaps his knee.*] There where I been missing it all the time. I carried two instead of one. Blame fool I is. [*He hits the side of his head with his knuckle. In his excitement he calls out.*] Puny, I'm getting that answer. [*But Puny is snoring away. In a moment Abe throws down his book with beaming face.*] I got it, folkses, I got it. Fifteen! That white man know what he's doing, he all time get them answer right. [*He turns expectantly toward Lije.*] I got it, Lije. [*Lije makes no answer. He turns toward Puny again, starts to speak, but sees he is asleep.*] Bud! [*But Bud makes no answer. The heavy breathing of the sleepers falls regularly upon his ears. His face sinks into a sort of hopeless brooding.*] Yeh, sleep, sleep, sleep your life away. I figger for you, for me, for all the black in the world to lead 'em up out of ignorance. They don't listen, they don't hear me, they in the wilderness, don't want to be led. They sleep, sleep in bondage. [*He bows his head between his knees.*] Sleep in sin. [*presently*] Time me to eat.

[*Abe reaches for his bucket and is about to open it when Puny springs high into the air with a squeak of terror and begins rolling over and over in the leaves and briers.*]

PUNY: Come here, folkses, come here and get this thing off'n me.

[*Puny clutches at his breeches. Lije and Bud start up out of their sleep.*]

LIJE: Who that run-mad man?
BUD: That damn Puny, something in his britches!
ABE: Be still, Puny, I get it out. [*He goes up to the frightened Puny, reaches down his trousers, and pulls out a mouse.*] Nothing but a little bitty old field mice.

[*Abe throws the mouse into the thicket. Lije and Bud break into roaring laughter. Puny sits down exhausted, fanning himself angrily.*]

PUNY: Laugh, laugh, all of you. That thing bite same as a mud turtle. Yeh, funny, funny like hell to you.

[*Puny snaps his mouth closed and fans himself the more furiously. A loud shout comes from off the left.*]

ABE: Stop your laughing, I hear somebody hollering.

[*A second halloo comes down the hill.*]

PUNY: That the Colonel and Mr. Lonnie!

BUD: Sound like 'em. That's who 'tis.

ABE: [*going off at the left*] Here we is, Colonel Mack, at the spring eating dinner! [*He comes back.*] Colonel Mack and Mr. Lonnie coming on down here.

PUNY: 'Course. Got to see how many boxes us cleaned up this morning.

ABE: He tell me about the school now. [*He stirs around him in his excitement.*] Mebbe that his main business here in the middle of the day.

BUD: Hunh, mebbe. Got some special work wants done. Wants to hurry us to it, that's what.

[*The sound of voices is heard approaching from the left, and almost immediately the Colonel and his son Lonnie come in. The Colonel carries a riding whip. He is a stout run-down southerner, past middle age, with all the signs of moral and intellectual decadence upon him. Lechery, whisky, and levity of living have taken their toll of him, and yet he has retained a kind of native good-naturedness. His shirt front and once pointed beard are stained with the drippings of tobacco juice. There is something in his bearing and in the contour of his face that resembles Abe. His son, a heavyish florid young man of twenty-three or four, walks behind him.*]

COLONEL: [*in a high jerky voice*] Snoozing, hanh?

ABE: Just finishing our dinner, suh.

PUNY: Us about to work overtime today, Colonel.

COLONEL: Not likely, I reckon. Say, I want you fellows, all four of you, to get over to the swamp piece on Dry Creek. Boxes there are running over, two quarts in 'em apiece, prime virgin. [*They begin to move to their feet.*] No, I don't mean to go right now. Gabe's coming by on the big road here [*jerking his whip toward the rear*] with a load of barrels and the dippers in about a half-hour. Meet him out there.

LONNIE: Yeh, we want to get the wagons off to Fayetteville tonight.

COLONEL: How you get on cornering this morning, Bud?

BUD: Purty good, suh. Us four done about all that pasture piece, suh.

COLONEL: Fine, fine. That's the way. Puny and Lije stay with you?

BUD: Right there every jump.

LIJE: Yes, suh, yes, suh!

PUNY: When he give the call we give him the response every time, suh. Yes, suh, us kept him crowded.

COLONEL: We got to get on, Lonnie. Want to see how the scrape's coming over on Uncle Joe's Branch. Be up on the road there in half an hour.

LONNIE: [*stopping as they go out*] Got so you doing any better work lately, Abe?

ABE: [*starting*] Suh?

LONNIE: You heard me.

ABE: I didn't understand you, Mr. Lonnie.

LONNIE: You understood me all right. [*pointing to the book on the ground*] Let them damned books worry you still?

COLONEL: Come on, Lonnie.

ABE: [*stammering*] I dunno—I—

COLONEL: Sill holding out on short rations, ain't you, Abe? [*There is the least hint of pride in the Colonel's voice.*]

ABE: [*somewhat confused*] I studying what I can. Slow go, slow go.

COLONEL: Stick to it. You're the first Negro I ever saw so determined. But then you're uncommon! [*The Colonel moves on.*] Come on, Lonnie.

ABE: [*following somewhat timidly after him*] Colonel Mack, did, di—you—what'd they say over there about that little school business?

COLONEL: Bless my soul, about to forget it. I talked it over with the board and most of 'em think maybe we'd better not try it yet.

ABE: [*his face falling*] When they say it might be a good time? I'm getting right along with that 'rithmetic and spelling and reading. I can teach the colored boys and girls a whole heap right now, and I'll keep studying.

COLONEL: [*impatiently*] Oh, I dunno. Time'll come maybe. Maybe time won't come. Folks are queer things, you know. [*He moves on.*]

ABE: Can't you get 'em to let me try it a while? Reckon—

COLONEL: I don't know, I tell you. Got my business on my mind now.

LONNIE: He's done told you two or three times, can't you hear?

ABE: [*his eyes flashing and his voice shaking with sudden uncontrollable anger*] Yeh, yeh, I hear him. Them white folks don't care—they—

LONNIE: [*stepping before him*] Look out! None of your sass. Pa's already done more for you than you deserve. He even stood up for you and they laughing at him there in town.

ABE: [*trembling*] Yeh, yeh, I know. But them white folks don't think—I'm going to show 'em—I—

LONNIE: [*pushing himself up before him*] Dry up. Not another word.

ABE: [*his voice breaking almost into a sob*] Don't talk to me like that, Mr. Lonnie. Stop him, Colonel Mack, before I hurt him.

[*The other Negroes draw off into a knot by the pine tree, mumbling in excitement and fear.*]

COLONEL: Stop, Lonnie! Abe, don't you talk to my son like that.

LONNIE: By God, I'm going to take some of the airs off'n him right now. You've gone around here getting sorrier and more worthless every day for the last year — sassy to my father. What you need is a good beating, and I'm going to give it to you. [*He steps backward and snatches the whip from his father's hand.*]

COLONEL: Stop that, Lonnie!

LONNIE: Keep out of this yourself. [*He comes toward Abe.*] I'll beat his black hide off'n him.

ABE: Keep him back there, Colonel Mack. I mought kill him! Keep him off.

LONNIE: Kill him! All right, do it, damn you!

[*He strikes Abe across the face with his whip. With a snarl Abe springs upon him, tears the whip from his hand, and hurls him headlong into the thicket of briers and bushes. Then he stands with his hands and head hanging down, his body shaking like one with a palsy.*]

PUNY: [*screaming*] You done killed Mr. Lonnie! Oh, Lordy, Lordy.

COLONEL: [*running to Lonnie who is crawling up out of the mud with his clothes and skin torn, sobbing and cursing*] Are you hurt? How bad are you hurt?

LONNIE: Let me get at that son of a bitch and I'll kill him dead. [*moaning*] Oh, I'll beat his brains out with one of them axes.

COLONEL: Yeh, and you'd better keep your hands off'n him. I'll fix him. [*He reaches down and picks up the whip — thundering.*] Get down on your knees, Abe! Get down, you slave! I'm going to beat you.

[*Abe jerks his head up in defiance, but before the stern face of the Colonel his strength goes out of him. He puts his hands up in supplication.*]

ABE: Don't beat me, Colonel Mack, don't beat me with that whip!

COLONEL: Get down on your knees! Get down! [*He strikes him several blows.*]

ABE: [*falling on his knees*] Oh, Lord, have mercy upon me!

[*The Colonel begins to beat him, blow upon blow. Puny, Bud, and Lije stand near the pine in breathless anxiety.*]

PUNY: The Colonel'll kill him!

BUD: [*seizing his arm*] Shut that mouth!

COLONEL: [*as he brings the whip down*] Let this be a lesson to you — keep to your place!

ABE: [*his back twitching under the whip, his voice broken*] Mercy, Colonel Mack, mercy!

COLONEL: You struck a white man, you struck my son.

ABE: [*raising his tear-stained face*] I your son too — you my daddy.

[*Abe throws himself down before the Colonel, embracing his feet. The Colonel lowers the whip, then drops it behind him.*]

LONNIE: [*his voice husky with rage*] You hear what he say? Hear what he called you? [*He seizes the whip and in a blind rage strikes the prostrate Abe again.*]

COLONEL: [*stepping between them*] Stop it! Give me that whip. [*Lonnie hesitates and then reluctantly hands him the whip.*] Go on back out to the road and wait for me. Trot! [*Lonnie in disgust and rage finally goes off at the left nursing his face in his arms.*] Get up, Abe. Get up, I say.

[*Abe sits up, hugging his face between his knees. The Colonel wets his handkerchief in the spring, and with his hands on Abe's head bathes the bruises on his neck and shoulders.*]

ABE: [*in a voice grown strangely dignified and quiet*] Thank'ee, thank'ee, Colonel Mack.

COLONEL: [*breathing heavily*] Thanky nothing. I had to beat you, Abe, had to. Think no more about it. Dangerous thing, hitting a white man. But this is the end of it. Won't be no law, nothing but this. Put some tar and honey on yourself tonight and you'll be all right tomorrow. And keep your temper down. It's crazy — crazy. [*The bushes are suddenly parted at the rear and a tall sinuous young mulatto woman bounds through. She carries a bucket in her hand. At the sight of the Colonel bathing Abe's head and neck she rushes forward with a low cry. The Colonel turns toward her.*] Now, Goldie, ain't no use cutting up. Abe's been in a little trouble. Nothing much.

GOLDIE: [*moaning*] I heard the racket and I 'fraid somebody being killed. Is you hurt bad, Abe, honey babe? [*She bends tenderly over him, her hand running over his hair.*] Who hurt you, honey, who hurt you?

COLONEL: [*handing Goldie his handkerchief*] Look after him, Goldie. [*He goes out at the left, calling.*] Wait a minute, Lonnie!

GOLDIE: What they do to you, Abe? Who hurt you? [*All the time she is rubbing his neck, dabbing his shoulders with the handkerchief, and cooing over him.*] Whyn't you kill them white mens if they hurt you? You can do it, break 'em like broom straws.

ABE: [*standing up*] Ain't nobody hurt me. I crazy that's what—he say so—crazy in the head. Ain't nobody hurt me.

GOLDIE: [*clinging to him*] You is hurt, hurt bad. Look at your poor neck and shoulders. Look at 'em beat with great wales on 'em.

ABE: [*growling*] Ain't nobody hurt me, I tell you.

GOLDIE: Lay yourself down here and let me smooth off your forehead and put some cold water on that mark across your face. Please'm, Abe.

ABE: [*suddenly crying out in a loud voice*] I ain't nothing, nothing. That white man beat me, beat me like a dog. [*his voice rising into a wail*] He flail me like a suck-egg dog. [*He rocks his head from side to side in a frenzy of wrath.*] Lemme get to him! [*He falls on his knees searching in the leaves and finds a stone. Goldie stands wringing her hands and moaning. He jumps to his feet, raising the stone high above his head.*] Lemme get to him, I scrush his God-damn head like a egg shell!

[*Abe moves to the left to follow the Colonel. Goldie throws her arms around his neck.*]

GOLDIE: No, no, you ain't gwine out there. Abe, Abe!

PUNY: [*crying out*] Stop him, Bud! Lije, keep him back!

LIJE: [*coming from the pine tree*] Here now, you Abe, stop that.

BUD: [*moving quickly before him and blocking his path*] Stop that, fool. You gwine fix it to get yourself hung up on a telegram pole. Body so full of holes, sift sand.

GOLDIE: [*sobbing*] Don't do it, Abe, sugar babe. [*She throws herself upon his breast.*]

BUD: [*reaching toward her*] Seem like you'd take yourself off'n that man!

ABE: [*pulling her arms from around him*] Lemme loose, lemme loose. [*After a moment he throws the stone down.*] I ain't going to do nothing. [*He sits down on the log at the left holding his head in his hands.*]

GOLDIE: [*bringing her bucket*] Here, eat something, Abe, you feel better. I got some pie and some cake in here for you.

PUNY: [*stepping back and forth in senseless excitement*] Somebody gwine get killed at this mess, somebody—

ABE: [*pushing Goldie away*] I ain't want nothing to eat. Ain't hungry.

LIJE: Better eat, Abe. Get your strength back.

ABE: [*savagely*] Ain't hungry. I keep telling you.

[*Goldie drops on her knees beside him and laying her head in Abe's lap clasps her arms around him.*]

GOLDIE: [*sobbing softly*] Oh, boy, boy, why they beat you so? What you do to 'em?

ABE: Fool, fool I is. Crazy, that's it.

BUD: [*sharply*] He given Mr. Lonnie and the Colonel back talk. Can't sass white mens and get away with it. Abe ought to know better.

[*Lije wanders over to the right blowing his harp softly and forlornly.*]

PUNY: [*sitting down on the ground*] Can't be done, Abe. Can't.

BUD: [*stripping leaves from a bush and watching Goldie as she carries on over Abe*] Here, woman, stop that rairing. [*muttering to himself*] Never see two bigger fools.

[*Abe puts his hands mechanically on Goldie's shoulders and begins stroking her.*]

ABE: Stop it, baby. Ain't no use to cry.

[*Puny sits with his mouth open in astonishment watching them. Lije lays himself back on the ground and blows his harp, apparently no longer interested in the scene.*]

BUD: [*jealousy raging within him*] Heigh, Goldie, get up from that man's lap. He ain't care nothing for you. [*Goldie's sobs die away and she is quiet.*] He say you foolish many a time. He look down on you.

GOLDIE: [*raising her tear-stained face*] How you know? You jealous, Bud Gaskins. He better man than you. Worth a whole town of you. [*catching Abe by the hand and picking up her bucket*] Come on, come on, honey, let's go off there in the woods and eat our dinner by ourselves!

BUD: [*coming up to her*] Here, you stay out'n that woods with him.

ABE: [*standing up*] Yeh, yeh, I come with you. [*He moves mechanically on, and reaches out and pushes Bud behind him.*]

GOLDIE: [*her face alight, a sort of reckless and unreal abandonment upon her*] I knows where there's a cool place under a big tree. And there's cool green moss there and soft leaves. Let's go there, boy. I gwine tend to you and feed you. [*She moves across toward the right, leading Abe like a child.*] We make us a bed there, honey. [*Lije sits up watching them.*] Us forget the 'membrance of all this trouble. [*a kind of ecstasy breaking in her voice*] There the birds sing and we hear the little branch running over the rocks.

Cool there, sweet there, you can sleep, honey, rest there, baby. Your mammy, your child gwine love you, make you forget.

ABE: [*moved out of himself*] Yeh, yeh, I come with you. I don't care for nothing, not nothing no more. You, just you'n me.

GOLDIE: Ain't no world, ain't no Lije and Bud, nobody. Us gwine make us a 'biding place and a pillow under that tree. [*in sweet oblivion*] Feel your arms around me, my lips on yourn. We go singing up to heaven, honey, together — together.

[*They go off, Goldie's voice gradually dying away like a nun's chant.*]

BUD: [*breaking a sapling in his grasp*] Gwine off, gwine off in the woods together there like hogs.

PUNY: [*bounding up, his body shaking in lascivious delight*] I gwine watch 'em — hee-hee — I gwine watch 'em.

LIJE: [*knocking him back*] Better stay out'n that woods. Abe kill you.

PUNY: [*standing up by the pine tree*] Can see 'em, her still a-leading him.

LIJE: [*standing up and peering off to the right*] There on the cool moss and the soft green leaves.

BUD: [*stripping the limbs from the top of the broken sapling*] There she go playing the hog. Didn't know she like that. God damn her, I could tame her down and take that spirit out'n her. [*He crowds out his chest and walks up and down.*]

PUNY: [*grasping Lije's arm*] Can't hardly see 'em no more, can you?

LIJE: Can hardly.

BUD: [*his anger and jealousy disappearing in physical emotion and vulgar curiosity*] Where they now?

LIJE: [*pointing*] There, there, they crossing the branch now.

PUNY: [*breathlessly*] I see 'em. I see 'em. His arm around her now, her head on his shoulder. [*He capers in his excitement.*] Lord! Lord!

BUD: [*with a loud brutal laugh as he slaps Lije on the back*] On the soft green moss.

LIJE: [*laughing back and dragging his harp across his mouth in a cascade of sound*] Where the leaves is cool.

PUNY: Can't see 'em no more! [*He whirls about and turns a handspring.*] Whoopee, folkses! Gwine run away with myself!

BUD: [*his eyes shining*] Down where the sweet branch water run. [*He shuffles a jig among the leaves.*]

LIJE: [*blowing upon his harp*] Singing right up to heaven! [*He blows more wildly as they all drop into a barbaric dance that gradually mounts into a Dionysiac frenzy.*]

PUNY: Heaven!

BUD: Jesus, Lord, Father and Son! [*shouting off*] Go to it, Abe Old Son, bring her home to glory!

LIJE: [*singing loudly as they dance, the music running into a quick thumping rhythm*]

My feets were wet with the sunrise dew,
The morning star were a witness too.
'Way, 'way up in the Rock of Ages,
In God's bosom gwine be my pillow.

[*They gambol, turn and twist, run on all fours, rear themselves up on their haunches, cavort like goats.*]

PUNY: In God's bosom—hanh!

BUD: In who bosom?

LIJE: In who bosom, bubber?

[*A loud halloo comes down from the hill in the rear, unnoticed by them.*]

PUNY: In Goldie's bosom. Hee-hee-hee.

BUD and LIJE: Hah-haw-haw! Hee-hee-hee! In Goldie's bosom gwine be his pillow.

[*The halloo is repeated.*]

LIJE: Here, there that Gabe calling us. Better get, or the Colonel have that stick on our back.

[*They gather up their buckets and axes. Puny clambers up the pine a few feet and drops to the ground.*]

BUD: Can see?

PUNY: See nothing. Hee-hee!

LIJE: Got to leave 'em now. Abe catch it again don't mind out. He not coming with us.

BUD: He done for now. That gal got him hard and fast. [*snorting scornfully*] Books! Books! Rise 'em up like hell!

LIJE: I done told you. Heart say this, head say that. Bad mixtry. Bad. Crazy!

PUNY: [*shouting*] Heigh, you Gabe! Coming!

[*They move out at the rear up the hill, singing, laughing, and jostling each other.*]

'Way, 'way down by the sweet branch water,
In her bosom gwine be his pillow!

Hee-hee-haw-haw! [*Their loud, brutally mocking laughter floats back behind them.*]

*Fade-out*

SCENE 2

[*A spring day about three years later, in a two-room cabin, the home of Abraham McCranie. The room is roughly built of framed material and is unceiled. To the right front is a fireplace with a lightwood-fed green oakwood fire going. A wood box is to the right of the chimney. To the left rear of the room is a bed, and at the left center rear a door leads out to the porch. To the right of the door a window gives a view of wide-stretched cotton fields. Below the window close to the wall is a rough homemade chest with several books on it, and hanging between it and the door is a sort of calendar, with the illustration of a slave leaving his chains behind and walking up a hill toward the sunrise. There is a caption at the top of the print in large letters— "We Are Rising." Several old dresses, bonnets, and coats hang on the nails in the joists in the right rear. A door in the right center leads into the kitchen. At the left front is a dilapidated old bureau, small pieces of wood taking the place of lost casters. The top drawer is open, sagging down like a wide lip, with stray bits of clothing hanging over the edge. A bucket of water and a pan are on the bureau. There are several splint-bottomed chairs and a rocker in the room.*

*When the curtain rises Muh Mack is sitting by the fire rocking a bundle in her arms. She is a chocolate-colored Negress of near sixty, dressed in a long dirty wrapper, and barefooted. Her graying hair is wrapped into pigtails and stands around her head Medusalike. A long snuff stick protrudes from her mouth. Goldie's long gaunt form lies stretched on the bed at the left, partly covered by a sheet, her head resting on her arm. She is constantly raising in her languid hand a stick with a paper tied to it to shoo away the flies. Muh Mack rocks and sings.*]

MUH MACK:
  Oohm — oohm — hoonh — oohm-oohm —
  This here baby the purtiest baby,
  Purtiest baby in the land.
  He gwine grow up champeen soldier,
  Mammy's honey, onliest man.
  Oohm — oohm — hoonh — oohm — oohm —
GOLDIE: [*in a tired voice*] How he coming now?

MUH MACK: [*shaking her finger and wagging her head at the bundle*] Done seen him grow. Look at me like he know me.

GOLDIE: [*with a long sigh*] I so tired, tired. Seem like I can sleep forever.

MUH MACK: Lie and sleep, sleep. Get your strength.

GOLDIE: I tired but can't sleep. [*She lapses into silence. The old woman rocks and sings. Presently Goldie raises her head.] raises her head.*] What day today?

MUH MACK: Saturday.

GOLDIE: Seem like I can't 'member nothing. What day he come?

MUH MACK: He come a-Tuesday.

GOLDIE: That make him—let's see, how old?

MUH MACK: Four day now.

GOLDIE: [*suddenly sitting up with a gasp*] Them other two die, one three days, other'n four.

MUH MACK: Nanh—nanh, lie back down. This here baby live to be a hundred. He strong, he muscled. Them other poor little 'uns puny, born to die. The mark was on 'em from the first.

GOLDIE: [*bending her head between her knees and weeping softly*] They was so pitiful and little. I can't forget how they feel and fumble for me with their little hands and they hungry.

MUH MACK: [*irritably*] Bless God, crying after them, and got this fine 'un here. Lay yourself down on that bed and rest.

GOLDIE: Can't forget 'em, can't.

MUH MACK: Hunh, mought as well and they done plowed in the ground.

GOLDIE: [*her tears beginning to flow again*] Yeh, yeh, they is! Abe didn't try to keep Mr. Lonnie from cutting down them plum bushes and plowing up that hedgerow. I hold it against him long as I live.

MUH MACK: Why for? The dead's the dead. Let the earth have 'em. Let cotton grow over 'em. No use moaning. Think on the living.

GOLDIE: Poor Abe, weren't his fault though. He proud, stand by and see white mens plow over 'em, say nothing, won't beg for his babies.

MUH MACK: Can't blame him! He stiff-neck. God break his spirit. Give him two dead 'uns to fetch 'im down. He better humble now. [*talking half to herself*] He talk proudlike, gwine raise up big son, leader among men. First 'un come thin, little like a rat. He hate him. He die. God call him. Then next year second come, Old Master keep him little, thin. He die too. Abe getting down to sackcloth and ashes. God see him down crying for mercy. He send this one, strong Israel man. He gwine flourish, he gwine wax.

GOLDIE: [*stretching herself out on the bed*] Abe says this 'un gwine die too, same like the others. He don't look at him, pay no attention.

MUH MACK: Hunh, he will though when he see 'im fleshen up with his sucking.

GOLDIE: Where's Abe?

MUH MACK: Went down in the new-ground planting corn. Won't make nothing though and it the light of the moon time. He be here directly for his dinner.

GOLDIE: Poor Abe work too hard!

MUH MACK: [*snorting*] Work too hard the mischief! Ain't work what ail him. He studying old books and mess too much. Crop shows it.

GOLDIE: He don't look well, neither.

MUH MACK: Can't look well and worry all time. [*A step is heard on the porch.*] There he now. Take this baby. Got to put dinner on the table.

[*She takes the baby over to Goldie, lays it by her side, goes out at the right, and is heard rattling dishes and pans in the kitchen.*]

GOLDIE: [*crooning over the baby*] Now you go sleep, rest yourself, get strong and grow great big.

[*Abe comes in at the rear carrying a hoe and a file. He is barefooted and dressed in overalls, ragged shirt, and weather-stained straw hat. Sitting down near the center of the room, he begins filing his hoe.*]

ABE: [*without looking around*] How you come on?

GOLDIE: Better, I reckon. [*with a sharp gasp*] Here, why you fetch that hoe in the house?

ABE: [*paying no attention to her query*] Baby still living, hunh?

GOLDIE: Abe, take that hoe out'n this house. Might bring bad luck on you. [*raising herself up in bed*] Might bring something on the baby.

ABE: Can't swub them new-ground bushes with no dull hoe.

GOLDIE: [*pleading*] Take it out'n the house, I say.

ABE: When I damn ready.

GOLDIE: [*calling*] Muh Mack!

MUH MACK: [*coming to the door at the right*] What ails you? [*She sees Abe filing his hoe.*] Lord help us! Throw that thing out, throw it out! Ain't got no sense. Goldie too weak to be worried up.

ABE: All right then. I finish with it now. Set of fools. Everything got a sign attached to it. Ignorant, blind! [*He throws the hoe out through the rear door and gets a book from the chest and begins reading.*]

MUH MACK: Back at them books. Lord, never see such. [*She goes scornfully back to the kitchen.*]

ABE: [*half growling*] Says here we got to get out'n them suspicions and being afraid. Ain't no signs with evil and good in 'em. I read that last night. [*reading and halting over the words*] "The Negro is a superstitious person. There are signs and wonders in the weather, some fraught with evil, some with good. He plants his crops according to the moon, works and labors under the eye of some evil spirit of his own imagining." [*closing the book with a bang*] Hear that?

GOLDIE: I hear but don't mind it. Mean nothing. White man wrote it, and he don't know.

ABE: That's just it, he do know. We the ones don't know. That book is wrote for you, Muh Mack, and all of the blind.

GOLDIE: Put up them old books. Seem like you care more for them than you do this here baby, and he a fine boychild.

ABE: [*throwing the book back on the chest*] What he nohow? Ain't interested in him. Ain't no use being. He be dead in a week. God done cuss me and my household. No luck at nothing. Can't raise children, can't raise crop, nothing. Ain't dry weather, wet. Ain't wet, dry. Here May month and cold enough for freeze. [*He stretches his feet to the fire.*] The damn crows down there on the creek pulling up my corn faster'n I can plant it. [*He rocks his head.*] Jesus!

GOLDIE: [*pleading*] Abe, honey, don't get down. Things coming better now. This boy gwine make you feel better. Here he lie now just smiling like he understand me. [*bending over the baby*] Yeh, you is gwine grown up and take trouble off'n your poor daddy. Yeh, you is.

ABE: [*holding his head in his arms*] Listen to that talk, listen there. [*bitterly*] Woman know. She know. Here I am with no money to buy me shoes. [*holding up his duststained foot*] There you is, foot, cut with glass, full of briers, wore out stumping the roots and snags, and I can't buy nothing to cover you with.

GOLDIE: The Colonel give you shoes, you ask him. [*She opens the bosom of her wrapper and begins to nurse the baby.*]

ABE: Ain't gwine ask him nothing, not nothing. [*suddenly clenching his fist and hitting his thigh*] That man beat me, beat me at the spring three year ago, I ain't forget. [*He gets up and strides over to the bed and looks down at the suckling infant.*] There you lie drinking your grub in. What you care? Nothing. [*He lays his hand roughly on the baby and pinches him. The child lets out a high thin wail.*]

GOLDIE: [*beating his hand off*] Quit that pinching that baby. Quit it!

ABE: [*laughing brutally as he walks up and down the floor*] Yeh, you fight over him now and he be plowed in the ground like the others in a month. Hee-hee! Ain't this a hell of a mess! It sure God is. And we ain't got enough to feed a cat. You'n Muh Mack cook and slay and waste fast as I make it. Note at the store done took up, crop done all mortgaged up ahead of time. Can't make ends meet, can't. [*throwing his hands out helplessly*] I ain't no farmer.

GOLDIE: [*wretchedly*] Oh, Abe, we get on somehow, we will. And Muh Mack and me don't waste. I be up with you in the fields by the middle of the week. Poor child, you need sleep, need rest.

ABE: Make no difference. Work our guts out do no good. I tell you, gal, we're down, down. The white man up there high. Sitting up with God, up there in his favor. He get everything, we get the scraps, leavings. [*flaring out*] Ain't no God for the black man, that's a white man's God. That come to me down in the new-ground. [*He sits down again, tapping his feet on the floor.*]

GOLDIE: [*wiping her eyes*] Honey, you got to stop talking like that. Can't be bad luck always. I's 'feared when you talk that wild talk. God hear it, He do. [*Muh Mack comes and stands in the door.*] He might be doing all this to make us good, make us humble down before Him.

ABE: Humble down, hell! Look at the other darkies then. They shout and carry on in the church, pray and pay the preachers in their blindness. They humble. What do God do? Starve 'em to death. Kill 'em off like flies with consumption. They dying along the river same as the children in the wilderness.

MUH MACK: You blaspheming, that's what you doing. No wonder God take your babies away, no wonder he make your mule die, blast down your plans, and send the crows and cold weather and root lice to destroy your crops. [*her eyes flashing*] You got to change your ways. Some day he gwine reach down from the clouds and grab you by the scruff of the neck and break you across he knee. He give you a fine baby-child, you don't thank him. You got to fall down, pray, get low, get humble. [*Her voice rises into a semichant.*] You there, Jesus, hear my prayer. This poor sinner, he wicked, he blaspheme. Save him and save this poor little baby.

GOLDIE: [*weeping over the child*] Do, Lord, hear our prayer.

[*Abe sits down in his chair and stares moodily into the fire.*]

MUH MACK: [*crying out*] Them there old books cause it, that's what. Burn 'em up, burn 'em with fire. Your wild talk gwine make the Upper Powers drop lightning on this house, gwine destroy all of us. [*She wraps her arms before her, mumbling and swaying from side to side. Suddenly she raises her head and striding over to the chest shakes her fist at the books and kicks them.*] You the trouble. I hate the sight of you, and I wish there weren't nary one of you in the world.

ABE: [*reaching out and pulling her back*] Look out, woman! Don't touch my books!

MUH MACK: You mash my arm! [*With a wail she goes out at the right and is heard sobbing in the kitchen.*]

GOLDIE: Oh, you struck her! Abe — Abe —

[*Goldie sits up in the bed rocking the baby and quieting him. A heavy step sounds on the porch. Abe sits before the fire smoothing out the leaves of a book as a voice calls from the outside.*]

COLONEL: Heigh, you, Abe!

GOLDIE: [*quickly*] That the Colonel out there, Abe.

ABE: [*going to the door*] Yes, suh, that you, Colonel Mack?

COLONEL: [*coming in*] Yes. How you come on, all of you? [*He looks around the room and at the bed. Three years have worked a great change in him. He is stouter, his face mottled, and he walks with difficulty, propped on a stick.*] Been wanting to see that fine baby, Abe.

ABE: [*quietly*] Yes, suh — yes, suh.

MUH MACK: [*coming in*] And he sure is a fine 'un. [*standing near the Colonel*] Fine and strong same like Abe when he were born.

COLONEL: What's the matter, Goldie? Ain't been fighting, have you all? Who was that making a racket in here?

GOLDIE: [*keeping her head lowered*] I'm all right, Colonel Mack.

MUH MACK: [*wiping her eyes*] Ain't no row, Colonel. Want you to persuade that Abe to get rid of them old books. Enough trouble come on us account of 'em.

COLONEL: [*laughing*] The devil, let him keep his books. He's the only darky in the whole country worth a durn. Let me see the baby. [*Goldie shows the baby.*] That's a fine 'un, Abe. He'll live. Let me feel him. [*holding him up*] Heavy, gracious!

[*Muh Mack looks at him intently and there is the vaguest touch of malice in her voice as she speaks.*]

MUH MACK: Lord, it all comes to me again. Just such a day as this nigh thirty years ago you come down here and hold Abe up that-a-way.

COLONEL: [*a little heavily*] Don't remember it — nah —

MUH MACK: And my po' sister Caroline turnt her face to the wall — her wet face to the wall.

COLONEL: [*looking through the window a long while*] Thirty years ago. Time hurries on, it goes by in a hurry.

[*Abe looks before him with an indefinable expression on his face. A constrained silence comes over them, and the Colonel takes a sort of refuge in gazing intently at the child. Once or twice he clears his throat as if about to speak. For an instant all differences are passed away and they are four human beings aware of the strangeness of their lives, conscious of what queer relationships have fastened them together.*]

MUH MACK: [*starting*] Yes, suh, we ain't got much longer down here.

[*Then the baby begins to cry and the Colonel smiles.*]

COLONEL: Here, take him, Goldie. Favors Muh Mack, don't favor you, Abe.

ABE: Yes, suh.

COLONEL: [*softly as if to himself*] Nor your mammy. [*then drawing a heavy folded paper from his pocket slowly and with weighty dignity*] I got a little surprise for you'n Goldie, Abe. [*He puts on his spectacles, opens the paper, and starts to read.*] "Whereas— [*He stops as if convulsed with pain, and presently goes on.*] I devise to Abraham McCranie a house and tract of land containing twenty-five acres and formerly known as the 'Howington place,' to him and his heirs forever." [*hesitating a moment and folding the paper together*] Then follows a description of the place in course and distance, Abe, which I won't read. It's all signed and recorded in the courthouse. [*He feels around him heavily for his stick.*]

ABE: [*incredulously*] What that? That for me?

COLONEL: Yes, for you. A deed to this house and twenty-five acres of land, yours. [*He holds out the paper to Abe.*]

ABE: [*taking it with trembling hands*] Lord, Colonel Mack, what I going to say?

COLONEL: Say nothing. Say thanky if you want to.

ABE: [*overcome*] Thanky, suh, thanky, suh.

COLONEL: Shake hands on it, Abe.

ABE: [*wiping his hand on his coat*] Thanky, suh.

[*The Colonel looks at his bent head with strange intentness and then drops Abe's hand.*]

GOLDIE: Oh, Colonel Mack! [*Her eyes are shining with thankfulness.*]

MUH MACK: Abe, you's got land, boy, you owns a piece of land! Glory! [*She runs up to the Colonel and covers his hands with kisses.*]

COLONEL: [*waving her off*] Nothing, nothing to do for him. He deserves it. [*looking straight at Abe*] You do, boy. I want to see you go forward now. You had a hard time the last two years.

GOLDIE: He has, poor boy. He had it hard since the day he married me.

COLONEL: Hunh, he couldn't a-done better nowhere. I know. [*The Colonel picks up his stick which he has laid across the bed.*] Well, I got to move on. [*He stops near the door.*] And, Abe, how's your book business coming on?

ABE: I—I'm studying and reading now and then. Most too tired every night to do much.

COLONEL: Don't give up like Lonnie. Sent him to school and sent him to school, even tried him at the university, won't stay. He ain't worth a continental, that's what. [*turning toward the door and stopping again*] Well, I've got another little surprise for you in celebration of that fine boy. [*He looks down and taps on the floor.*]

ABE: [*excitedly*] What is it, Colonel Mack, suh?

COLONEL: How'd you like to try your hand at teaching a little school next fall?

[*Muh Mack throws up her hands.*]

GOLDIE: [*breathlessly*] Oh, me!

ABE: [*in confusion*] Teach school? Yessuh, I—

COLONEL: I'm going to have that old Quillie house fixed up and put some benches in it and a blackboard. I'll get two Negroes to serve with me on the school board and we'll try you out. [*smiling queerly*] I want to see you try it before I die.

ABE: [*with a great breath*] I'm going to teach school—at last!

COLONEL: [*going shakily out at the door*] Yes, at last. Now don't forget your crop, Abe, and study yourself to death.

ABE: [*following him*] Colonel Mack, you, you—I—I—

COLONEL: Take care of that baby. Raise him up right And, Abe, don't forget you ain't going to have no easy time. I'll get a lot of cussing for this, well as you. Go on eat your dinner. [*He stops on the porch and calls.*] Here, Goldie, take this fifty cents and buy the boy a stick of candy. [*He steps to the door and throws a coin on the bed.*] Take care of him and don't kill him on collards and beans. [*He goes off.*]

ABE: [*calling after him*] I ain't, Colonel, I'm going to raise him, going to make a man— [*He stops and stands watching the old man going up the lane. Then he turns and stumbles into the room with shining face.*] I—I forgives him all. I don't remember that beating by the spring no more.

GOLDIE: [*reaching out from the bed and grasping his hand*] Oh, honey babe, our troubles is ended. We gwine—we gwine have enough to eat and you be happy. [*She turns over in the bed and begins to cry softly.*]

ABE: [*patting her shoulders*] There, there, don't you cry, child. [*He wipes his *eyes with his sleeve.*] I been mean man. [*in a husky voice*] I treat my gal mean, blaspheme against the Lord, I'm going to do better, I — [*a sob chokes in his throat*]

MUH MACK: [*coming up to him and clasping her arms around him*] Bless the Lord, you gwine do better now. [*She sits down in a chair and bows her head in her lap.*]

GOLDIE: He good man, the Colonel. He too good to us. Raise us up, help us.

ABE: [*vaguely*] Up! Lift me up! Up! Up toward the sun! [*He glances at the calendar.*] That whip don't hurt no more. The remembrance is passed away. [*thumping on his breast*] Ain't no more bitter gall in here. Peace. It come all sudden over me. [*He suddenly falls on his knees by the bed in a sobbing burst of prayer.*] O God, God of the poor and of the sinful!

MUH MACK: Yea, our God.

ABE: The black man's God, the white man's God, the one and only God, hear me, hear my prayer.

MUH MACK: [*swaying and moaning*] Hear him, Jesus!

GOLDIE: [*softly*] We thy chillun, Lord.

ABE: Thy little chillun, and you powerful. You the Almighty, us the dust in thy hand. Us poor and weak, us nothing. Like the grasshopper, like the poor field lark, swept away in the storm. Man got no strength in him, no muscle can raise him, 'cepting your power. He walk in the wind, the wind take him away. Let there be fire, and fire burn him. It devour him. Same like the broom straw he fall before it. Man can't stand. He lost, lost. Shut in the grave, shut till the judgment.

MUH MACK: Jesus! Jesus!

GOLDIE: [*piteously*] Jesus!

ABE: He fall in the winter. He lie down in the summer. The spring come and find him gone.

MUH MACK: Have mercy, our Father.

GOLDIE: [*whispering*] Jesus, forgive him.

ABE: [*his voice rising into a chant*] The dirt stop up his poor mouth. Peace come to him in the ground. And the friends do cry, they wail and beat their breast. They call for their loved ones, and they don't answer. Their tongue make no more speech, from the graveyard, from the deep grave.

MUH MACK: Yea, Lord!

ABE: They gone at the planting, gone at the harvest. The hoe dull with rust, the harness wait on the peg, the bridle hang still, the collar hang there useless. They ain't no more hoeing, ain't no more plowing, no shoe track in the furrow. Man gone, same like a whisper, hushed in the graveyard, in the deep grave.

MUH MACK: Oh, have mercy upon us!

GOLDIE: Mercy!

ABE: [*raising his head up, his eyes closed*] Hear us, hear us, hear me this day, hear my poor prayer. Forgive me my sins, my blasphemy. Wipe out the evil of my wicked days. Purify, make clean, forget the remembrance of my transgression. Now here I do humble down, I do confess. Lift me, raise me, up, up!

MUH MACK: Hallelujah!

GOLDIE: Amen.

ABE: [*bowing his head in a storm of grief*] Reach down your hand and gimme strength. Now I draw nigh, I feel your spirit. Save me, save me now. [*Muh Mack and Goldie pray and moan aloud. Presently Abe stands up and cries out exultantly.*] He save me, he done save me! He done forgive me!

MUH MACK: [*clapping her hands wildly*] Bless the Lord, bless him!

GOLDIE: [*faintly*] Do, Jesus, save my baby and my husband.

[*Abe is silent a moment, his face working with emotion. He turns and bends down over the bed.*]

ABE: Poor little fellow. He sleep and rest. [*He puts his arms around Goldie and she clings to him.*] Honey child, I changed. I'm going to take new hold. From this day I begins. I'm sorry for all the past. [*He loosens her arms from around his neck and stands up, a strange set look on his face.*] I'm going to keep heart now, look up, rise. I'm going to lead. [*looking down at the baby*] I'm going to raise him up a light unto peoples. He be a new Moses, he bring the chillun out of bondage, out'n sin and ignorance.

[*Abe turns suddenly and goes to the bucket at the left, pours some water out in a pan and sets it on the bed. Then he bends down and lifts the baby in his hand. Muh Mack looks up, drying her eyes.*]

GOLDIE: What that, Abe? What that you doing?

ABE: [*dipping his hand in the water and holding the child aloft, his face lighted up in a beatific smile*] On this day I name you Douglass. You going to be same like him. Yeh, better. You going to be a light in darkness, a mighty man. [*He dips his hand into the water and sprinkles the child.*] I baptize you and consecrate you to the salvation of my peoples this day! Amen!

[*The women stare at him transfixed, caught out of themselves. Abe bends his head and stands with the child stretched before him as if making an offering to some god.*]

*Fade-out*

# SCENE 3

[*Winter of the same year. The old Quillie house, a Negro cabin of one bare room, now fitted up as a schoolhouse. At the left center is a squat rusty cast-iron stove, the pipe of which reels up a few feet and then topples over into an elbow to run through the wall. A box of pine knots rests on the floor by it. Four or five rough pine benches, worn slick by restless students, stretch nearly the length of the room, ending toward a small blackboard nailed to the wall in the rear center. Between the benches and the blackboard is the teacher's rickety table with a splint-bottomed chair behind it. A heavy dinner bell with a wooden handle is on the table. To the right rear is a small window, giving a glimpse of brown broom sedge stretching up a gentle hill, and beyond, a ragged field of stripped cornstalks, gray now and falling down in the rot of winter rains. To the left rear is a door opening to the outside.*

*The curtain rises on the empty room. Presently Abe comes in, carrying a tin lunch bucket and two or three books. He is wearing an old overcoat and a derby hat, both making some claims to a threadbare decency. He sets the bucket and books on the table and hangs his coat and hat on a nail in the wall at the right, then comes back to the stove, revealing himself dressed in baggy trousers worn slick with too much ironing, heavy short coat, cheap shirt, and celluloid collar with no tie. With his pocketknife he whittles some shavings from a pine knot and starts a fire in the stove. He looks at his watch, beats his hands together from cold, and stirs about the room, his brow wrinkled in thought and apparent worry. Again and again he goes to the door and stares out expectantly. Looking at his watch the second and third time, he takes up the bell and goes out and rings it.*]

ABE: [*shouting toward the empty fields*] Books! Books! Come in to books! [*He returns and sits down by the stove.*] No scholars in sight. [*with a sigh*] Ahem. [*He goes to the board and writes laboriously across the top —* "January 21. An idle brain is the devil's workshop." *While he is writing, three Negro Students come in carrying a bucket and a book or two each — a lazy slumbrous girl of eighteen or twenty, a stout thick-lipped youth about the same age, and a little serious-faced ragged boy of ten. Abe's face brightens at the sight of them.*] Good morning, chillun. Late. Everybody's a little late.
STUDENTS: [*standing uncertainly around the stove*] Good morning, Mr. Mack.
ABE: [*finishing his writing*] This will be our motto for today. [*Abe's speech has improved somewhat. He addresses the little boy.*] Read it, Eddie, out loud.
EDDIE: [*eagerly*] I can read it, Mr. Mack. [*In a slow and halting voice he reads.*]
   "An idle brain is the devil's workshop."
ABE: Good, fine. Can you read it, Neilly?

NEILLY: [*boldly*] Yes, suh, read it right off.

ABE: And how about you, Lanie?

LANIE: [*dropping her heavy-lidded eyes*] I can too.

[*She and Neilly look at each other with a fleeting smile over some secret between them. Eddie gazes up at them, his lips moving silently as if over something to be told which he dare not utter.*]

ABE: [*pulling out his watch*] Twenty minutes to nine. Where the other scholars? [*No one answers. Neilly gives the girl a quick look and turns deftly on his heel and kicks the stove, sticking out his lips in a low whistle.*] You see the Ragland chillun on the road, Lanie?

LANIE: [*enigmatically*] Yes, suh. I see 'em.

[*Abe goes to the door and rings his bell again.*]

ABE: Books! Books! Come in to books! [*He puts the bell on the table and stands pondering.*] How about the Matthews chillun?

NEILLY: Ain't coming!

ABE: They say so?

NEILLY: Yes, suh.

ABE: [*shortly*] Take your seats. We'll go on with our lessons if nobody else don't come. [*He turns to his table.*]

EDDIE: [*pulling excitedly at Lanie's dress*] Go on, ask him what he gwine do.

LANIE: [*snatching herself loose from him*] Shut up. Ain't my business.

ABE: Put your buckets up and take your seats and listen to the roll call. All the late ones catch it on the woodpile and sweeping up the schoolyard. [*eyeing them*] I said take your seat.

[*Eddie hurries to his seat.*]

NEILLY: Ain't gwine have no school, is we?

ABE: Hunh?

NEILLY: Ain't gwine be no more school.

[*Lanie giggles.*]

ABE: [*with a worried note in his voice*] Going to have school same as usual. Seem like all of 'em late though. Take your seats, time for the spelling lesson. Won't have the Scripture reading this morning.

NEILLY: The rest of 'em done quit school.

[*Lanie giggles again.*]

ABE: Stop that giggling and go to your seat.

[*Lanie moves to her seat sulkily.*]

EDDIE: [*in a high frightened quaver*] Mr. Mack, they all say the school ain't gwine run no more and they ain't coming.

ABE: How they hear it? I ain't heard it. [*No one answers.*] Where'd you folks get all this news, Neilly?

NEILLY: They was all talking it down the road. We wouldn't a-come neither, but Eddie there beg me and Lanie so hard to come with him. Ain't no more folks coming though.

ABE: [*hitting the table with his fist*] Something up. They got to show me before I quit, they got to show me. Put up your buckets and things, we're going to have school. [*They reluctantly set down their buckets near the wall and stand waiting.*] Take your seats, I say, and listen to your name. [*He pulls out a cheap memorandum book and begins calling the roll.*] Lanie Horton.

LANIE: Present. [*She looks around at the bare seats and gives her senseless giggle.*]

ABE: Jay Gool Jones, absent; 'Ona May Jordan, absent; Jane Matthews, absent; Sister Matthews, absent; Jennie McAllister, absent; Neilly McNeill.

NEILLY: Present. [*He smiles at Lanie.*]

ABE: Arthur Ragland, absent. Didn't 'spect him back nohow. Dora Ragland, absent; Nora Ragland, absent; Eddie Williams.

EDDIE: Present.

[*Abe sits drumming on the table and staring before him. The students twist about on their seats in embarrassment.*]

ABE: [*roughly*] Spelling lesson! [*The three move out and stand in line before him.*] How many of you been over it at least four times?

EDDIE: [*raising his hand*] I been over it nine times forward and six backward.

ABE: You, Neilly?

NEILLY: I been over it once and part twice, Mr. Mack.

ABE: Lanie?

LANIE: I dunno hardly.

ABE: Have you studied it any?

LANIE: [*pouting*] I done lost my book somewhere.

ABE: And you were supposed to be head today. You'n Neilly can clean up the paper and sweep around the well at recess. Let's see your book, Eddie. [*Eddie hands him his book.*] Eddie, you got a head-mark yesterday, so you foot today. [*opening the book*] The first word is chew, chew like vittles, Lanie, chew.

LANIE: C-c — c-u, chew.

ABE: One more trial.

LANIE: [*pondering a long while*] I can't spell that.

ABE: Yes, you can. Try it.

LANIE: C-h-u, chew.

ABE: Next.

NEILLY: [*smiling ruefully*] Too hard for me. Just well pass on.

ABE: [*working his jaws up and down*] Watch me work my jaws. That's chew, chewing. Spell at it, Neilly, chew.

NEILLY: [*scratching his head and nervously boring the floor with the toe of his shoe*] Can't do it, can't form no letters in my head.

ABE: I'll have to pass it on then.

NEILLY: [*taking a hopeless shot at it*] S-s — s-u, chew. No, that wrong. I seed that word on the page, but can't remember it now. I can't spell it. Give it to Eddie, he can.

ABE: All right, Eddie.

EDDIE: C-h-e-w, chew. [*He darts around Neilly and Lanie and stands triumphantly at the head of the class.*]

ABE: I'm going to send you back to your seats to study twenty minutes. Then come back here and don't make no such mess of it. I'll put the writing lesson up while you study. [*They go to their seats.*] Lanie, you look with Eddie in his book. [*He turns to the board and begins to write down the copy models. As he writes, the students mumble over their words in a drone. Neilly and Lanie begin talking to each other in low whispers. Eddie is lost in his book. Lanie suddenly giggles out loud, and Abe turns quickly from his board.*] Heigh, you, Lanie, stand up in that corner over there. School isn't out yet.

LANIE: I ain't done nothing. [*half audibly*] "Isn't!"

ABE: Don't talk back. Stand in the corner with your face to the wall. Here, Eddie, you read in this reader and let her have your book.

[*Lanie creeps over to the corner and mouths over her lesson. Abe finishes his apothegm — "A wise man will rise with the sun, or before it." He is finishing another — "Wise children will imitate the manner of polite people," when there is a stir at the door and Puny Avery comes in, swallowed up in a teamster's coat and carrying a long blacksnake whip in his hand.*]

PUNY: Good morning.

ABE: Good morning, Mr. Avery.

[*At the appellation of "Mister" Puny stuffs his cap against his mouth to hide a grin.*]

PUNY: How you come on, Mr. McCranie? Can I warm my hands a minute? Freezing cold sitting on that wagon seat. [*He moves up to the stove and stretches his hands above it.*]

ABE: Help yourself. Be a snow before night, I believe.

PUNY: Yeh, or — look like it.

[*Puny warms himself, and Abe sits at the table watching him questioningly. Now and then his gaze drops upon the whip.*]

ABE: Hauling lumber over the river?

PUNY: Is that. [*looking at Lanie in the corner*] What she do?

ABE: Misbehaved.

PUNY: Seem like your school kinder thin. [*Abe says nothing.*] Been getting thinner every since Colonel died last fall, ain't it?

ABE: Been dropping off some since then.

PUNY: Where all the rest of the scholars?

ABE: Haven't showed up yet.

PUNY: Uhm.

ABE: Why you want to know, might I ask?

PUNY: [*authoritatively*] Already know. And for your own good I come by to tell you and to bring you a message.

ABE: [*looking at him intently and then waving his hand at the three students*] You chillun can go out and have recess now. Mr. Avery wants to see me on a little business. [*Lanie and Neilly get their coats and walk out. Eddie remains crouched in his seat, unconscious of his surroundings.*] What message you got for me?

PUNY: You just well quit the school business right here and now. They ain't gwine send to you no more.

ABE: What's the trouble?

PUNY: Trouble! You gone and done it, you has, when you beat Will Ragland's boy yesterday. Will so mad he can kill you.

ABE: [*his anger rising in his voice*] Needn't think I'm scared of him.

PUNY: I know you ain't. But Will went around last night and got everybody to say they weren't gwine send to you no more.

ABE: [*angrily*] I had a right to beat him. I couldn't make him work no other way, and besides he told a lie to me. Said he didn't eat poor little Sis Matthews' dinner. Several of 'em seen him do it.

PUNY: Can't help it. You beat him so Will done gone to the sheriff to get out papers for you.

ABE: [*starting out of his chair*] Going to have me arrested?

PUNY: He is that. And more, I reckon. And my advice to you is to get from here. As a member of the school board I say, better leave.

ABE: He think he can run me away?

PUNY: Don't know what he think. Know I wouldn't like to lie in no white man's jailhouse, that's me.

ABE: The other members of the board know about it?

PUNY: Us had a meeting last night.

ABE: What they say?

PUNY: [*fumbling in his pockets*] They all side with Will, account of the beating and account of that speech you make in church last Sunday.

ABE: Were Mr. Lonnie there?

PUNY: He there and he send this here writing to you.

[*Puny pulls a note from his pocket and hands it to Abe, who opens it excitedly.*]

ABE: [*clenching his fist*] That man say here — God — he say the board done all decided the school got to stop. [*He tears the note to pieces and throws it toward the stove.*] He say there he know a good job in Raleigh at public work he can get me. [*bitterly*] Say I do better at that than farming or school. [*Pacing the floor, he throws his hand above his head.*] Nanh-anh-suh, I sets a oath on high. I ain't going let 'em run me off. They can't scare me. They can't run me off like I stole something. [*He turns on Puny with blazing eyes, and Eddie now watches him, terrified.*] Why you all vote that way? Whyn't you stand up and vote for me? You know I'm trying to do right. You weak, coward, no backbone.

PUNY: [*backing toward the door*] I ain't got nothing against you, Abe. Why you 'buse me?

ABE: Get out of here. All of you down on me. That speech was so. It was right. That beating was right. [*crying out*] They can't run me. You can't run me. I fight 'em. I stay here. Let 'em put me in the jail. I last till the jail rot down. [*He moves menacingly toward Puny who flees through the door and slams it after him.*] I come through their bars, their iron won't hold me. I'll get there, I'll come. My flesh will be as tough as their iron! [*He goes to the table and picks up his books. He opens the Bible and stands thinking. Dropping into his chair, he sits with his elbow on the table and his chin in his hand, gazing into the distance. The anger and bitterness gradually pass from his face.*] That man's talk, proud. Can't push through without help — [*putting his hand on the Bible*] without help from up there. [*He bows his head on the table. Eddie begins to sob and, leaving his seat timidly, approaches Abe's bent form, gulping and wiping his nose and eyes with his sleeve. Abe looks up and puts his arm around him.*] Son, this here's the last of this school. But we can't stop, we got to keep on. [*Eddie leans his head against him, his sobs increasing.*] Got to keep studying, got to keep climbing. [*After a moment he stands up and writes across the board, "This school is stopped for a while." Lanie and Neilly come inquiringly in.*] Chillun, ain't going to be any more school till maybe next year. You can go home. [*Lanie giggles and Neilly looks at him with familiar condescension.*] But I wants to dismiss with a word of prayer. [*At a sign from him, Eddie falls on his knees by the table. Abe gets down at his chair.*] Our Father, where two or three is gathered — [*Neilly and Lanie look at him, pick up their buckets, and scurry out giggling and laughing loudly. Abe springs to his feet, his face blank with astonishment. He calls after them furiously.*] Heigh, heigh, you! [*They are heard going off, their sharp laughter softening in the distance.*]

*Fade-out*


## SCENE 4

[*Fifteen years later. A room in the poverty-stricken Negro section of Durham, North Carolina. When the curtain rises, Goldie is washing at a tub placed on a goods box at the left of the room. Muh Mack is seated at the fireplace at the right, bent under a slat bonnet and dozing. Pots and pans are piled around the hearth and a kettle is singing on the fire. Several garments are hanging on chairs before the fire, drying.*

*To the left rear is a bed with a pile of rough-dried clothes on it. A door at the center rear leads into another room. To the right of the door is a low chest with books and dishes upon it. At the right front by the chimney is a small window letting in the sickly light of a dying winter day. In the center of the room is a small eating-table covered with a greasy spotted oilcloth.*

*Goldie washes heavily at the tub, her body bent and disfigured with the years of toil and poverty and the violence of childbirth. Her movements are slow, oxlike, and in her eyes now and then comes a sort of vacant look as if some deadening disease has had its way within her brain, or as if trouble and worry have hardened her beyond the possibility of enthusiasm or grief any more. Between her eyes a deep line has furrowed itself, a line often found on the foreheads of those who think a great deal or those who are forgetting how to think at all. And her mouth has long ago fastened itself into a drawn anguished questioning that has no ease-*

*ful answer in the world. She washes away at the tub, the garment making a kind of flopping sound against the board. After a moment she calls to Muh Mack.*]

GOLDIE. Getting near about day-down, Muh Mack. Time to start supper.

MUH MACK: [*whom age and poverty have made meaner than before*] Yeh, yeh, it is, and I got to get it, I reckon.

GOLDIE: [*making an effort to hurry*] Yeh, Mis' Duke got to have her clothes tomorrow, I done said.

MUH MACK: [*getting slowly to her feet*] What I gwine cook?

GOLDIE: Make some corn bread, and there's a little piece of Baltimore meat in the chest. [*Muh Mack arranges her pan on the fire with much grumbling and growling, and goes over to the chest.*]

MUH MACK: [*knocking the pile of books off with a bang*] Here them old books of Abe's piled right in the way. I'm a mind to burn 'em up. Always where they ain't got no business.

GOLDIE: [*abstractedly*] Yeh, yeh. Always a mind to burn 'em.

MUH MACK: [*opening the chest and pulling out a small piece of white meat*] Hunh, look at this, will you? Ain't more'n enough to fill my old hollow tooth. Can't us get something else for supper? I et that old meat and corn bread till it makes me heave to look at it.

GOLDIE: That all they is.

MUH MACK: That won't make a mouthful for Abe. What we gwine eat, I ask you?

GOLDIE: Abe won't eat it nohow, and I don't want nothing. You'n Douglass can eat it.

MUH MACK: Both of you gwine die if you don't eat. That Abe been living off'n coffee and bread two weeks now. No wonder he look like a shadow and can't half do his work.

GOLDIE: Can't eat when you ain't got it.

MUH MACK: Well, starving ain't gwine give you strength to get no more. How you gwine keep washing for folks and you don't eat?

GOLDIE: [*bowing her head in weariness over the tub, her voice rising with sudden shrillness*] Oh, Lord God in heaven, I don't know!

MUH MACK: Calling on God ain't gwine help you get no supper either. [*throwing the meat back into the chest and slamming the lid*] Well, I won't cook that old mess. I'll sit right here by this fire and starve with you and Abe.

GOLDIE: [*drying her hands on her apron*] I got just one more fifty-cent piece in that pocketbook. I'll get it and run out and buy some pork then. Poor Abe got to live somehow. [*She goes out at the rear and returns immediately holding an empty ragged purse in her hand.*] Where my half dollar? Where is it?

MUH MACK: How do I know?

GOLDIE: [*sitting down and rocking back and forth*] Somebody stole it. [*turning upon Muh Mack*] You done given it to that Douglass.

MUH MACK: Ain't.

GOLDIE: Yeh, you has, you has.

MUH MACK: [*beating the floor with her foot*] Ain't, I tell you.

GOLDIE: [*staggering to her feet*] And he off somewheres spending it for ice cream and mess.

MUH MACK: Don't care if I did. Poor boy do without all the time.

GOLDIE: [*falling on the tub with renewed vigor*] Can't cry now!

MUH MACK: Go on down there and get that man to let you have something on a credit. You can pay him tomorrow when Mis' Duke pay you.

GOLDIE: He done said he ain't gwine let us have no more without the money.

MUH MACK: Maybe Abe fetch something when he come.

GOLDIE: How can he and they don't pay him off till tomorrow evening?

MUH MACK: [*suddenly crying out with a whimper*] I wants to go back home. I wants to go back home. Mr. Lonnie won't let us starve.

GOLDIE: I been wanting to go back for fifteen year, but Abe's gwine die 'fore he go back.

MUH MACK: [*beating her hands together in her lap*] Crazy, crazy! He the biggest fool in the whole world. He getting down lower every day. Getting sick worse all the time. Oh, me, what'll become of us all!

GOLDIE: [*hopelessly*] The Lord maybe'll provide.

MUH MACK: [*snorting*] Hunh, he mought. He ain't gwine provide nothing less'n us do something. [*her voice falling into a sort of hysterical whine*] Here I is all laid up with rheumatiz and can't see how to travel no more and about to starve. Starve, hear me!

GOLDIE: [*dropping into her chair again*] You ain't the only one.

MUH MACK: Reckon I knows it. But that don't keep my stomach from cutting up.

GOLDIE: We doing the best we can by you.

MUH MACK: [*somewhat softened*] I knows it, child, but that Abe, that Abe, I say! He the trouble at the bottom of it all.

GOLDIE: Needn't keep talking about Abe. Why don't you say that to his face? He doing the best he can.

MUH MACK: [*her anger rising*] I will tell him. There you sit, Goldie McCranie, and say that, after he done drug you from pillar to post for fifteen year.

Doing the best he can! He ain't nothing, just worse'n nothing! He just a plumb fool. But my sister Caroline were a fool before him. That's how come she mammied him into this world the way she done.

GOLDIE: Stop that. He's sick, been sick a long time, poor fellow, and he keeps trying.

MUH MACK: Sick! He weren't sick back there when he got into court and lost all his land trying to get them lawyers to keep him out'n jail, and he beat that Will Ragland's boy half to death. [*Goldie bows her head in her hands, swaying from side to side.*] The devil in him! That's what. And were he sick, and he cutting up a rust in Raleigh and the white folks running him out'n there? It was old Scratch in him there too, I tells you.

GOLDIE: [*wretchedly*] They didn't treat him right over there.

MUH MACK: Hunh. No, they didn't. And they didn't treat him right in Greensboro, did they? Same old tale there, getting in a row with somebody and have to leave. He's mean, mean like something mad at the world.

GOLDIE: [*tossing her head about her*] I dunno, I dunno. He ought to never married me and got tied down. Seem like things all go wrong, crosswise for him.

MUH MACK: [*staring at her*] Hunh. Things'll be crosswise with him till they straighten him out in the grave. Them's my gospel words. [*blowing her nose in her skirt and half weeping*] If all that shooting and killing in Wilmington wouldn't make him do better, nothing in God's world can.

GOLDIE: [*moaning*] Stop that talking. I can't bear it.

MUH MACK: That's just what you ought to stop doing, stop bearing it. Gather up your duds and take me'n Douglass and whop off'n leave him, that's what you ought to do.

GOLDIE: [*beating herself with her fist*] I ain't. I ain't. I gwine stay by him.

MUH MACK: 'Course you gwine stay by him — and starve too. For that's what you'll do. What he don't spend on medicine he do on them old lodges and such and books and newspapers. And gets turned out'n every one of 'em for his speeches and wild talk, he do. [*with grim satisfaction*] Shoveling that coal down at the powerhouse reckon'll hold him for a while. [*with an afterthought*] Hold him down till somebody crack his head with a shovel and turn him off. [*stirring the fire and then folding up her hands*] I done said my say-so now. Do no good, 'cause you so wrapped up in the fool.

GOLDIE: [*flaring out*] No, it won't do no good. I gwine stick by him. [*rising and turning to her work again*] They ain't never done him right. They all been down on him from the first.

MUH MACK: [*shrilly*] And'll be till the last. Other colored folks make a living for their family. Why don't he? Always got his eyes on something else.

GOLDIE: He gwine be a big man yet. Them others do the dirty work and take what they can get. They the low-down trash. [*her voice trembling*] He gwine get him a big school some these days.

MUH MACK: [*laughing scornfully*] Hee-hee—hee. Listen at her. He can't teach nothing. The colored teachers round here know more in a minute than Abe do in a week. They been to college at Raleigh and Greensboro and no telling where. And they got some sense besides their learning. That little Eddie Williams has. He done gone through that Shaw school in Raleigh and is off doing big work. Why couldn't Abe do something like that! [*pulling a walking stick from the chimney corner*] I gwine go down to Liza's and ax her to give me some supper. [*She groans and creaks to her feet.*]

GOLDIE: Wait'll Douglass come from school and I'll get him to go down to the corner and get some meat from that man — maybe.

MUH MACK: Done past time for Douglass to be here. Mought not come till late.

GOLDIE: [*drying her hands again and patting her hair*] I'll go then. You put the kettle on for some coffee and set the table and I'll be right back. [*Far off a muffled whistle blows.*] There's the powerhouse whistle. Abe be here soon. Light the lamp. [*She goes out.*]

MUH MACK: [*somewhat mollified, calling after her*] All right — and you beg that meat man — keep begging till he have to give in.

[*Muh Mack puts her stick back in the corner, fills the kettle and stirs stiffly about her, bringing plates to the table and laying out the knives and forks. She hobbles into the room at the rear and returns with a lamp without any chimney, which she lights at the fireplace and places on the table. While she is engaged in making coffee over the fire, Douglass strolls in. He is a young Negro in short trousers, fifteen or sixteen years old, black as Muh Mack and with something of a wild and worthless spirit already beginning to show in his face. He carries two ragged books under his arm.*]

DOUGLASS: [*dropping the books by the door and kicking them near the chest*] Heigh!

MUH MACK: [*jumping*] Who? Hee-hee, you scared me, honey. [*She stands up and looks at him indulgently.*] Where you been so late?

DOUGLASS: Oh, round and about. Stopped by the hot-dog stand a while, chewing the rag with some fellows.

MUH MACK: How many them sausage things you eat?

DOUGLASS: Dunno. Several.

MUH MACK: [*leaning forward, her eyes shining with anticipation*] What you fotch me to eat?

DOUGLASS: I wanted to bring you something, but —

MUH MACK: You mean you ain't brung me nothing with that fifty cents?

DOUGLASS: I fool-like matched with some of 'em down there and had to set 'em up.

MUH MACK: And I so hungry my stomach just hollering.

DOUGLASS: [*nonchalantly*] I can't help it.

MUH MACK: [*threateningly*] I gwine tell your daddy on you.

DOUGLASS: [*looking at her*] Hunh, you better not. Do and I won't play nary piece for you in — in two weeks maybe.

MUH MACK: [*turning to her cooking*] Your muh know about it.

DOUGLASS: Why you tell her?

MUH MACK: She guessed at it. She knowed you tuk that money soon's she found it gone.

DOUGLASS: [*alarmed*] Pap don't know, do he?

MUH MACK: Not yet. He ain't come from work. [*Douglass turns back into the room at the rear and reappears with a guitar. Sitting down, wonderfully at ease, he begins strumming.*] Lord, Lord, honey give us a piece 'fore your daddy come. [*He falls to playing and Muh Mack begins to pat the floor and skip happily now and then as she moves about the fireplace.*] Hee-hee — that's better'n eating.

DOUGLASS: [*hugging up the "box" and throwing back his head in abandon*] Hee-hee — ain't it though! [*He turns and scowls at the books lying on the floor and begins singing to them.*]
Them old books [*strum, strum*]
Lying in the corner. [*strum, strum*]
Them old books [*strum, strum*]
Lying in the corner — [*strum, strum*]
Lie there, babies, lie there!
Hee-hee — Muh Mack, I can make music right out'n my head. [*He goes on throwing his fingers across the strings.*]

MUH MACK: You can, honey, you surely can.

[*Muh Mack sits listening happily. Douglass wraps himself over the guitar, his fingers popping up and down the neck of the instrument with marvelous dexterity. His bowed head begins to weave about him rhythmically as he bursts into snatches of song.*]

DOUGLASS: [*singing*]
Look down, look down that lonesome road,
    The hacks all dead in line.

Some give a nickel, some give a dime
To bury this poor body of mine.

MUH MACK: [*staring at him*] I declare! I declare! Listen at that child.

DOUGLASS: Never mind, never mind me. [*modulating with amazing swiftness from key to key*] And there was poor Brady, poor old Brady.

MUH MACK: Yeh, Brady, they laid him down to die.

DOUGLASS: [*singing*]

Oh, Brady, Brady, you know you done me wrong,
You come in when the game was a-going on!
And they laid poor Brady down.
Womens in Georgy they heard the news,
Walking about in their little red shoes,
They glad, they glad poor Brady dead.
When I close my eyes to catch a little sleep,
Poor old Brady about my bed do creep,
One more, just one more rounder gone.

[*While Douglass is singing and playing, Abe comes in suddenly at the rear dragging a heavy wooden box in one hand and carrying a dinner pail in the other. He is dirty and begrimed with coal dust.*]

ABE: [*shouting*] Put up that box! [*Douglass bounds out of his chair as if shot and backs away from him.*] Put down that damn guitar, you good-for-nothing!

[*Abe hangs his cap and dinner pail on a nail by the door and comes heavily across to the fire. His face is haggard and old and his shoulders have grown humped with the going of time. Douglass slips out with his guitar and presently creeps in and sits stealthily on the chest. Abe lays the goods box on the floor and breaks it up and places pieces of it on the fire. Then he sits down and stretches out his feet and stares moodily before him. Muh Mack hurries around making bread, frying the hated side meat, and arranging the table.*]

MUH MACK: [*tremulously*] How you feeling? You come quick after the whistle —

ABE: Ah, feel like I'll stifle in here. [*He strikes his breast once and then follows it with a fury of savage blows.*] Can't get no wind down in that boiler house. [*He drags his hand wearily across his brow and shakes his head as if clearing his eyes of a fog.*] Where's Goldie?

MUH MACK: Gone out to the corner to beg some meat. Time she back.

ABE: How long 'fore supper?

MUH MACK: Soon's she gets back and we can cook the meat — if they is meat.

ABE: [*pulling off his shoes and setting them in the corner*] I'm going to lie down a minute till my head clears up. Feel like it'll blow off at the top. [*Grasping his chair, he staggers to his feet and goes across the room. At the door he stops and looks down at Douglass.*] I'm going to tend to you in a little bit.

[*Douglass quails before him. Abe goes out and slams the door.*]

MUH MACK: What the name of God ail him now? Worse'n ever.

DOUGLASS: [*whimpering*] He gonna beat me! He'll kill me.

[*The bed is heard creaking in the rear room as Abe lies down.*]

MUH MACK: What'n the world for? [*She stands tapping her hands together helplessly.*]

DOUGLASS: He done heared sump'n on me. Oh, he gonna beat me to death.

[*Abe is heard turning in his bed again, and he immediately appears in the door.*]

ABE: Shut up that whimpering. Get over there and start washing on them clothes for your poor mammy. [*Douglass darts over and begins rubbing at the board and sniffling.*] Dry up, I tell you. [*Abe turns back to his bed.*]

MUH MACK: [*sitting to the fire and rocking back and forth in her anxiety*] Oh, Lord—Lord!

[*She hides her head in her skirt grumbling and moaning. Presently Goldie comes in.*]

GOLDIE: [*coming over to the tub*] Look out, son, lemme get at 'em. [*She falls to washing feverishly.*]

MUH MACK: [*looking up*] Where that meat, Goldie?

GOLDIE: That man look at me and laugh—he laugh. [*Turning angrily toward Douglass.*] You went and—

MUH MACK: [*throwing out her hand in alarm*] Nanh, nanh, Goldie. [*Lowering her voice and nodding to the rear.*] Abe in there. He find out about that, he kill the boy. Done say he gwine beat him for sump'n or other.

GOLDIE: When he come?

MUH MACK: He just this minute got here.

GOLDIE: [*in alarm*] He worse off, I bet. [*She hurries into the room and is heard talking softly and kindly to Abe. He answers her with indistinct growls. In a moment Goldie returns.*] Put what you got on the table and let's eat. [*She goes on with her washing.*] Abe ain't feeling well. Have to eat what he can, I reckon.

[*Muh Mack puts the bread, coffee, and meat on the table.*]

MUH MACK: Come on, you all.

GOLDIE: Come on in, Abe. [*Abe enters in his undershirt and trousers.*] Go on and eat. I don't want nothing.

ABE: [*almost falling in his chair*] Come on and set whether you can or not. [*Goldie takes her place at the table.*] Come on, Douglass.

DOUGLASS: I don't want nothing either.

[*Muh Mack draws up her chair.*]

ABE: Don't make no difference. I said come on. [*Douglass gets a chair and takes his place. Abe surveys the fare before him.*] This all you got for a working man and he sick?

GOLDIE: I didn't have no money, and— [*She gulps and drops her head to hide the tears.*]

ABE: [*kindly, as he reaches out and touches her shoulder*] Never mind, honey child. [*He closes his eyes with weariness and sits brooding. Presently he raises his head.*] Well, never you mind, I ain't hungry. [*looking at her sadly*] But you must be plumb wore out with all that washing and all. [*dropping his head*] Let's have the blessing. Oh, Lord, we thank Thee for what we have before us. Make us truly thankful for all Thy gifts and save us at last, we humbly beg, for Christ's sake, Amen! [*After the blessing Goldie still keeps her head bowed, her shoulders heaving with repressed sobs. Muh Mack pours out the coffee and hands it round. Abe calls to Goldie.*] Come on eat sump'n, Goldie, you feel better, you git your strength back. Drink some this coffee.

[*Goldie, bursting into wild sobs, goes and sits by the fire.*]

ABE: What's the matter, child?

MUH MACK: She done worked to death and nothing to work on, that's what.

ABE: [*drinking down a cup of steaming coffee at a gulp*] Pour me some more of that! [*Goldie's sobs gradually die away.*] Come on, honey, don't cry no more!

[*Goldie stands up and looks toward the table with anguished face.*]

GOLDIE: Abe, Abe, honey babe, what us gwine do? [*She buries her face in her hands.*]

ABE: You done heared sump'n, ain't you?

GOLDIE: Yeh, yeh, Liza told me. Jim done come from the powerhouse and told her.

ABE: [*dully*] Never mind. Come on, drink some coffee. We talk about that directly. I got sump'n else to tell you too.

MUH MACK: [*staring at him in fear*] What that happen at the powerhouse?

ABE: I tell you when I get good and ready. Come on, Goldie child. [*Goldie wipes her eyes and returns to the table to drink her coffee.*] Before we gets on what happened with me, I got a question to ax this young gentleman. [*looking across at Douglass*] Why don't you eat?

DOUGLASS: [*falteringly*] I ain't hungry.

ABE: Try and see do you want anything.

DOUGLASS: I can't eat nothing.

ABE: How come?

DOUGLASS: I just don't want nothing.

ABE: [*bitterly*] I reckon I know how come. This evening I pass on the other side of the street and see you down there at that drink stand setting up them worthless fellows with your mammy's good money. [*savagely*] Oh, yeh, I know that's where you got it. I see you last night watching her put it away.

GOLDIE: Please don't have no more row, Abe.

ABE: I ain't going to beat him for that, nunh-unh. Sump'n else he's going to catch it for. [*raging out*] The teacher stop me on the street and tell me you doing worse'n ever in your books and she done had to put you back in the third reader. [*Swallowing another cup of coffee down with a hunk of bread, he stands up and stares into the distance.*] Here we done labor and sweat for you, fix for you to rise up and be sump'n. Eight year you been going to school and you won't work, you won't learn. [*He strikes the table with his fist, and the lamp flickers and almost goes out.*] You ain't no good. Once I thought you going go on, climb, rise high, and lead. [*He seizes Douglass by the collar and, lifting him from the floor, shakes him like a rag.*]

DOUGLASS: [*sputtering and choking*] Pap, Papa!

MUH MACK: [*shrieking in terror*] Stop that! You kill him!

ABE: I teach you to fool with low-down trash! I get you out'n them trifling ways or I'll break your back in two. [*He sits down and jerks the boy across his knee and begins beating him blindly.*] I name you for a great man, a man what stand high like the sun, and you turn out to be the lowest of the low! Change your name, that's what you better do. [*With a cuff on the cheek he hurls him across the room, where Douglass falls sobbing and wailing on the floor.*] Shut that fuss up! [*Douglass' sobs gradually cease. Goldie starts toward him, but Abe jerks her back.*] Let him lie there, the skunk and coward.

[*Goldie turns despairingly to her washing again. Abe moves to the fire and sits down, pulling a wrinkled newspaper out of his pocket, while Muh Mack rocks and slobbers and moans.*]

MUH MACK: You need the law on you, Abe McCranie. You beat that poor baby—

ABE: Shut up! You what ruin him. He takes after you and your trifling.

MUH MACK: Oh, I gwine leave here, find me another place to stay.

ABE: We all got to get another place to stay.

GOLDIE: Let's go back home, Abe! Let's go back.

MUH MACK: Have we got to leave 'cause of what you done down at the powerhouse? [*wringing her hands*] What you do down there? Oh, Lord!

ABE: Ain't no use waking up the neighborhood with your yelling. I didn't do nothing but stand up for my rights. A white man sass me and I sass back at him. And a crowd of 'em run me off. Won't be able to get no other job in this town, God damn it! [*standing up and shaking his fist*] God damn the people in this town! Them with their tobacco warehouses, and cotton mills, and money in the bank you couldn't handle with a shovel!

MUH MACK: Let's go back home. The Colonel fix it in his will so us could have a place to come back to. Mr. Lonnie'll rent us some land.

GOLDIE: [*coming over to Abe's chair and dropping on her knees beside him*] Abe, Abe, let's go back. Please do. Let's go back where we growed up. Ain't no home for us in no town. We got to get back to the country. That's where we belong. [*She lays her head in his lap.*]

ABE: [*looking down at her tenderly*] Yeh, yeh, honey. We is going back. After all these years I knows now the town ain't no place for us. Fifteen year we been trying to make it and couldn't. That's what I was going to tell you. All the signs been against us. I ought to knowed it after three or four years. Back home the place for us. Back in our own country. [*staring before him and a smile suddenly sweetening the hardness of his face*] We go back there and take a new start. We going to build up on a new foundation. Took all these years to show me. [*his voice rising in nervous exultation*] There's where my work is cut out to be. It come to me this evening while I walked on the street. [*standing up*] Seem like sump'n spoke to me and said "Go back down on the Cape Fear River." I heared it plain like a voice talking. "These streets and these peoples ain't your peoples. Your'n is the kind what works and labors with the earth and the sun. Them who knows the earth and the fullness thereof. There's where your harvest is to be." And then when I come face to face with the ruining of my boy, in my anger I see the way clear. We going back, we going back. And there at last I knows I'm going to build up and lead! And my boy going to be a man. [*looking at Douglass with a hint of pleadingness*] Ain't it so?

[*But Douglass only stares at him coldly.*]

GOLDIE: [*looking up at him*] I knows you will. I feel it just the way you do. I keep telling Muh Mack some day you gwine get there.

ABE: [*gazing down at her*] These years all been sent for our trial, ain't they, honey?

GOLDIE: Yeh, yeh, we been tried all for a purpose.

ABE: And now we ready, ain't we, honey?

GOLDIE: We ready to go back and start all over.

MUH MACK: [*repeating uncertainly*] To start all over.

ABE: To build us a monument from generation unto generation.

GOLDIE: [*softly, the tears pouring from her eyes*] Yeh, yeh.

ABE: And all this sin and tribulation and sorrow will be forgot, passed away, wiped out till the judgment, won't it, child?

GOLDIE: It will, oh, I knows it will. We done suffered our share and Old Master gwine be good to us now.

ABE: Good! Yeh, good! [*He sits with bowed head.*]

*Fade-out*

## SCENE 5

[*Three years later. The same as Scene 2, in Abe's cabin on the McCranie farm. The room shows some sign of improvement over its former state. There is a lambrequin of crepe paper on the mantel, a wooden clock, and at the right a home-fashioned bookcase with books and magazines. On the rear wall is the same colored print with the caption of the rising slave.*

*Abe is seated at a table near the front, writing by a lighted lamp. He is better dressed and more alert than formerly. Farther back and to the left of the fireplace sits Muh Mack dozing and quarreling in her rocking chair. Her head and face are hid under the same slat bonnet, and a dirty pink "fascinator" is draped over her bony shoulders. Her huge snuff brush protrudes from her lips and now and then describes a sort of waving motion when she moves her jaws in sleep. Between her knees she clasps her walking stick.*

*Through the window at the rear come bright streaks from the orange afterglow of the west. The November sun has set and the sky near the horizon is fading into a deep gloom under an approaching cloudiness. In the oaks outside the house the sparrows going to roost pour out a flooding medley of sharp calls resembling the heavy dripping of rain from eaves. For a moment Abe continues his writing and then lays down his pencil and replenishes the fire. He returns to his chair and sits drumming absently on the table.*]

ABE: When's Goldie coming back, Muh Mack? [*His speech is gentle and more cultivated.*]
MUH MACK: [*starting out of her sleep*] What you say?
ABE: When Goldie coming back from Mr. Lonnie's?
MUH MACK: When she get done of that washing and ironing, poor thing.
ABE: Seem like it's time she was back.
MUH MACK: What you care about her and you sitting there all day working at that old speech mess.
ABE: You going to cook any supper?
MUH MACK: Supper! You ax that and know I can't get out'n my chair with the stiffness and misery. You'll have to eat cold.
ABE: I've done looked. Ain't nothing cold.
MUH MACK: Then you'll have to wait till she come. Poor, poor thing, with all her trouble wonder she able to cook or work or do anything.

[*She turns to her snoozing, and Abe picks up his pencil again and gnaws at it as he works on his speech. Soon he stops and begins tapping on the table.*]

ABE: What trouble she got now?
MUH MACK: [*astounded*] You ax that and you fixing to bring more trouble on us with your schooling and mess. And with Mr. Lonnie down on you about the crop again. Lord, Lord! And who that won't let his own poor boy put foot in the home? Keep him driv' off like a homeless dog. [*She wipes her eyes with a dirty rag.*]
ABE: You whine, but this time they won't be no failing. The school is going through. Then I can talk to Mr. Lonnie. Six men done already promised a thousand dollars. Can't fail this time, no, suh.
MUH MACK: You don't deserve nothing, and won't let poor Douglass come back to see his mammy—and his old auntie that loves him. [*brightly*] Them men maybe ain't promised. They talking.
ABE: [*sharply*] I know—you needn't say another word about it. [*concerned with the speech*] And that Douglass—I won't let him darken my door.

[*Muh Mack stirs from her doze and sniffles into her rag, wiping the rheumy tears from her eyes. Abe turns to his writing. He writes more and more rapidly as he nears the end. Presently he throws down his pencil and stretches his arms back of his head with a weary yawn. He looks toward Muh Mack and speaks exultantly.*]

ABE: That's the best I've ever done. They can't go against that, they can't this time.

MUH MACK: [*sleepily, rubbing her eyes and speaking coldly*] Thank God you's finished your speech and'll soon be out'n my sight and I can get a little nap.

ABE: [*not noticing her*] That crowd's going to listen to me tonight.

MUH MACK: Maybe they will, but you's talked your life away, and it ain't come to nothing.

ABE: [*looking at the speech*] I've done my best this time. All I got from books and experience is there, and the truth's in it. [*He gathers the closely written sheets together.*] I tell 'em — [*He turns to his speech and begins to read as he rises from his chair.*] I say, "Ladies and gentlemen — [*He does not notice the movement of disgust Muh Mack makes as she turns away from him.*] this night is going to mean much in the lives of each and every one of us, big and little."

MUH MACK: Hit won't if they treats they chillun like you treats your one.

ABE: [*hurrying on*] "It marks the founding of the Cape Fear Training School, an institution that will one day be a light to other institutions around and about. It is to be our aim here, with the few teachers and facilities we can provide, to offer education to the colored children amongst us and offer it cheap. [*He turns toward Muh Mack and speaks with more spirit, as if his audience were directly before him. But she turns her back to him and blinks at the fire.*] Looking over the country, ladies and gentlemen, we see ten million souls striving in slavery, yea, slavery, brethren, the slavery of ignorance. And ignorance means being oppressed, both by yourselves and by others — hewers of wood and drawers of water." [*He picks up his pencil and crosses out a word.*]

MUH MACK: [*sarcastically*] They hain't nobody been in slavery since the surrender. If they is, how come? And I reckon the hewers of wood and the drawers of water is about free as anybody.

ABE: [*continuing his speech without noticing her*] "Ignorance means sin, and sin means destruction, destruction before the law and destruction in a man's own heart. The Negro will rise when his character is of the nature to cause him to rise — for on that the future of the race depends, and that character is mostly to be built by education, for it cannot exist in ignorance. Let me repeat again, ladies and gentlemen. We want our children and our grandchildren to march on toward full lives and noble characters, and that has got to come, I say, by education. We have no other way. We got to live and learn — and think, that's it. [*He strides in front of the old woman, who has dozed off again under his eloquence. She raises her head with a jerk when he thunders at her.*] A few short years ago the white man's power covered us like the night. Through war and destruction we was freed. But it was freedom of the body and not freedom of the mind. And what is freedom of the body without freedom of the mind? It means nothing. It don't exist. [*throwing his arm out in a long gesture*] What we need is thinking people, people who will not let the body rule the head. And again I cry out, education. I been accused of wanting to make the Negro the equal of the white man. Been run from pillar to post, living in poverty, because of that belief. But it is false. I never preached that doctrine. I don't say that the colored ought to be made equal to the white in society, now. We are not ready for it yet. But I do say that we have equal rights to education and free thought and living our lives. With that all the rest will come. [*pointing to the bookcase*] Them books there show it. [*Caught up in the dreams of his life, he pours out a roll of words and beats the air with his fist.*] Ladies and gentlemen, what's to hinder us from starting a great center of learning here, putting our time and our hope and money and labor into it and not into the much foolishness of this life. What little education I got was by lightwood knots, and after reading and studying all these years, I am just a little ways along. We must give the children of the future a better chance than we have had. With this one school building we can make a good start. Then we can get more teachers later on, more equipment, and some day a library where the boys and girls can read about men that have done something for the world. And before many years pass we will be giving instruction in how to farm, how to be carpenters, how to preach, how to teach, how to do anything." [*Forgetful of his written page, he shouts.*] And what will stop us in the end from growing into a great Negro college, a university, a light on a hill, a place the pride of both black and white! [*He stands a moment, lost in thought. Turning through the leaves of his speech, he looks toward Muh Mack, who sits hidden under her bonnet.*] Ain't that the truth, Muh Mack? Ain't it? [*anxiously*] They can't stand out against that, can they? Ain't that a speech equal to the best of the white, ain't it? [*He coughs.*]

MUH MACK: Lord Jesus! You's enough to wake the dead. And you brung on your cough again.

ABE: [*fiercely*] I tell you it's going through. I believe the people here are with me this time.

MUH MACK: Sounds like the same old tale. [*bitterly*] You's made them there speeches from Wilmington and Greensboro to I don't know where. It's foolishness, and you knows it. [*Abe arranges the leaves of his speech without listening to her.*] Time you's learning that white is white and black is black, and God made the white to allus be better'n the black. It was so intended from the beginning.

ABE: [*staring at her and speaking half aloud*] We been taught and kept believing that for two hundred years. [*blazing out*] But it's a lie, a lie, and the truth ain't in it.

MUH MACK: [*going on in her whining, irritating voice*] Yeh, all your life you's hollered Lord and followed Devil, and look what it's brung you to. If you'd a-put as much time on picking cotton lately as you has on that speech, you wouldn't have Mr. Lonnie down on you the way he is. The truth's in that all right.

ABE: [*trying to control his nervousness and anger*] I ain't a farmer. My business is with schools. [*Hotly.*] Can't you learn nothing? You dribbling old — Here for twenty years you've heard me talk the gospel and it ain't made no impression on you. [*He turns away and speaks to himself and the shadows in the room.*] That speech is so! It's so, and I got to speak it that-a-way. [*He looks about him with burning eyes and pleads as if with an unseen power.*] The truth's there. Can't you see it? [*His nostrils quiver and he goes on in a kind of sob, calling to the unbeliever hiding within the dark.*] God Almighty knows they ain't no difference at the bottom. Color hadn't ought to count. It's the man, it's the man that lasts. [*brokenly*] Give us the truth! Give us the truth! [*He coughs slightly, and a queer baffled look creeps over his face. For a moment he seems to sense ultimate defeat before a hidden unreachable enemy.*]

MUH MACK: [*looking at the clock and snapping*] Thought you's bound to be at the Quillie house by six o'clock. It's near about time. Get on, I wants my nap.

[*She pours snuff into her lip and turns to her snoozing again. With a hurried look at the clock, Abe crams his speech into his pocket, gets a plug hat from the desk, and blows out the lamp. The room is filled with great leaping shadows from the darting flames of the fireplace.*]

ABE: [*at the door*] You remember what I said about Douglass.

MUH MACK: Get on, get on. [*whining sarcastically*] Sure you'll be a light on the hill and the pride of the land — and you won't even let a poor old woman see her boy.

ABE: [*turning back*] Damn him! If he puts his foot in this house he'd better not let me get hold of him. They ain't no man, flesh of my flesh or not, going to lie rotten with liquor and crooks around me. That's what I been talking against for twenty years. I drove him off for it, and I'd do it again. Just because a little time's passed ain't no reason I've changed.

MUH MACK: He mought a-changed and want to do better.

ABE: [*coming back into the room*] Changed enough so he like to got arrested in town yesterday and it his first day back.

MUH MACK: [*pleading in a high quavering voice*] But I got to see him. He's been gone two year.

ABE: Let him come if he dares. You ruint him with your tales and worthless guitar playing and I don't want nothing more to do with him.

MUH MACK: [*mumbling to herself*] I's gwine see him before he goes 'way back yonder if I has to crawl slam over the river.

ABE: [*with brightening eye*] You heard me. He ain't no longer mine, and that's the end of it.

MUH MACK: [*bursting into a rage*] And you ain't none o' mine nor your mammy's. You's got all the high notions of old Colonel Mack and the white folks and don't care nothing for your own. Get on. [*He stands looking at the floor, hesitating over something.*] What you scared of, the dark?

ABE: [*shuddering and going across the room and getting an old overcoat from a nail*] Yes, I'm afraid of it. You're right, I'm none of yours, nor my own mother either. You know what I am — no, I dunno what I am. Sometime I think that's the trouble. [*sharply*] No, no, the trouble's out there, around me, everywhere around me. [*The despondent look comes back to his face and he speaks more calmly.*] I'll cut across the fields the near way. And tell Goldie not to worry. I'll be back by ten with the school as good as started. [*At the door he turns back again and calls to the old woman earnestly.*] Muh Mack, don't let her worry, don't. [*But the old woman is asleep.*] Let her sleep, let us all sleep. [*He goes out softly, closing the door behind him.*]

*Fade-out*

SCENE 6

[*An hour later, the same evening. A sandy country road twists out of the gloom of scrubby oaks and bushes at the rear and divides into a fork, one branch turning sharply to the left and the other to the right. The moon has risen in the east, casting a sickly drunken light over the landscape through the flying clouds. To the left in a field of small loblolly pines the dim outline of a barn can be seen. The tops and the branches of the larger trees move like a vast tangle of restless arms, and the small bushes and grasses hug the earth under the wind's blustering. Down the road in the distance come the sounds of running footsteps, and farther off, almost out of hearing, a halloo as of someone pursuing. The footsteps thump nearer, and presently Abe staggers up out of the darkness and falls panting in the edge of the bushes at the right. His hat is gone and his clothes torn. The shouts sound fainter in the night and gradually die away. Abe crawls to his knees and stares back at the road, his breath coming in great gasps.*]

ABE: Reckon — reckon they leave me alone now, the damn cutthroats! [*holding his sides with his hands and rocking his head in pain*] Oh, my breast feel like it'll bust. Yeh, I outrun you, you poor white trash. [*clambering wildly to his feet and staring up the road*] But you done fix me now. You done got all the underholt and lay me on the bottom. [*looking up at the sky and raising his fist above his head*] There that moon looking on it all so peaceful-like. It don't know, it can't feel what they done to me. [*bursting out with a loud cry*] Them white sons of bitches! They don't give me no chance. They stop every crack, nail up every door, and shut me in. They stomp on me, squash me, mash me in the ground like a worm. [*his voice breaking into a sob*] They ain't no place for me. I lost, ain't no home, no 'biding place. [*He throws himself down on the ground and lays his cheek to the earth. Unseen by him a light begins to twinkle at the barn. He sits up and looks intently at the ground.*] Seem like this earth feel sweet to me. It warm me like it feel sorry. [*Laying his hand on it as if it were a being.*] Ground, you is my last and only friend. You take me in, you keep me safe from trouble. Wish I could dig me a hole now and cover me up and sleep till the judgment day, and nobody never know where I gone.

[*Lonnie, stout and middle-aged, comes in at the left with a heavy lantern.*]

LONNIE: Heigh there!

ABE: [*bounding up*] Keep back, whoever you is. Stay back there, white man.

LONNIE: [*peering forward*] Who's that cutting up crazy here in the night?

ABE: Ain't nobody, nobody.

LONNIE: Well, by God, Abe, what's the matter?

ABE: That you, Mr. Lonnie?

LONNIE: Yeh. What'n the world's the matter? I was out there at the barn and heard the awfullest racket. Somebody talking like they was crazy.

ABE: Trouble, Mr. Lonnie, trouble.

LONNIE: Trouble? What sort of trouble? [*coming closer and holding up his light before Abe*] Great goodness, you're wet as water.

ABE: [*straightening up*] I all right now. Got to go on.

[*He takes a drunken step on the road toward the right. Lonnie gets quickly before him.*]

LONNIE: Where you going?

ABE: I going to leave here, going clean away.

LONNIE: No, you're not. Tell me what's the matter.

ABE: Them white men run me away from the Quillie house.

LONNIE: That's what the shouting was about, was it?

ABE: Maybe so, suh.

LONNIE: Uh-huh. You were down there about your school business, anh?

ABE: I weren't doing no harm. I was going to talk to the folks about our school for next year, and when I got there they was a crowd of low-down white men there—

LONNIE: Look out, mind how you talk.

ABE: I minding all right. When I got there they done run them lazy darkies off and told me I had to go. [*grimly*] They couldn't scare me, though. I went on in the house and started my speech. And then— [*throwing out his arms wildly*] Mr. Lonnie, help me get back at 'em. Help me get the law on 'em.

LONNIE: What'd they do?

ABE: They fell on me and beat me and told me I got to get out of the country. And they run me off. But I reckon some of 'em got they heads cracked. [*his body swaying with weakness*] What I going to do? I don't know what to do.

LONNIE: Go on home and behave yourself.

ABE: [*his voice almost breaking*] I ain't done nothing, I tell you.

LONNIE: [*roughly*] Serves you right. I've told you time and again to quit that messing about and look after your crop and keep in your place. But you won't, you won't. I reckon you'll stay quiet now a while.

ABE: [*pleading with him*] But I done right. I ain't done nothing to be beat for.

LONNIE: The devil you ain't! I've been off today all around the country trying to get hands to pick your cotton. It's falling out and rotting in the fields.

ABE: But I ain't lost no time from the cotton patch, 'cepting two or three days and I was sick then. I been sick all today.

LONNIE: You needn't talk back to me. If you're sick what are you doing out tonight and getting yourself beat half to death? Yeh, I reckon I know such tales as that. And you needn't fool with the crop no more. I done levied on it and am going to have it housed myself.

ABE: [*moving toward him*] You mean you took my crop away from me?

LONNIE: Don't talk to me like that, I tell you. [*A fit of coughing seizes Abe.*] Call it taking away from you if you want to, I'm done of you. Next year you can hunt another place.

ABE: [*his face working in uncontrollable rage*] Then you're a damn thief, white man.

LONNIE: [*yelling*] Stop that!

ABE: [*moving toward him*] Now I'm going to pay somebody back. I going to get even.

LONNIE: Stop! I'll kill you with this lantern.

ABE: [*with a loud laugh*] Yeh, yeh, hit me. Your time done come.

[*He makes a movement toward Lonnie, who swings his lantern aloft and brings it crashing down on Abe's head. The light goes out and the two rocking forms are seen gripping each other's throats under the moon.*]

LONNIE: Let go — let go —

[*Abe gradually crushes him down to the ground, choking him.*]

ABE: [*gnashing his teeth and snarling like a wild animal*] I choke you, I choke your guts out'n your mouth. [*He finally throws Lonnie's limp body from him, and then falls upon it, beating and trampling the upturned face.*] There you lie now. Dead! [*His voice trails high into a croon.*] I wipe out some the suffering of this world now! [*standing up and drawing away from the body*] I — I — get even, I pay 'em back. [*He begins wiping his hands feverishly upon his trousers.*] Blood! Blood, the white man's blood all over me. [*screaming out in sudden fear*] I done killed somebody! Oh, Lord, Mr. Lonnie! Mr. Lonnie! [*He falls on his knees by the body.*] What's the matter? Wake up, wake up! Pshaw, he's asleep, fooling. [*springing to his feet*] He's dead, dead! [*The wind groans through the trees like the deep note of some enormous fiddle and then dies away with a muffled boom across the open fields. Abe stands frozen with horror.*] Listen at that wind, will you! Mercy, that his spirit riding it and crying! [*He falls prone upon the earth moaning and rocking. In a moment he sits up and holds his head tightly in his hands.*] Oh — oh, seem like my head done turned to a piece of wood, seem like cold as ice. [*He slaps his forehead queerly with his own palms.*] The whole world done seem turned upside down, everything going round me like a wheel. [*As he stares wonderingly around and gropes before him like one dreaming, the branches of the trees seem to change their shape and become a wild seething of mocking, menacing hands stretched forth from all sides at him. He snatches up a piece of broken fence rail and snarls at them.*] Don't touch me, I kill you! [*He stands in an attitude of defense and the branches seem to regain their normal appearance. Stupefied, he lets the rail fall to the ground and then wraps his arms spasmodically across his face.*] O Lord, I going crazy, that's what! [*He bends over, jerking and shivering.*

*Presently out of the underbrush at the left steal two shadowy figures dressed in the fashion of the late fifties. One is a young good-looking Negress of twenty, the other a dandified young white man about thirty. As they move across the scene at the rear, the man looks guiltily around him as if in fear of being surprised. The woman stops and points to the thicket at the right. He nods and motions her to move on, his arm around her. Abe looks up and sees them stealing away. He leaps to his feet and stares at them.*] Who that woman and white man? [*With a joyous cry he rushes forward.*] Mammy! Mammy! That you! This here's Abe, your boy! Mammy Caroline! [*The figures begin entering the thicket.*] Mammy! That you, Colonel Mack? Where you going? Stay here, help me, I — [*The man and the woman disappear into the bushes. Abe stands with his mouth open, staring after them.*] What's all this? Must be another dream — a dream. Sump'n quare. [*He moves cautiously forward and parts the bushes and starts back with a loud oath.*] God damn 'em! There they like hogs! [*The fearful truth breaks upon him and he shrieks.*] Stop it! Stop that, Mammy, Colonel Mack! [*Rushing toward the bushes again and stopping as if spellbound.*] Stop that, I tell you, that's me! That's me! [*He stumbles backward over the body of Lonnie and, shrieking, rushes down the road at the left.*]

*Fade-out*


### SCENE 7

[*Thirty minutes later Douglass has arrived and, with Muh Mack before the cabin fire, is giving an account of his travels. He is now about nineteen years old, and has developed into a reckless dissipated youth dressed in the cheap flashy clothes of a sport.*]

DOUGLASS: [*turning toward Muh Mack with a bitter smile*] Yeh, I says it and I says it again. Let them there Norveners put Pap in print for what he's trying to do for the colored. If they could see him now, down a poor dirt farmer they'd not think he's such a smart man. Let him read his books and get new idees. They won't change the black in him, not by a damn sight. He's right down working a tenant and that's where he belongs. Get me? And him off tonight making his speeches. I bet to Christ this here's his last 'un.

MUH MACK: For God's sake don't carry on so. Come on and tell me some more about the places you been since you left here. [*He sits looking in the fire.*] What—what's the matter? You hain't been usual so ficeylike with your Pap. You been drinking?

DOUGLASS: [*laughing sweetly*] Yeh, I been drinking. And I got cause to cuss the whole works out. [*looking at her fiercely*] Listen here. Let this slip in your ear. For you'd hear it soon enough. You never has swung a eight-pound hammer, steel-driving day after day in the broiling sun, has you? And you hain't never done it with a ball and chain on you 'cause you is marked dangerous, has you? And that for a whole year long? Well, I has.

MUH MACK: [*in astonishment*] You been on the roads since you left?

DOUGLASS: [*recklessly*] I has that, and wore the convict clothes just 'cause in my drunkenness I begun to preach some of his doctrines about there being no difference 'twixt the colored and the white. I knowed better. But I was drunk and had heard so many of his speeches. The judge in Wilson said he'd just stop my mouth for a month, and show me the difference. And I got a knife one day and stabbed a guard to the hollow. And they give me twelve months for that.

MUH MACK: [*admiring his prowess*] You always was one what fought at the drap of the hat.

DOUGLASS: [*disgustedly*] Yeh, a damn fool, and I ain't forgit how he run me off'n here and beat me! [*bursting out with shining eyes*] Hain't I got cause to hate him and want to get him down?

MUH MACK: Getting on the roads ain't much, Douglass.

DOUGLASS: No, it ain't much to lie in the jug, is it? You do it and you ain't never gwine have no more peace. The cops is allus watching you. You gets the look and they knows you. They tried to arrest me yesterday over there in Lillington, and I hadn't done nothing. And the old man was knowing to it too. But I's learnt what he'll never learn and it's this—that we belongs down with the pick and the sledge hammer and the tee-iron and the steam shovel, and the heavy things—at the bottom doing the dirty work for the white man, that's it. And he ain't gonna stand for us to be educated out'n it, neither. He's gonna keep us there. It pays him to. I sees it. And after all these years Pap keeps on trying to teach that men is men. Some white man's gonna shoot his lights out one these days, see if they don't. [*with reckless forgetfulness*] And so I says gimme a fast time, a little gin to drown down all my troubles in, and then— [*He goes over to the door and gets his guitar.*] a little music to top it off with. How about it, Muh Mack?

MUH MACK: [*straining her eyes through the shadows*] What you got there? [*jubilantly*] Lord, Lord! If you ain't brung your box with you! And I ain't heared nothing but them sparrows by the door and that old rain crow in the hollow since you left two year back. Play her, boy, play her.

[*By this time Douglass has sat down by the fire, strumming.*]

DOUGLASS: [*tuning up while Muh Mack sits in a quiver of excitement*] Lemme play your old piece. My woman in Rocky Mount said 'twas the onliest tune.

MUH MACK: That's it! That's it! Lord, gimme the "Band." I used to be put in the middle every time for that step. Dance all day, dance all night, just so I's home by the broad daylight. Child, I could natch'ly knock the wool off 'n 'em.

[*As Douglass plays she chuckles and whines with delight and almost rises from her seat. He starts in a quiet manner, gradually working up to a paroxysm of pantomime and song. Muh Mack begins doing the Jonah's Band Party step with her heels and toes while sitting. Douglass spreads his wriggling feet apart, leans forward with closed eyes, and commences the "call," with the old woman's quavery slobbering voice giving the "response."*]

DOUGLASS: [*giving the "call"*] Such a kicking up sand!

MUH MACK: [*giving the "response"*] Jonah's band! [*This is repeated; then comes the command to change steps.*]

Hands up, sixteen, and circle to the right,
   We's gwine get big eatings here tonight.

Such a kicking up sand! Jonah's band!
   Such a kicking up sand! Jonah's band!

Raise your right foot, kick it up high,
   Knock that Mobile buck in the eye.

Such a kicking up sand! Jonah's band!
   Such a kicking up sand! Jonah's band!

Stand up, flat foot. Jump them bars.
   Karo backward like a train of cars.

Such a kicking up sand! Jonah's band!
   Such a kicking up sand! Jonah's band!

Dance round, woman, show 'em the p'int,
   Them other coons don'ter how to conj'int.

[*By this time Douglass is playing a tattoo on the wood of his box and carrying on the tune at the same time. Muh Mack has risen from her chair. With her dress to her knees, defying her years, she cuts several of the well-remembered steps. At sight of her bare and thin dry shanks the delirious Douglass bursts into loud mocking guffaws and only plays faster. The door opens at the right and Goldie comes timidly in. Her face is worn and haggard, and the strained vacant look in her eyes has deepened. Muh Mack stops and creeps guiltily to her chair. Douglass tapers off his music and stops. For a moment Goldie stands astonished in the door, holding a bulky tow sack in her hand. She drops the sack and hurries over to Douglass.]*

GOLDIE: Mercy me! I knowed 'twas you soon's I heard the guitar. And such carrying-ons!

DOUGLASS: [*rising confusedly as she comes up to him*] How you, Mom?

[*Goldie puts her hand shyly on his arm and then clings convulsively to him, her shoulders heaving with restrained sobs. He lays one arm around her and stands looking tenderly and somewhat foolishly down at her. It is evident that in his way he cares for her. She suddenly raises her head, dries her eyes with her apron, and fetches wood from the box.*]

GOLDIE: [*punching the fire*] Whyn't you let me know Douglass had come, Muh Mack?

MUH MACK: He just come.

DOUGLASS: [*laying his box on the bed*] Mom, you set in this chair. You must be cold.

[*Goldie sits down wearily and Douglass stands with his back to the fire. Muh Mack picks up her snuff brush and slyly begins to dip from her tin box.*]

GOLDIE: [*with a sudden start of terror*] You ain't seed your pap, has you?

DOUGLASS: No'm, I ain't seed 'im. I found out he done gone to the Quillie house 'fore I come. I slipped in here and found Muh Mack asleep. Lord, I scared her with a fire coal.

GOLDIE: [*suddenly reaching out and clutching his hand to her face*] Don't you and your pap have no trouble. Don't egg him on. He—he—ain't well and might rile easy. We—we can see one 'nother off—you and me.

DOUGLASS: Oh, I'm gonna be partic'lar. Now don't worry no more. It's all right.

GOLDIE: [*slowly getting up*] You all set while I fix some supper. I got something good for Abe and the rest of us. Lemme show you. [*She brings the bag, sits down in the chair and takes out a big meaty ham bone. Muh Mack eyes it hungrily—naively.*] Ain't that the finest though? And I got a hog head, too, and collards and cracklings.

DOUGLASS: [angrily] That's the way with them damn—with them white folks. They works you to death and then shoves they old skippery meat off on you for pay.

GOLDIE: [*a worried look coming over her face*] You hadn't ought to say that, Douglass. Mr. Lonnie gave me it — all of it. And he paid me cash for my work. Abe'll have a new bottle of medicine Monday. [*She fingers the food childishly, and Douglass turns away with a smothered oath. Putting the food back into the bag, she stands up.*] Now I'll get you some supper.

DOUGLASS: I can't stay for no supper. I promised to eat down the road with Joe Day. Let's sit and talk, 'cause we don't have much time and you can cook after I'm gone.

GOLDIE: [*hesitating*] Well — lemme put these here in the kitchen then. [*She goes out at the right.*]

DOUGLASS: [*turning sharply to Muh Mack*] What's the matter with Mom?

MUH MACK: Weren't we just a-having of a time when she broke in?

DOUGLASS: Cut out the damn jowing. What makes Mom act so quare?

MUH MACK: [*surprised*] Do how? She acts all right.

DOUGLASS: She don't. She acts sort of lost-like — wrapped up in something. [*He scratches his head, perplexed.*]

MUH MACK: If they's anything wrong with her it's 'count of trouble, I reckon.

DOUGLASS: The hell-fired fool! He's drug her to death with his wildishness.

MUH MACK: And if it's trouble that ails her, I reckons as how you's done your share in bringing it on.

[*Douglass swallows his reply as Goldie comes in. She lights the lamp, then sits down and begins staring in the fire.*]

DOUGLASS: [*after turning from one side to the other*] Mammy, what's the matter with you?

GOLDIE: [*brushing her hand across her face and looking up as she wipes the tears from her eyes*] Lord bless you, child, they ain't nothing. I's just happy to be with you.

[*She catches his hand and holds it a moment, then drops it and begins to look in the fire again. Douglass watches her intently and then turns away as if somewhat awed by her manner. There is a noise of someone coming up on the porch.*]

MUH MACK: [*crying out in fear*] That's him, Douglass! I know his step. That's your pap.

[*Goldie stands up, wringing her hands, as Douglass gets his guitar and hurries into the kitchen. The door at the left opens and Abe enters.*]

GOLDIE: [*leaning forward and rousing the fire*] Did everything turn out — [*Muh Mack suddenly screams. Goldie looks up and cries out.*] Oh!

[*Abe comes toward the fire. His face is bruised and bloody, his clothes torn to shreds, and he sways as he walks.*]

MUH MACK: [*rising from her chair*] They's been after him! They's been after him!

ABE: [*snarling at her*] Shut up your damn yowling, will you? And don't be rousing the neighborhood. I'm not dying yet.

[*Goldie stands a moment terror-stricken and then runs up to him.*]

GOLDIE: You's hurt, hurt bad, Abe, poor baby!

ABE: [*pushing her back*] Ain't hurt much. No time to doctor me now. [*He stands before the fire as Muh Mack collapses in her chair. He is no longer the reformer and educator, but a criminal, beaten and hunted.*] I come to tell you to get away — [*panting*] to — to leave, leave!

GOLDIE: [*sobbing and burying her face in her hands*] What's happened? What's happened?

MUH MACK: [*teetering in her chair and crying to herself*] Lord-a-mercy on us! Lord-a-mercy!

[*For a moment Abe stands before the women, silent, with closed eyes.*]

ABE: [*looking at the motto on the wall and repeating the words dully*] We are rising! [*echoing*] We are rising! He didn't know what he said, he didn't. [*He staggers and grips the mantel and stands listening as if to faraway sounds. He turns desperately to the cowering women.*] Get your clothes and leave. You got to go, I tell you everything's finished at the end.

GOLDIE: [*wailing*] What happened at the schoolhouse?

ABE: [*pushing his bruised hand across his forehead*] I can't, can't quite think — yeh, they was a crowd of white men at the door with masks and dough-faces on. Said weren't going to be no meeting. They beat me, run me off. And they give me till tomorrow to get out'n the country. You got to get away, for it's worsen' that — oh, it is! [*calmly and without bitterness*] Who you reckon set 'em on me? Who you think it was told 'em about the trouble I been in before? Yeh, and he made it out terribler'n it was. Douglass told 'em. He done it. My own flesh and blood. No! No! He was but ain't no more! [*gloomily*] But I don't blame him — they ain't no blaming nobody no longer.

GOLDIE: [*fiercely*] He didn't — he wouldn't turn against his own pa.

ABE: [*sternly*] Hush! He did though. But it don't matter tonight. And you got to leave. [*half screaming and tearing at the mantel*] Now! Now, I tell you!

GOLDIE: [*between her sobs*] Did you—who hurt you?

ABE: I tell you I've done murder, and they's coming for me.

[*Muh Mack sits doubled up with fear, her head between her arms. With a sharp gasp Goldie ceases weeping and sits strangely silent.*]

MUH MACK: Murder! Oh, Lord-a-mercy! [*She mumbles and sobs in her rag.*]

ABE: They drove me away from the meeting. I come back by the road, mad. [*He gasps.*] Every white man's hand against me to the last. And Mr. Lonnie come out to the road when I passed his house and begun to abuse me about the crop. He struck at me, and I went blind all of a sudden and hit him with my fist. Then we fought. [*his voice growing shrill*] And I hit him and hit him. I beat his head in. I killed him dead, dead! I beat on and on until all the madness went out of me and the dark was everywhere. Then I seed a sight. [*He stops, aghast at the remembrance.*] I left the dead man there in the night on the ground. They done found him—I hear 'em crying on the road. They's coming to get me. [*He holds out his bruised hands.*] His blood's still shining on them hands. [*He turns his head away in fear.*]

MUH MACK: [*in a high whine of terror*] My God amighty! You kill't your own flesh!

ABE: [*turning wrathfully upon her*] Yeh, yeh, some bitch went a-coupling with a white man! My mother. I seed it—seed it—a soul being conceived in sin—me—and the curse of God upon me! [*He drops his hands helplessly. A sort of terror comes upon him.*] Oh, Lord God! I'm another Cain, and killed my brother. I tell you I—I scrushed his head in and beat it till I put out the stars with blood. Mercy! Mercy! [*With his hands still held before him, he stands with bowed head. After a moment he looks up and speaks calmly, almost resignedly, his dignity coming back to him.*] This is the way it was meant to be, and I'm glad it's ended. [*He stands with his fist to his temples and then flings out his arms in a wide gesture.*] Oh, but damn 'em! Don't they know I want to do all for the best. [*shaking his fist at the shadows*] I tell you, I tell you I wanted—I've tried to make it come right. [*Lowering his head.*] And now it's come to this.

[*Douglass comes in from the kitchen and stands away from him, his face filled with shame and fear. Abe looks at him without interest.*]

DOUGLASS: Before God, Pap, I—I didn't mean no such happenings. I never thought—

ABE: [*eyeing him coldly*] Who you? [*more loudly*] A leader, a king among men! [*to the women*] Here's Douglass and you can go with him.

[*Douglass turns back into the kitchen and instantly runs out. His eyes are staring with fear.*]

DOUGLASS: [*in a throaty whisper*] Come on, Mom! [*twisting his cap in terror*] They's coming. I heared 'em from the kitchen door. They's coming. Run, Pap! God have mercy!

[*Muh Mack hobbles to Douglass and tries to pull him through the door at the right. He looks back toward his mother.*]

MUH MACK: Come on! Come on!

DOUGLASS: Mom, Mom, don't stay here!

ABE: [*raising Goldie from her chair*] Go on with him. You ain't to blame for nothing.

[*Abe pushes her toward Douglass. But she turns and throws her arms around him, clinging silently to his breast.*]

MUH MACK: [*pulling at Douglass*] I hears 'em. That's them coming.

[*With an anxious look at Goldie, Douglass hurries with Muh Mack through the door and into the fields. Abe places Goldie back in her chair and stands looking at her. He catches her by the shoulders and shakes her.*]

ABE: Tell me, what is it, Goldie! What ails you, gal? [*She sits looking dumbly at him and he draws away from her. Presently there is a sound of stamping feet outside, and voices slip into the scene like the whispering of leaves. A stone is thrown against the house, then another and another. One crashes through the window and strikes the lamp. The room is left in semidarkness. Abe, with a sob of overwhelming terror, falls upon his knees. Twisting his great hands together, he casts up his eyes and cries in a loud voice.*] God, God where is you now! Where is you, God! [*He begins half sobbing and chanting.*] You has helped me before, help me now. Is you up there? Hear my voice! [*Fear takes possession of him.*] Blast me, Lord, in your thunder and lightning, if it is your will! Catch me away in the whirlwind, for I'm a sinner. Your will, your will, not mine. Let fire and brimstone burn me to ashes and scatter me on the earth. [*gasping*] I've tried, I've tried to walk the path, but I'm poor and sinful. Give me peace, rest — rest in your bosom — if it is thy will. Save me, Jesus. save me! [*He falls sobbing on the floor.*]

VOICE: [*outside*] Come out of there, Abraham McCranie! [*A shudder runs through Abe, and his sobs grow less violent.*] Come out! Come out!

[*Another stone crashes through the room. As if ashamed of his weakness, Abe rises from the floor. He speaks firmly to the shadows.*]

ABE: In the beginning it was so intended. [*looking around him*] And I end here where I begun. [*He bursts out in a loud voice.*] Yet they're asleep, asleep, and I can't wake 'em!

VOICES:
He's in there.
I hear him talking.
He's done talking now, Goddam him!
We'll show him the law all right.
He's got a gun!
Shoot him like a dog.

ABE: [*wiping his brow and again speaking in the role of the educator trying to convince his everlastingly silent hearers*] But you'll wake, you'll wake — a crack of thunder and deep divided from deep — a light! A light, and it will be! [*Goldie still sits hunched over in her chair. As Abe speaks he goes to the door at the left.*] We got to be free, freedom of the soul and of the mind. [*shouting*] Freedom! Freedom! [*lifting up his voice*] Yea, yea, it was writ, "Man that is born of woman is of few days and full of trouble." Like the wind with no home. Ayh, ayh, sinner man, sinner man — [*He opens the door.*] I go talk to 'em, I go meet 'em —

VOICES: Hell! Lookout! There he is!

ABE: Yea, guns and killings is in vain. [*He steps out on the porch.*] What we need is to — to — [*His words are cut short by a roar from several guns. He staggers and falls with his head in the doorway.*] and we must have — have —

[*At the sound of the guns, Goldie springs to her feet. For an instant everything is still. Then several shots are fired into Abe's body.*]

VOICE: Quit the shooting. He's dead as a damned door! Now everybody get away from here — no talking, no talking. Keep quiet — quiet.

[*There is the sound of shuffling footsteps and men leaping the fence. Voices come back into the room.*]

VOICES:
Yeh, mum's it.
He won't raise no more disturbances!

[*The voices grow more faint.*]

What a bloody murder he done!
He's still now, by God!
It's the only way to have peace, peace.
Peace, by God!

[*Goldie moves toward the door where Abe lies. Halfway across the room she stops and screams and then drops down beside his body. The wind blows through the house, setting the sparks flying.*]

*Curtain*

# Hymn to the Rising Sun

## *A Drama of Man's Waste*

In One Act

Green wrote *Hymn to the Rising Sun* in 1935 in response to a prisoner abuse case recently uncovered in the North Carolina prison system. During the winter of 1934–35, two black convicts (their family names were Shropshire and Barnes; their given names were never used in newspaper accocunts), in prison on minor charges, had been placed on the chain gang, then for working too slowly had been chained in an unheated building for two weeks in frigid January weather. Their feet froze, gangrene set in, and prison officials had the feet of both men amputated. As part of a prison reform effort, which included the abolition of chain gangs among other initiatives, Green wrote the play over the summer and fall of 1935 while a trial of the prison officials directly responsible for the treatment of the convicts was under way (the five officials were acquitted but later discharged by the state). Late in the play there is a passing reference to Shropshire and Barnes, but instead of generating outrage over a particular case, Green wanted the play to raise a general question: How could anyone think that such brutal treatment as existed in the prison system would send convicts back into society better prepared for responsible citizenship?

## CHARACTERS

PEARLY GATES

BRIGHT BOY

TWO CONVICTS

RUNT

A WHITE MAN

FIRST GUARD

THE COOK

THE CAPTAIN

SECOND GUARD

HOPPY

CARELESS LOVE

A NEGRO CONVICT

OTHER CONVICTS

TIME: *some years ago*
PLACE: *somewhere in the southern part of the United States*

[*The rising curtain discloses a convict stockade. It is the hour before sunrise, and in the gray twilight of the upheaving dawn a tent with the lips of its opening snarled back stands silhouetted against the paling stars. A line of posts like Indian palisades passes behind the tent, and stretched across them are the faint horizontal streaks of close barbed wire. At the left front is a barrel, and beside it a rough square table, and at the right front a box structure much like a small privy, some four feet high and about two feet wide. A smoky tin lantern set on top of the box casts its bilious eye over the scene and into the mouth of the tent where the convicts are sleeping in their double bunks.*

*For a moment after the curtain rises nothing is heard except the deep breathing of the sleepers and the occasional clink of a chain as some convict moves his weary body on a hard shuck mattress. And then far away from the other side of the round world comes the snug crow of a rooster in salute to the waking day. A huge half-naked middle-aged Negro lying in the bottom bunk at the left smacks his lips and mutters in his sleep.*]

PEARLY GATES: [*the sound growling up from the deep cavern of his belly*] Ah — oom.

[*His long arms slide off the bunk and hang limpfully down to the ground. The top bunk at the right creaks, a chain rattles, and a white BOY about seventeen years old, with shaved head, haggard face, and hollow eyes props himself up on his elbow and looks over at the Negro. He also is naked from the waist up.*]

BOY: [*calling in a husky whisper*] Pearly Gates. [*But there is no answer from the Negro. He calls again — softly and with a careful look about him.*] Pearly Gates.

[*The Negro stirs in restless fitfulness, pulls his long arms back up across his body, and with a deep sigh goes on sleeping.*]

A CONVICT'S VOICE: [*from the depths of the tent, angry and guttural*] Pipe down-n-n!

[*The Boy waits a moment and then turns and stares at the box. A long while he gazes at it as if listening, and then with a sort of moan stretches himself out on his mattress. For a while everything is quiet again—no rattling of chains, no clank of iron on iron, cuff on cuff, no muttering is heard. A deep and dreamless sleep once more seems to pervade the scene. But the sickly rheumy eye of the lantern does not sleep. Steadily it watches, waits, and watches, while the night gnats and bugs whirl dizzily around it. Now it begins to wink, for the box on which it sits has started shaking. Something is imprisoned there. A scurried drumming is heard inside as if a huge bird were beating at the plank walls with bony featherless wings. The Boy at the right front raises himself up in his bunk again and stares out at the box, then looks over at the Negro at the left.*]

BOY: [*in an agonized whisper*] Pearly Gates, Pearly Gates!

[*The Negro at the left shakes himself like a huge chained animal, sticks his great hands up, and grasps the side rails of the bunk above him.*]

PEARLY GATES: [*muttering*] Ah—oom.

[*His hands release the rails and drop to the ground with a thud. The drumming in the box grows louder, and a voice inside is heard calling piteously.*]

VOICE: [*in the box, as if embedded in a thick quilt*] Water—water!
BOY: [*now sitting bolt upright and wagging his head in anguish*] Somebody do something! Oh, do!

[*A tremulous shaking of iron chains passes through the tent, and the Convicts turn in their bunks.*]

ANOTHER CONVICT'S VOICE: [*from the depths of the tent*] Go to sleep!
BOY: Yeh—yeh—who can sleep? [*calling softly again*] Pearly Gates!
CONVICT'S VOICE: [*in savage mockery*] Pearly Gates—Pearly Gates! What can he do?

[*One of the great hands of the Negro at the left begins waving in the air around his face as if shooing off pestering mosquitoes or flies.*]

PEARLY GATES: [*groaning and smacking his lips in his sleep*] Lemme 'lone, lemme 'lone, I say.

VOICE: [*in the box*] Water, water—!

BOY: [*moaning*] Pearly Gates.

[*In the bunk below the Boy a dropsical brutal-faced White Man of fifty-five turns wrathfully over.*]

WHITE MAN: Shet your face, Bright Boy, shet it! [*muttering*] A man's got to git his sleep, ain't he, if he swings them picks? What with you and the bugs and the heat—[*He suddenly lunges upward, shoots his hand out around the rail of the Boy's bunk, and grabs him fiercely in the side. The Boy lets out a low wail and pulls loose from him, and the White Man lies down again.*] Next time I get hold of you I'll tear out a whole handful of your guts. [*The Boy bends his head on his knees and begins to weep silently. Presently he chokes down his sobs, wipes his eyes with the palm of his hand, and sits staring before him. For an instant everything is silent once more, and then the drumming in the box begins again. The Boy moans, and the White Man jerks up his leg to kick at the mattress above him, but a groan bursts from his lips as the shackle bites down on his ankle.*] Great God A'mighty—I've ruint my leg! [*He bends far over and rubs his leg, and then snarls around at the box.*] Stop it, Runt! Stop it!

[*He turns his face away from the lantern light and stretches himself out for a nap. Pearly Gates suddenly sits up in his bunk. He wriggles his fingers in the air, waking them to life, and opens his mouth in great gapes.*]

PEARLY GATES: [*scratching his close-cropped head and staring about him*] Who that called my name?

BOY: Runt's dying in that box. Oh, he is! Get the Cap'n, I tell you.

PEARLY GATES: [*thinking a while and then showing his white teeth in a grin*] How I gonna git the Cap'n and me chained to this here bunk?

BOY: Call him—he'll come.

PEARLY GATES: Nunh-unh.

WHITE MAN: [*turning over on his back and chuckling*] Reckon when Runt gets out of that box he'll quit going behind the tent to love hisself. [*Pearly Gates begins to laugh softly.*] What's tickling you?

PEARLY GATES: Bull of the woods, he said he was. Ah—oom—a hundred pounds of skin and bones—wimmen's ease.

RUNT: [*in the box*] Help me! Help me!

BOY: [*vehemently*] You got to do—

[*His voice stops dead in the air as the First Guard comes in from the left. He is a dissolute-looking fellow about thirty years old, dressed in overalls, a wide*] *field straw hat, and a homespun shirt. He carries a double-barreled shotgun in the crook of his arm. Everybody grows silent, and Pearly Gates lies down again in his bunk.*]

FIRST GUARD: [*quietly*] Cut out the talking. [*looking over at the Boy*] Lie down, sonny. [*He starts on out at the left rear.*]

BOY: Please, sir, please, sir—

FIRST GUARD: [*stopping*] What you want?

BOY: [*trying to control the trembling in his voice*] It's the Runt—water—give him a drink.

FIRST GUARD: [*sauntering back and stopping in front of the tent*] So Bright Boy don't like the way we treat the Runt, huh?

BOY: Give him some air. [*raging thoughtlessly out*] No, I don't like it! Nobody likes it.

FIRST GUARD: [*peering at the Boy*] Maybe you forgot what the Cap'n told you yesterday.

BOY: But he's smothering to death in there I tell you.

FIRST GUARD: It's Runt in old Aggie's belly, not you.

BOY: [*half hysterically*] And you're killing him—killing—

PEARLY GATES: [*interposing warningly*] Heah, heah, boy.

FIRST GUARD: So you think this is a Sunday school, huh? [*suddenly roaring at him*] Stop that whimpering! [*then quietly*] The Cap'n said keep your tongue to yourself, didn't he? Ah-ha, seems like we can't please you, son. But we'll learn to please you.

[*He turns and saunters on out at the left rear. The Boy flings himself back on his mattress and stuffs an old ragged blanket over his ears to keep out the low sound of Runt's whimpering in the box.*]

PEARLY GATES: [*looking out and whispering*] Jesus, child, you gonna git hurt if you don't mind. Heah me?

WHITE MAN: [*whispering likewise up toward the mattress*] It's hard at first, Bright Boy. But don't you worry. You'll forget your mother's love-song at evening—all of that. Yeah, after while you will. [*Now once more from that other side of the world far away comes the proud crowing of the rooster. The White Man mutters to himself.*] Whisht that chicken had a ball and chain around his neck. Oh, God, I do! [*He turns over again and hides his face under his arm.*]

PEARLY GATES: [*singing in a whisper to himself*]
Good morning, Mr. Rooster,

I wisht I had your wing,
I'd fly across the ocean —

[*He stops as an alarm clock goes off somewhere at the left, its little sharp daggers of sound stabbing the quiet scene. The Convicts lie still a moment and then twist and mutter in their bunks, and the rattle and clink of chains accompany them. The Cook enters from the left front, carrying a steaming tin tub in his hands which he sets on the table. He is an elderly bent white fellow with a sad monkeylike face. His close-shaven head gives him a strange youthful appearance around his forehead and ears which contrasts sharply with the gnarled eldishness of his mouth and jaw. As the tub thumps down on the table, the prisoner in the box at the right front drums and thunders with a last despairing burst of energy. The lantern reels crazily and falls to the ground, filling the scene with plunging grotesque shadows. A flood of clinking sounds rises from the tent, and the muffled faces and shoulders of the Convicts can be seen as they rear up in their bunks to look out. With the slow waddling movement of an old duck the Cook goes over, picks up the lantern, and replaces it on top of the box. Then he turns and pokes his way out at the left front, mopping his sweaty face with his apron as he goes. The Convicts lay themselves down again to their rest. By this time the slaty gray of the approaching dawn has changed to a pearly gray, and the outlines of the bunks in the tent, fifteen or twenty of them, show up somewhat more distinctly, as do the posts and barbed wire across the rear.*

*The convict boss comes walking slowly in from the right front. In the morning gloom he shows to be a heavy-set man, dressed in sombrero, khaki shirt, bow tie, and khaki trousers. Jammed down in one of his heavy boots is the snakelike form of Old Jeff, as the convict lash is called. In a holster at his waist he carries a forty-five automatic. Stopping by the box a moment he listens and then raps on it with his knuckles.*]

CAPTAIN: [*in a husky pleasant voice*] How is it, old Love Powder?

RUNT: [*faint and faraway*] Water, water!

CAPTAIN: Sure you're going to get your water — your piece of bread too — at feeding time. [*He walks on toward the mouth of the tent and speaks cheerily as he enters.*] Morning, boys, morning. [*Without waiting for a reply he continues.*] Hope you all slept well. [*Pulling a key from his pocket he begins unlocking the shackles with a cool, deft sound.*] I've let you sleep late today — half an hour extra. Now ain't that nice? I say, ain't that nice?

SEVERAL SCATTERED VOICES: Yes, sir, Cap'n, yes, sir.

CAPTAIN: In honor of the occasion, I did. Now stir yourselves. [*As each prisoner is unlocked, he slips his shoes on, steps out into the aisle, and stands with his face to the front waiting. The Captain goes on talking pleasantly.*] I've been up an hour. Already had my breakfast. [*click, click*] Yes, sir, couldn't sleep. Responsibility, worry, thinking about you fellows — how to handle you, how to keep you happy. [*chuckling*] Happy, you heard me. I'm the one that really wears the ball and chain in this camp. [*his voice dropping down into a sudden hard note and then rising to a pleasant pitch again*] Ha-ha, that's right. Oh, yes, it's right. [*Passing along the tier of bunks to the left he continues unlocking the shackles — click, click.*] I hope Runt's cutting up in that box didn't hinder your beauty sleep. [*He is now unlocking the shackles of Pearly Gates.*] I say, did it keep you awake?

PEARLY GATES: [*showing his white teeth in a sudden spasmodic grimace which is meant for a grin*] No, sir, no, sir.

[*The Captain steps back two or three paces toward the front and draws himself up in a military pose.*]

CAPTAIN: [*his voice barking through the morning air*] Hep — hep! [*The line of white Convicts on the right marches out and stands facing toward the left. There are ten of them — two elderly men, three middle-aged men, and five boys from seventeen to nineteen years of age. They are all naked to the waist, wearing dirty striped trousers and carrying their jackets and convict caps in their hands. The Negroes led by Pearly Gates come out and join the end of the line. There are eight of these, four young bucks, an old bent mulatto, and three middle-aged fellows. The Captain counts them.*] Two-four-six-eight-ten-twelve-fourteen-sixteen-eighteen — [*adding with a gesture toward the box behind him*] nineteen. All right, get over there and purty up your faces. [*They move over to the barrel at the left and begin washing themselves in turn. As each one steps up to the barrel, he sticks his jacket and cap between his knees, lifts out a cupped handful of water, dashes it on his face, and moves on, drying himself with his jacket. The Cook brings in a dishpan from the left, sets it on the table by the tub, and returns the way he came. The Convicts begin putting on their jackets and caps and forming in a line before the table, the ten whites in the same order as before and the Negroes behind them. The Captain pulls out a heavy gold watch, looks at it, snaps the lid to, and sends a brazen shout toward the rear.*] Guard Number One!

FIRST GUARD: [*answering from the right rear*] Yay-hoo!

CAPTAIN: Guard Number Two!

SECOND GUARD: [*from the left rear*] Yo-ho!

CAPTAIN: Four o'clock!

[*The Cook comes rolling a wheelbarrow in from the left. It is loaded with tin pans and spoons. He stops it by the table, steps behind the tin tub, and picks up a dipper.*]

COOK: [*croaking out to the tune of the Army mess call*] Greasy, greasy, greasy! Greasy, greasy, greasy!

[*The Convicts shuffle toward the wheelbarrow, and the white man who is in the lead picks up a plate with a spoon and holds it out for his helping. The Cook loads him down with a dipperful of cabbage, fatback, grits, and a hunk of bread. He passes on, goes over to the right rear, squats down on his haunches, and begins eating ravenously. The second man follows with his helping, takes his place by the first, and so on in turn until all have ringed themselves across the scene in a squatting semicircle, showing in the half light like a row of grotesque animals. Some of them eat with the rapacity of dogs — their pewter spoons going scrape, scrape against the bottoms of their tin plates — others slowly and with no interest in their food. The middle-aged and elderly ones seem to have the best appetites. The younger ones eat little, and the Boy nothing at all. While the Convicts are busy getting their food and settling down, the Captain stands watching them indulgently like a circus master with his trained pets. Now he moves over to the right front and leans against the box. As he faces us we get a better view of him in the lantern's glow. His face is swarthy, heavy jowled, clean-shaven and set off with a close-cropped gray mustache. When he is in an easy-going mood as he seems to be now, the pupils of his slumbrous brown eyes are cut across by the drooping curtain of two heavy eyelids. But when he gets mean, these same eyelids have a way of snapping back like the hinged flap of a box, and the gleaming forked light from his eyes looks holes through a man.*]

CAPTAIN: [*scanning the row of figures and listening to the scrape, scrape of the pewter spoons*] Go to it, boys, I like to hear you eat — and you need it. [*looking off by the tent toward the horizon where the red of approaching sunrise is beginning to dye the sky*] It's going to be a fine day. Clear as a bell. And hot — clear and hot. We ought to move many a yard of dirt on that fill, hadn't we? I say hadn't we?

SEVERAL SCATTERED VOICES: Yes, sir, Cap'n.

PEARLY GATES: Yea, Lord, let the buggies roll!

CAPTAIN: That's right, Pearly, old wheelhorse.

PEARLY GATES: Just watch me wheel, Cap'n.

CAPTAIN: [*tapping on the box and addressing the prisoner within*] And if you'll be a nice boy, Runt, we might give you your shovel back.

BOY: [*Squatting over his untouched food, he looks joyously up, his voice half breaking in a fervent sob.*] Thank God!

CAPTAIN: [*his glance drifting lazily over toward the Boy*] Son, you hurt my feelings. You oughta thank me — not God. [*his gaze coming back to the box*] And besides, Runt, we might need this bedroom of yours, who knows? [*The scraping of the spoons suddenly stops. The Captain laughs.*] Oh, I'm joking, boys, unless — [*His voice dies out, and a low aimless whistle begins to sound through his full lips. The scraping of the spoons begins again. Suddenly the air is rent by the sound of two shotguns fired off almost simultaneously in the distance. The Convicts spring to their feet with a howl and stand trembling with fear, some of them dropping their pans and food in the dirt. The Captain speaks soothingly to them.*] Never mind, boys, the guards are just celebrating a little. They ain't shooting nobody. [*calling off in his great voice*] Ready to ride!

FIRST GUARD: [*from the back*] Yay-hoo!

SECOND GUARD: [*likewise*] Yo-ho!

[*The Convicts settle down again on their haunches, some of them holding empty pans disconsolately in their hands. The Captain walks over toward the row of figures. He stops before Pearly Gates who is getting his hunk of fatback out of the dirt.*]

CAPTAIN: Why, Pearly, you let a gun firing off scare you, too? I'm surprised.

PEARLY GATES: [*grinning and gulping*] Me too, Cap'n. Seem like I can't help it. [*now showing his teeth in the same spasmodic grin and with a half-teasing unctuous begging*] Bet they ain't no seconds for a good boy, is they Cap'n?

CAPTAIN: [*to the Cook*] What say, Greasy?

COOK: [*croakingly, as he stares out before him with his batlike eyes*] Ain't no seconds.

[*Pearly Gates begins eating his meat, dirt and all. The Captain smiles and moves on.*]

CAPTAIN: [*stopping in front of the Boy*] What's the matter, son?

BOY: [*struggling to make his tongue speak and at last getting out a few words*] Not hungry, Cap'n.

CAPTAIN: Not hungry?

BOY: No, sir.

CAPTAIN: Sick?

BOY: Yes, sir, yes, sir.

CAPTAIN: Sorry to hear that. Wish I could fix you up a nice featherbed. Yes, sir, and give you a pretty little nurse to hold your hand and smooth your forehead. But we can't do that, son. [*suddenly bending over him, his voice chilly as steel*] Eat them God-damn rations! [*With a terrified look the Boy grabs up his plate and begins shoveling down the hated cabbage and side meat. And then suddenly his mouth flies open and he vomits them out again. The Captain backs away from him, bends over with his hands resting on his knees, and peers at him.*] That little shooting upset you, huh?

BOY: [*teetering back and forth on his heels and choking*] I just can't eat it, Cap'n, I can't.

CAPTAIN: Not good enough, eh?

BOY: [*watching him with ashy face*] Yes, sir, it's all right, but I just can't eat it.

CAPTAIN: And how the hell you 'spect to roll your wheelbarrow, if you don't eat?

BOY: [*his words sputtering from him like a shower of crumbs*] I'll keep it rolling, Cap'n, I'll keep it turning—I'll—

CAPTAIN: [*sorrowfully*] You didn't do it yesterday, son.

BOY: [*whimpering*] Yes, sir, yes, sir, I did.

CAPTAIN: Well, never mind, maybe you did. Anyhow, don't worry over your appetite, son. In a week or two you'll think fatback and cabbage are angel cake. [*He straightens up, laughs quietly as if dismissing the subject, and then addresses them.*] You boys know what today is? [*No one answers.*] Hey, you, Pearly Gates, what is today?

PEARLY GATES: Lawd, Cap'n, I don't know.

CAPTAIN: What, my right-hand man and he don't know? [*to the bloated-faced white man at his left*] You, Hoppy, what day is it?

HOPPY: Dunno, sir.

CAPTAIN: [*to a tall sad-faced young fellow*] You know, Careless Love?

CARELESS LOVE: Thursday, I think.

CAPTAIN: I'm ashamed of you fellows. Ain't you got no interest in your country? [*snarling out to the Boy, who jumps nervously*] What's today, son? What sets it apart from all other days?

BOY: [*fearfully*] It's the Fourth of July.

CAPTAIN: That's right, Bright Boy. Independence Day. [*shouting at them*] Attenshun! [*They all spring to their feet and stand with their tin pans in their hands.*] Forward, march! [*They move over toward the left and, passing by the wheelbarrow, lay their utensils down, then form in a line as before. The two Guards enter, one from the left, one from the right. The Second Guard is dressed like the first, is about the same age, and also has a double-barreled shotgun in the crook of his arm. They are both gnawing sandwiches. The Captain calls out to them.*] Well, gentlemen, I thought you'd fell into the latrine and got drowned. [*A staccato burst of laughter is fired off among*

Hymn to the Rising Sun   89

*the Convicts and then dies suddenly away as the Captain looks at them.*]
I was just saying that this is the glorious Independence Day, the great day when Old King George got his tail bit off. Hum — hum. I used to shoot thunderbolts in my mammy's yard on Fourth of July. Years ago, years ago, I did. My daddy beat me half to death once for doing it. [*holding up his left hand from which two fingers are missing*] Got them fingers blown off that way. [*Pearly Gates snickers. The Captain looks over at him.*] I forgot you knew all about it, Pearly. [*to the Convicts*] Well, he's right. A nigger bit 'em off long ago when I tried to arrest him for stealing a bushel of corn from old man Tyler. [*reminiscing as he drops his hand*] Hum — hum, and when I drilled him with the cold steel, he spit 'em out again — kerdab right in my face. And now, boys, since you know how it happened you needn't keep looking at my hand after this. [*his voice cracking out an order to the First Guard*] All right, clean up!

FIRST GUARD: [*adopting the authority of the Captain*] Fall out!

[*The Convicts fall out of line and begin policing the ground around the tent. The Second Guard finishes his sandwich and stands by the box. The Captain wanders toward him.*]

CAPTAIN: [*in a low voice*] Anything stirring?
SECOND GUARD: [*likewise in a low voice*] Looks like he's got to have it, Cap'n.
CAPTAIN: Hum.
SECOND GUARD: Can't seem to quiet him down. Talk — talk — cry, cry. Nobody couldn't sleep last night.
CAPTAIN: [*softly*] Bright Boy?
SECOND GUARD: Ah-hah, Bright Boy.

[*In the background the Boy bends over for a bit of paper, then stops and looks questioningly around. The First Guard touches him in the rump with the nozzle of his gun.*]

FIRST GUARD: Step along, Buster.

[*The Boy darts forward, grabs up the bit of paper, and begins searching the ground in front of him.*]

SECOND GUARD: [*to the Captain*] Been here a week and worse than ever.
CAPTAIN: He wants his mammy.
SECOND GUARD: Three days now and he says he's sick.
CAPTAIN: He ain't really sick.
SECOND GUARD: Oh, no, the thermometer said he weren't.

CAPTAIN: Ah-hah. He thinks we run a hospital.

SECOND GUARD: It ain't no hospital, is it?

CAPTAIN: Hell, no, it ain't that at all.

SECOND GUARD: And he thinks other things too. [*pulling a spoon from his pocket*] Found that in his mattress last night.

CAPTAIN: [*chuckling*] Thought he'd make him a pewter file, did he?

SECOND GUARD: Looks like it.

CAPTAIN: [*taking the spoon and looking at it*] They will try them little tricks at first. [*He throws the spoon over into the wheelbarrow.*]

A NEGRO CONVICT: [*in a high melodious call from the rear*] Wanter void, Cap'n, wanter void!

CAPTAIN: [*without looking around*] You can do it at the job — we're late now.

FIRST GUARD: [*singing out*] That's about all, Cap'n!

CAPTAIN: Okay, line up! [*The Convicts who have finished cleaning up resume their places as before. The Captain moves out and stands before them, and the two Guards stand at the right and left front facing toward the back. For a while everyone waits as the Captain's eyes study the pitiful motley crew before him. Presently he breaks into a low musical laugh. The Convicts look at him with a mixture of perplexity and fear. And then he speaks in an easy voice*] I was just wondering, boys, whether I ought to make you that Fourth of July speech or not. What the hell good will it do? What say, Pearly?

PEARLY GATES: [*with his everlasting grin*] Yes, sir, Cap'n, we'd sure like to hear you, suh.

CAPTAIN: I ain't had a chance to make you a speech since last Easter when I talked on the Resurrection. But orders from headquarters say I must call your attention to the occasion. [*clearing his throat*] Well, boys, orders is orders, as some of you ain't never found out and I take the privilege on our Independence Day of once more addressing a few words unto you. [*He waits a moment and then begins his flow of words.*] According to statute number six hundred and forty-two of the penal code duly proved and entered in the House of Representatives, so I'm told, by a vote of ninety-six to four, the punishment for constant trifling and bellyaching is twenty-nine blows with the whip. [*stopping and eyeing them*] But did I ever whip a man that much? I say, did I?

PEARLY GATES: No, sir.

CARELESS LOVE: No, Cap'n.

CAPTAIN: You're damn right I didn't. Also it prescribes old black Aggie over there, and the goat, and chaining you up for various offenses, such as trying to escape, plotting a mutiny, sex perversion, and crimes against nature. Yes, sir, that's what they tell me to do to you, and I'm nothing but the instrument of the voters' will. The voters say so, and what the voters say is law, ain't it?

HOPPY: [*shifting his weight*] It sure God is.

[*Some of the others nod their agreement, and all watch the Captain with roving blinking eyes, except the Boy who stands with his head bowed.*]

CAPTAIN: Yes, sir, they've got the power, for this is a democracy and democracy means the voice of the people. And the people—well who are the people? Why they are the grand old Daughters of the Revolution, and the Confederacy—and the bishops and ministers of the gospel— Episcopalians, the Baptists, the Methodists, and the Presbyterians, and all the Elks and the Kiwanis Clubs, the Rotarians, the Lions, the college presidents, the professors in the great institutions of learning, the folks that write books, and the lawyers—don't forget them. They are the people. They march to the polls and elect representatives and say pass the laws to keep the peace, and they pass the laws and they hand the laws over to me and say "Twenty-nine blows!" Ain't it so? And they tell me to put Runt there in that sweatbox in solitary confinement for messing with his private organs. Yes, sir, they're the folks that fasten chains and shackles around your legs, ain't it so?

SEVERAL CONVICTS: [*with more feeling*] Yes, sir, Cap'n.

CAPTAIN: [*with a snarl*] The hell it is! You fellows put the chains around your own legs. You don't pass the laws, but you break 'em. [*He quiets his voice down and goes on more pleasantly.*] I reckon some of you think I'm hard, that I ain't got no feeling, that I'm a brutal slave driver. Well, I ain't enjoyed beating any one of you the whole time you been here. And I don't enjoy hearing Runt drumming inside that box no better than you do. But you're undergoing a course of training, and I'm the teacher, and I got to call it to your attention again that this ain't no life for a human being to stay in. Behave yourselves, I say. Do what you're told, and get out of here quick as you can. Go back to the other world and start a new life. [*more persuasively*] Some of you boys have killed folks. You've robbed filling stations, burnt houses, stole, and raped and violated screaming women. Every one of you is in here for some reason. They didn't put you in here just because they liked to go around and ketch you the way boys do birds and wring their necks. The great commonwealth of this state wishes every one of you was out of here. And I do too—wishes you were good upright citizens. Yeh, citizens—you heard me. And that's what you're here for—to see if I can make citizens out of you. And how you going to do that? Not by lying in bed and eating chocolate candy and having a 'lectric fan blowing over you. No, sir. If they made jails like that everybody'd be in jail and there'd be nobody outside of it. [*with a barking laugh*] Then what'd happen to me? I wouldn't have no job, would I?

[*The Convicts relax their stony attitude a bit, for now the Captain is feeling his speechmaking power and his voice has grown mellow.*]

VOICES: Yes, sir, Cap'n, that's right.

CAPTAIN: And I try to be a good Cap'n to you, don't I?

VOICES: [*more heartily*] Yes, sir, Cap'n.

CAPTAIN: You're damn right I do. And I have a hard time of it, 'cause there are a lot of folks on the outside who keep snooping about, messing around, trying to tell me how to run things. Them university fellows come down here and leave their books, and I been reading one of 'em written by a fellow named Green. And what does he say? Why, the man weeps tears, he does. He goes on page after page crying about the po' Negro, how we got to do this and that for him, got to raise him up. A lot of crap, every word of it. A nigger's a nigger. Ain't that so, Pearly Gates?

PEARLY GATES: [*with his puppetlike spasmodic grin*] That's the gospel, Cap'n.

CAPTAIN: Right. And you niggers that's in here didn't have sense enough to know that, and so you went around trying to stir up trouble, thinking maybe you were just sunburnt white men and could do as you pleased. Well, you got away easy. A lot of you ought to have been strung up to telegraph poles and the limbs of trees, and you know it. Well, when you get out of here, go back home and keep to your place, a nigger's place. And as for you white fellows, look at you. I been bossing convict camps for twenty years. More'n half the prisoners under me has been boys like Bright Boy there — hardly loose from their mother's apron strings, just in the marble stage. What the devil's the matter with you? Well, I reckon it's them same mothers — they didn't know how to train you, petted and spoiled you. Well, I say it again — you won't be petted here. The course of sprouts I'm putting you through is a course of rawhide sprouts, as the Scriptures say. And when I turn you loose you'll be hard as iron, you'll be men. You won't be wanting to go home to suck your mammy's sugar tit, no sir. Hard did I say? You heard me. For when the judge sentenced you here he said at hard labor, and that's what I aim to make it. [*his voice now taking on an oratorical sonorous sweep*] For this ain't no boat trip on the river, this ain't no little gang of girls playing doll-babies. No, sir, not a bit of it. This ain't no circus full of hootchy-kootchy mommas strutting their hot stuff before your watery mouth. This ain't no riding on a Ferris wheel or eating peanuts and popcorn and drinking cold drinks at a lemonade stand. No it ain't, you bet your life. This is the chain gang, the chain gang. This is the ball and chain, the nine-pound hammer, the wheelbarrow, the shovel, the twenty-nine lashes, the seventy-two lashes, the sweatbox, the steel cage, the rifle and the shotgun. You've heard about them two niggers, Shropshire and Barnes, in the next camp down the road. They didn't want to work. Well, old boss Jackson chained 'em up to the bars till their feet froze and rotted with gangrene, and the doctor had to cut 'em off. Ain't that hard? Yes, that's a little bit hard. Shows you how hard I could be if I wanted to. Compared to that, the Runt is having an easy time of it in that sweatbox. [*the hard note coming suddenly back into his voice*] But some of you don't think so, do you? Bright Boy there—he says it's killing the Runt. I hear that he lies awake all night making himself sick—worrying and moaning over poor Runt. Why that's a pity, for I'm looking after Runt myself, and there ain't no use of both of us trying to do the same job. Is there? No, sir, there ain't. And Bright Boy will have to learn better. He'll have to get hard. I say it again and that wise old judge he knew. Hard, he said. You heard me. For if you don't get hard you can't make your time, and if you don't make your time you can't pay your debts to the state. And the only way you can pay it is by work. You can't pay by playing sick, by getting beat, by being shut up in the sweatbox, by being chained up till your feet fall off. That don't do nobody no good. It's work we want. Work the state wants. It's for that the great railroad company has hired you from the governor. Yes, sir, the governor has rented you out the way he would a mule or a shovel or a dragpan—hired you out to build that railroad. And, boys, you got to build it. 'Cause they need coal down in Florida, and they need oranges and mushmelons and bananas up there in New York. And the cotton has to get to the seaport, and the tobacco's got to get to the factory. And there's a world of shipping and trade got to happen, boys. And it all depends on you. [*Now his voice drops to a low singing croon.*] I know it's a hell of a life. It's a hell of a life for all of us—the shackles and the iron pin, the hammer and the ball. But damn your son-of-a-bitching souls, I'm going to see that you wear 'em till the end! [*His voice dies out and he stands staring at the Convicts, who shift themselves uneasily about. Then he smiles pleasantly at them.*] Well, boys, that's about all I've got to say. So we'll get on with the rest of the exercises as per the orders.

[*By this time the light has spread up the sky, and the figures of the raggle-taggle crew stand illuminated in it. The Captain moves around to the right and begins walking slowly behind them, studying each man as he passes.*

*They feel him there apprehensively, some of them swaying nervously on their feet like saplings in a gentle wind. The Captain stops behind Hoppy.*]

CAPTAIN: Anything to complain of?

HOPPY: [*stuttering and like the other Convicts staring straight ahead of him*] No, sir, no, sir, everything's fine.

CAPTAIN: Seems like yestiddy that little Georgy buggy needed greasing, huh?

HOPPY: [*swallowing and gulping*] I kept her rolling from sun to sun.

CAPTAIN: [*pleasantly*] Like hell you did! Didn't the wheel get stuck every once in a while and wouldn't turn?

HOPPY: No, sir, no, sir. But just watch me, boss, watch me today. [*And his great trembling hand goes up and wipes the popping sweat from his forehead.*]

CAPTAIN: Don't mind we'll have to grease it for you, son, the first thing you know. [*And as he looks at Hoppy's shaking form, a half-affectionate smile plays on his swarthy face. For a moment longer he stares at him and then moves on to the next man. A sigh, a long half-inaudible sigh escapes from Hoppy's lips. The Captain turns and gazes at him.*] Don't let me scare you, snowbird! [*And now he stops behind the Boy.*] So you're sick, hah?

[*His voice is brittle and steely, a new note in it, and a shiver seems to run the length of the dirty gray-striped line. The Boy looks out before him with wide frightened eyes and face the color of ash-tree wood.*]

BOY: Yes, sir, yes, sir, I'm sick.

CAPTAIN: [*now looming above him*] Hum. When a man's sick he's got a fever, ain't he? And when he's got a fever the thermometer says so, don't it? Well, the thermometer says you ain't got no fever. Therefore you ain't sick.

BOY: [*in a low agonized pleading*] Please, sir, please.

CAPTAIN: [*suddenly pulling Old Jeff out of the cuff of his boot and touching the Boy on the shoulder*] This way, son.

BOY: [*terror-stricken*] But I been doing all right, Cap'n. They ain't been any complaint has they, none you've heard of?

CAPTAIN: [*kindly*] This way, son.

[*The First Guard comes up in front of him and touches him in the stomach with his gun.*]

FIRST GUARD: You heard him.

BOY: [*his hands suddenly fluttering aimlessly in the air, his breath sucked through his lips with a gasp*] Oh, Lord, have mercy! Mercy!

CAPTAIN: So, you're callin' on the Lord? Well, the Lord ain't here. The Lord is far away. In fact you might say this ain't no place for the Lord.

BOY: [*whispering*] Cap'n, Cap'n!

CAPTAIN: I know you need medicine, son. That's what we're going to give you. Maybe after that you won't be sick. Maybe you won't talk so much either.

BOY: [*wailing and bobbing his chin against his breast*] I'm sick, bad sick, I tell you!

CAPTAIN: [*snarling*] And I reckon the man you killed was sick too, when you soused that knife in him.

BOY: [*gasping*] I didn't kill him. I didn't, I tell you. They put the blame on me!

CAPTAIN: Oh, you didn't? But the jury said so. This way, son.

[*With the lash of the whip clasped against the butt, he reaches out, hooks the loop over the Boy's neck and jerks him backward. The Boy shakes as if with ague and stands with half-bent knees, about to fall. The Second Guard moves through the gap in the line and takes him by the arm.*]

SECOND GUARD: Step back! [*He pushes him toward the rear.*]

CAPTAIN: Pull your pants down, son.

BOY: [*moaning*] Cap'n, Cap'n!

CAPTAIN: Don't call on me 'cause I'm like the Lord. I can't hear you either. Unbutton your pants. [*snarling*] I say unbutton your pants! Don't let me tell you thrice, as the Son of God said to the rooster.

[*With a wild and desperate look around and with a sudden vague gesture in the air, the Boy slowly begins to undo his belt. The Cook at the left front, who has continued cleaning up unconcernedly, piles the tub on the pans in the wheelbarrow and rolls it away to the left. And now the First Guard steps several paces to the front and lays his gun at the menacing ready across his forearm.*]

SECOND GUARD: Bend over, son.

[*The Boy's knees sag, he falls forward, and lies with his face in the dirt, his arms outstretched. The Convicts stand in a stiff line, their eyes staring straight ahead of them, their lips tightly shut.*]

CAPTAIN: [*calling*] Come hold his feet, Pearly Gates!

[*Like frightened animals before an approaching storm the Convicts suddenly shrink closer together and the Boy's prone body is hidden from our view.*]

PEARLY GATES: [*twisting his shoulders and flinging his hands together in front of his stomach*] He'll be good, Cap'n, he'll lie still.

CAPTAIN: [*yelling*] Come hold his feet! [*Pearly Gates leaves his place at the end of the line and goes gingerly around to the rear. The Convicts stand like a row of stony-faced Indians, outlined against the red light of the approaching sun, the Captain's head showing above them as he speaks.*] Boys, let this be another warning to you. It's a month now since I had to use the lash. But some of you keep trying to dead-beat me, don't you?

[*The lids of his eyes are snapped back and his dark brown pupils are filled with a fiery demoniac light. Suddenly like a flash he whirls back toward the recumbent figure, raises himself up on the balls of his feet, and brings the whip down with a whistling, tearing sound. Though we don't see it, the Boy's body bounds from the ground like a rubber ball, and with a cry Pearly Gates flings himself upon the plunging feet. But no sound comes from the Boy's lips. At this first blow a gust of horror seems to sweep the line of Convicts, and they waver back and forth and then stand still, their eyes lifted and set toward the vast and empty sky. Once more the Captain brings his whip down, and the Convicts flinch as if their own backs had felt the lash. Then at the third blow, a wild hysterical scream bursts from the Boy's lips.*]

BOY: [*with a shriek*] Mama! Mama!

[*At the fourth blow he begins to whimper. And at the fifth and sixth blows the wild animal scream tears once more from his body. At the seventh and eighth blows he begins whimpering again like a baby, the sound of his piteous crying rising and then sinking again like a child crying itself to sleep. And then at the tenth blow the Captain suddenly stops and doubles up his whip.*]

CAPTAIN: [*curtly*] Button his diaper. [*thundering*] Turn him loose, Pearly Gates!

[*A moment passes and then the huge Negro backs toward his position at the end of the line, staring hypnotically before him where the gasping figure lies. Presently the Captain comes around to the front, crams the whip into his boot, and stands gazing at them in silence. The Second Guard now pushes the shuddering boy back to his place and helps him fasten his belt across his jerking quivering stomach. As he moves away from him, the Boy spins drunkenly about, and as he is falling the Guard catches him and steadies him on his feet. The Boy stands there moaning and shaking, his eyes closed, the tears wetting his cheeks. The Second Guard moves over to the right front, holding his gun before him. For a while the Captain is silent, as if his mind*] *were wrapped away from the scene. Then as the Boy's weeping dies down to an almost inaudible whimper, he looks up.*]

CAPTAIN: I let him off easy this time, boys, because it's the Fourth of July. [*gesturing to the two Guards*] All right, gentlemen, give us another little salute to the morning sun. For this is the day the Thirteen Original States freed themselves from the bloody Englishmen. Fee-fi-fo-fum. [*The Guards raise their guns and fire a volley toward the sunrise. The Convicts tremble and shudder, their eyes rolling in their haggard faces. The Captain laughs softly, then pulling off his hat gives it a rolling wave around in the air.*] Hooray.

FIRST GUARD: [*loudly*] Hooray for the Fourth of July!

SECOND GUARD: [*more loudly*] Hooray for the United States!

CAPTAIN: That's right. [*to the Convicts*] Come on, boys, give us a cheer for your country. [*A feeble cheer finally breaks from their pallid lips.*] Damn it, don't you love Uncle Sam better'n that? Come on — once more.

[*The cheer is given a bit more loudly, but by empty wooden voices.*]

FIRST GUARD: [*calling out*] All right, Bright Boy, we ain't heard from you.

[*The Boy tries to control his quivery shoulders.*]

CAPTAIN: [*interposing*] Never mind, he'll do it next Fourth of July. [*Pulling a crumpled sheet of paper from his pocket, he smooths it out and looks over at the Convicts pleasantly.*] Order of the day further certifies that before we set forth to work it shall be the duty of the boss to have a rendition of "America" sung by the prisoners. [*He puts the sheet of paper back into his pocket.*] Any you fellows know the tune? [*No one answers.*] I say do any of you know it? [*The Convicts shake their heads.*] How about you, Bright Boy? [*The Boy stands staring at the ground.*] I say do you know the hymn?

[*The Boy's figure gives a spasmodic jerk.*]

BOY: [*in a muffled voice*] Yes, sir.

CAPTAIN: All right, lead it off.

[*The boy hesitates, gulps once or twice, and then, lifting his eyes toward the sky, begins to sing in a clear beautiful voice.*]

BOY:
My country, 'tis of thee,
Sweet land of liberty,
Of thee I sing.

CAPTAIN: [*thundering at the other Convicts*] Take off your caps!

[*They pull off their caps. The Captain raises his hand in a salute, and the two Guards present arms. The Boy continues singing, some of the Convicts mumble along with him, and the Captain brays out a stave or two.*]

VOICES: [*led by the Boy*]
Land where my fathers died,
Land of the pilgrim's pride,
From every mountainside
   Let freedom ring.

[*At the end of the first stanza the Captain drops his hand, the two Guards set their guns down, and the Convicts stop singing. But the Boy continues.*]

BOY:
My native country, thee—
Land of the noble free,
   Thy name I love.

CAPTAIN: [*sharply*] All right, you can stop now. [*The Boy stops singing, drops his head on his breast, and stares at the ground again. The Captain turns and goes over to the box at the right front.*] And now, boys, as another honor for the occasion I'm going to do a good turn for Runt. And I'm going to break the law to do it. The voters prescribe twenty-one days for the Runt. Yes, sir, that's what they prescribe in the House of Representatives. But I'm letting him out on the eleventh day. [*He unlocks the door to the box and flings it open.*] All right, Runt, roll out. [*Inside the box we can see a little skinny Negro doubled up like a baby in its mother's womb, his head stuck between his knees.*] Roll out, Runt.

[*But there is no movement from the doubled-up form. The Captain reaches in, takes the Negro by the collar, pulls him out, and drops his head against the ground. The figure lies still. The Captain stares at it. A murmur of fear runs among the Convicts. The Second Guard steps over and peers at the bundle of rags.*]

SECOND GUARD: [*feeling the bony chest*] Say, you better—

[*The Captain drops down on his knees, lays his hand on the Negro's heart. He squats there a moment and then rises abruptly to his feet and stands staring thoughtfully at the body.*]

CAPTAIN: Ain't that a hell of a note!

FIRST GUARD: [*now coming forward*] He was okay a few minutes ago.

CAPTAIN: Yeh, but he ain't now. Yeh, that's right, I remember—I ain't heard him making no fuss since I first come in. Hum—hum. [*turning toward the Convicts*] Well, boys, the Runt's gone from us. He's dead. [*A mumble runs through the line, and the prisoners take off their caps in awed respect. But the Boy's cap remains on his bowed head, for he is paying no attention to what goes on around him. The Cook comes in at the left with a glass of water and a piece of bread held priestlike before him. The Captain looks up.*] Runt won't need his breakfast today, Greasy.

[*The Cook stops and gazes impassively down at the body.*]

COOK: [*croakingly*] Didn't think he'd make it.
CAPTAIN: The hell you say! Then why didn't you tell me he was getting sick in there?
COOK: [*impassively*] I did. Yesterday I said let's take him out, Cap'n—I said.
CAPTAIN: You fool! When did you feed him last?
COOK: [*with his old man's toothless snicker*] Feed him, Cap'n?
CAPTAIN: Well, give him his bread and water, then?
COOK: Yestiddy—the way the orders say. He cried a little bit and said he was gonna die in that box, and I told him I reckon he would.
CAPTAIN: Yeh, and the bastard did. [*He stands thinking a moment.*]
COOK: And he said you could bury him up on the railroad fill, 'cause he didn't have no home and no folks.
CAPTAIN: He told you that?
COOK: Yes, sir. And I said I didn't think you would on account of the law.
CAPTAIN: What law?
COOK: I dunno, Cap'n, just some law, I reckon.
CAPTAIN: [*wrathfully*] I'll bury him where I damn please.
COOK: Yes, sir, he said he wanted to be buried up there so he could hear the trains run at night. [*He turns and goes on out at the left, carrying the glass of water before him.*]
CAPTAIN: [*to the Convicts*] That's right, boys, you remember how Runt liked to hear the trains blow. What you say? Shall we take him up there and bury him? [*The Convicts look at him with dull cold eyes.*] Well, I don't blame you for feeling bad over it. I do myself. All right, we will. It's his last wish and the wishes of the dead are sacred. We all know that. [*now standing over Runt and looking sorrowfully down at him*] You know me, Runt, I didn't have no grudge against you. It was the law said do it. [*with sudden blinding rage*] Yeh, the law! [*then after a moment, more quietly*] All right, we'll put you away like you wanted. [*with a chuckle*] But how the hell you gonna

hear them trains running at night and your ears packed full of clay? [*looking pensively beyond the Convicts, at the light flooding up the eastern sky*] Yeh, we'll put him up there in a hole. And soon the crossties will be laid — the rails strung out, and the steel-driving men sink the spikes on down. And Runt won't care, will he? Runt won't care [*beginning to make his speech again, but this time more lyrically, more singsong, with something of a hedge priest's evangelical fervor*] Night and day the great trains will be running over old Runt's bones, running from the big cities up north to the Floridy pleasure grounds and back again, carrying the President, and his folks maybe, the big bosses from France and Rooshy, and the tobacco kings, pimps and bawds, the gamblers and the bridal couples and the congressmen, the lieutenants and the generals, all pulled along by the fiery iron horse with its one eye. "Hah, hah, hah," it snorts. "Get out of my way. You can harness down the earth and the sun and the moon but you can't put a check rein on me. 'Cause I'm bound for Key West, and I'm going to run right off the deep end and drown the whole God-damned load in the Atlantic Ocean." Yes, by Christ, and I hope it does! [*The Cook comes in at the left with a pail of water and a mop and begins to wash off the table. The Captain bends down and picks up Runt's frail little form in his arms. He looks along the line of Convicts a moment and then steps toward Pearly Gates who draws back with a shudder.*] All right, Pearly, take him. He's crapped all over himself and stinks like a skunk, but he can't hurt you now. [*Pearly Gates still draws back, but the Captain drapes the crooked body over the huge Negro's shoulder. Pulling a whistle from his belt, he blows two sharp blasts, then barks out.*] R-i-g-h-t face! [*The Convicts obey, but the Boy stands staring at the ground as before. Careless Love pushes him around in line, and we can see the seat of his trousers showing sopping wet with blood.*] Forward, mar-ch! Hep-hep— [*The Convicts start marching out at the right, the Second Guard going before. The Captain calls back to the First Guard.*] Better fill out the death certificate.

FIRST GUARD: [*dropping the butt of his gun lazily to the ground*] Regular form?

CAPTAIN: Hep-hep — Hell, yes! [*And now Pearly Gates, the last of the line, goes out, carrying Runt's dead body like a sack on his shoulder. The Captain follows after, his heavy boots marching in step, and his voice calling rhythmically.*] Hep-hep-hep!

[*The Cook goes on mopping the table. The First Guard yawns and stretches his arms, gun and all, above his head.*]

FIRST GUARD: Well, I better get busy on that certificate — old Doc Jones might want it today. Uhm — And then some sleep. [*He starts out at the left rear, then stops and calls back.*] What was Runt's name?

COOK: [*still intent on his scrubbing*] Just Runt, I reckon.

FIRST GUARD: I remember now — Johnson. [*with a snicker*] Vanderbilt Johnson. What you reckon he died of? [*The Cook makes no answer.*] Heart failure maybe — [*with certainty*] Sure — his heart give out on him — weak heart — natural causes. Hum. [*looking off toward the east*] Golly, today's gonna be another scorcher.

[*He goes on out. The Cook finishes scouring the table, then brings his utensils over to the sweatbox. Dipping his mop into the pail, he starts cleaning out the fouled insides. In the distance the faint sound of the Captain's "Hep-hep" is heard dying away.*]

COOK: [*suddenly beginning to sing in a flat froglike voice as he works*]
Land where — my fathers died,
Land of — the pilgrims' pride —

[*And now peering up over the rim of the world at the back comes the smiling face of the sun.*]

*Curtain*

# The Lost Colony

## ACT II

Act I focuses on Sir Walter Raleigh's attempt to establish an English colony in the New World during the years 1584 to 1587, and the action, guided by the Historian as narrator, moves back and forth between England and Roanoke Island. The Raleigh of this play, unlike his historical counterpart, is motivated by a dream of founding a democratic society. Such a dream, seemingly inappropriate for a member of the nobility, is at the heart of Green's play, where it is articulated through several characters and carried out through the play's action. Early in Act I the Historian, speaking to the audience, says, "Friends, we are gathered here this evening to honor the spiritual birthplace of our nation and to memorialize those brave men and women who made it so. . . . England—ever in competition with the growing power of Spain—determined to start her own colonization in the new world. On this Roanoke Island and at this very site a beginning was finally made, and from this beginning there has grown in time a new nation and a new form of government in the world" (p. 3).

While the play concentrates on the establishment of a new social order in the New World, it does not neglect the other side of the coin—the impact on the people whose land is taken over. The Historian sets up this line of consideration early in Act I when he interprets an Indian dance as a prayer for a good harvest from land and sea, then adds that the Indians' "god deceived them. Instead of plenteous crops and bounteous fish from the waters for the year ahead, these trusting people receive the Englishman" (p. 6).

The attempted colonization had three phases. In 1584 Raleigh sent out an expedition to find a suitable place along the east coast of North America, and the explorers chose Roanoke Island for its mild climate and natural defenses. In 1585 a second expedition went to Roanoke Island to build houses, clear land for fields, and ready the site for a permanent settlement. Unfortunately, the leader of that expedition, Ralph Lane, lacked judgment and good will, and one night, with his men, he surprised a neighboring Indian village and killed many of the inhabitants. In retaliation the Indians began attacking Lane's encampment, and by the time the third group arrived from England in July 1587, they had killed or driven off all of Lane's men. This third group, comprised of women and children as well as men, was intended to form the basis of a permanent colony and is the focus of *The Lost Colony*.

Raleigh himself had wanted to lead the expedition, but in Act I his social superior, Queen Elizabeth, because she fears an invasion by Spain, refuses him permission to leave England. The group is therefore led by Governor John White, and the military commander is Captain Ananias Dare. In Act I Dare is engaged to Eleanor White, daughter of Governor White, and the two are married shortly before the company sails from England in May. Eleanor, who is pregnant at the opening of Act II, had been in love with John Borden, a bright, courageous, and public-spirited young man, but she has followed her father's wishes and married for social advancement. (Unlike Dare, who was an officer in the army, Borden was only a tenant on one of her father's farms.) Although Eleanor conforms to social expectations in her marriage, however, she does not acquiesce in the gender expectations of her day. In Act I, when the Queen herself tries to dissuade Eleanor from going to the New World by arguing that Englishwomen should leave such hard and dangerous work to their men, Eleanor's determined individuality comes out in her reply: "If England's men have dreams, so have her women" (p. 17).

Borden, who becomes the dominant character in Act II, concludes Act I by rallying the fainthearted among the colonists. At Plymouth harbor, ready to set sail for the New World, some of the colonists begin to lose their nerve as they listen to tales about the dangers and hardships they will face. The spinner of these tales is Simon Fernandes, hired by Raleigh to pilot the ship to Roanoke Island. Taking a cue from the Spanish-sounding name, Borden accuses Fernandes of being a Spanish agent who wants to prevent England from opening a colony in America. He alleviates everyone's fears by reminding the gathered people that they are going out "to conquer [an] unknown wilderness—to build a nation there—our nation," a nation for the common people (p. 40).

Old Tom, another character who plays a prominent role in Act II, is introduced in Act I as he is being thrown out of a London tavern. A beggar and drunkard, Tom has no standing, friends, or self-respect in England's stratified society, where he is on the bottom rung.

Act II opens with the colonists' arrival at the fortified village built by Lane and his men.


SCENE 1


[*After the intermission, the audience is summoned back to the amphitheatre by a flourish of trumpets. After a pause this is repeated. Presently the house lights die out and the chorus, only dimly seen at the left front, begins a chant, the music accompanying.*]


CHORUS:
We commend to thy almighty protection, thy servants
For whose preservation upon the great deep
our prayers are desired.
Guard them, we beseech thee, from the dangers of the sea,
From sickness and death,
And from every evil.
Conduct them in safety
To the haven where they would be. — Amen.

[*As the chorus chants, a great shaft of light comes up back of the main structure of the center stage, and the tall masts of the ship can be seen in its rays, moving from left to right like something in a dream. The shaft of light dies out, and the lights come up on the chorus as its chant strengthens.*]

God is our hope and strength, a very present help in trouble.
Therefore will we not fear, though the earth be moved,
And though the hills be carried into the midst of the sea;
Though the waters thereof rage and swell,
And though the mountains shake at the tempest of the same.
Be still then and know that I am God.
I will be exalted among the nations
And I will be exalted in the earth.

[*The light fades from the chorus and now rises on the historian who is standing at left center stage, his book in his hand.*]

HISTORIAN: After a long and stormy voyage the colony arrived at Roanoke Island on July 23, 1587. Landing parties were at once sent out for the relief of the fifteen men who had been left behind the year before. The party with John Borden and Captain Dare was the first to reach the fort.

[*The light dies from the historian, as he moves left up the walkway, and comes in full on the center stage, revealing the interior of the fort as Lane and others had built it. At the center back is a little chapel, topped by a cross, and with the wrecked interior open to the audience. To the left of that is a little cabin and to the right another little cabin. Jutting in from either side at the front are the roof edges of still other cabins. A few boxes, casks and bales are scattered about, rude furniture overturned, and in general the scene shows signs of having been recently plundered. And now the sound of an English snare drum is heard coming in at the right. Ananias Dare enters at the head of some eight or ten armed men—John Borden and Manteo among them. At a gesture from Dare, the small cortege stops, grounds arms and looks curiously about, and the flagbearer rests the butt of the flag staff against the earth. The drum is silent.*]

DARE: [*calling loudly*] Hooah! Show yourselves! Heeoh—friends!

[*At another gesture from him, the drummer drums a tattoo beat. Presently from the direction of the woods at the right front a wild whoop is heard. Uppowoc, the medicine man, bounds from the thicket there with his rattle in his hand. He shakes it menacingly in the air and lets out a loud call behind him.*]

UPPOWOC: Yona — yona — ee — Wankees! [*He shakes his rattle once more, then turns and darts away as he came. Borden has lifted his musket at the ready.*]

BORDEN: Stop him, Captain Dare! Stop him! [*He starts forward. Dare throws up his hand.*]

DARE: [*with a sort of schoolmaster manner*] Soldier John Borden, once more I command you to your place — in the ranks. [*Borden starts to reply, then bows his head and resumes his place.*] We will now advance to the end of the island in search of our friends.

BORDEN: What think you of the fifteen men, Chief Manteo?

MANTEO: [*slowly and gravely*] Maybe all dead — gone. [*He gestures toward the sky.*]

DARE: Advance at guard!

[*The drummer begins to beat his drum again, and they march out at the left, the flag going gaily before. They have hardly disappeared when a voice is heard calling off at the right.*]

VOICE: Wait, comrades, wait for me!

[*Old Tom comes puffing in, his doublet undone, and his ancient musket hanging loosely in the crook of his arm. He stops and stares off at the left.*]

OLD TOM: Leave me, do they, all in the heat of their youth and great marching, and me with the weight of years upon me back. Across this wild territory they tear, like their hose were girt with garters of fire, and me hacked and slashed to bits with a power of thorns and godless briars! [*He sinks down on a box and wipes his hot face with his sleeve, after which he looks curiously about him.*] Ah, I could do with a mug of Plymouth ale! — Bah! — What a wilderness and desolation! So this is Roanoke Island in the new world, this is the land of Sir Walter's great visioning and Mistress Dare's wise words of encouragement. What a woman, and she to be the mother of a new babe in two weeks or three! Ah, poor babe. *(rocking from side to side)* Heave, ship, blow storm, and always the same. We are sailing to the new land of freedom, we are pioneers of a dream, me hearties. Ah, well, the blind man eats many a fly. [*spitting and half-singing*] O the stormy winds may blow, and the raging seas — [*with a sickened shudder*] Urck! Eight weeks shut up in the belly of that little ship — and me swearing a great oath on the mercy seat of God — Give me dry land again and I would be Christian flesh from then on. Well, this is dry land — but nothing more. [*He lifts a handful of sand and lets it trickle through his fingers, then climbs wearily to his feet.*] Ah, how green the grass grows in England! And I could already wish me back there tasting of good mutton on the Devon hills. [*He walks gingerly about the scene, peering into the cabins and pushing over boxes. Suddenly he grips his gun and whirls about as if he felt an enemy creeping up on him from behind. He breaks into a laugh.] Hah-hah-hah, what a fool I am! [looking off at the left again and calling] Captain Dare, Captain Ana-ni-as Dare! Where is every soul? [striking his breast] Peace, you organ of wind! After all they are near at hand, and Governor White is approaching. I am sworn to bravery and great endeavor. Sir Walter depends on me. Then he shall hear of my deport — [His voice dies out with a gasp and he stands staring at the cabin to the right front. He begins to shake like a man with a chill. With a loud cry, he tears out at the left, calling as he goes.] Help! Help! [at the same moment voices are heard hallooing off at the right]

VOICES: Heigh-ya! Hoo-ee!

[Immediately John White, with Simon Fernandes, Reverend Martin and soldiers, enters. Old Tom re-enters and runs up to John White.]

OLD TOM: Master White, good Governor White, look, look!

[He points to the cabin at the right. White, Fernandes and the soldiers hurry over to the cabin, stand a moment in silence and then turn back toward the center of the stage.]

A SOLDIER: One of our countrymen.
WHITE: He has been dead very long. [shaking his head] The Indian method — they broke his bones.
FERNANDES: As they will yours and your followers.
WHITE: Peace! [looking off at the left] Look ye, how bravely my son Captain Dare marches. The Indians could ambush the whole of them.
FERNANDES: And they will.

[A murmur arises among the men.]

WHITE: Rest.

[They drop down and squat about on the ground. Dare comes in with his little group of men, drum, flag and all. Accompanying Manteo now are his little son Wano and his wife Meeta. She is weeping with happiness as she clings to his arm.]

DARE: Halt! [His troop stops, and he salutes Governor White.] We have sorrowful tidings, sir, from Manteo's wife.
MANTEO: [indicating his wife] She see — Indians come kill white men last moon — some drown — all dead.

[*White stands with his head bowed in thought.*]

FERNANDES: [*satirically*] Shall we unload the women from the ships, Governor? They are over-weary in their cramped quarters.

WHITE: First we must remove the dead. Borden, take three soldiers. [*Borden and three soldiers go off into the shadows at the right rear. White turns to the others.*] Later we will inter the broken body decently. [*to the group*] We have arrived too late to aid those brave men who held this fort in the queen's name. But thankful still we are to Almighty God that he in his kindness has brought us safely to our new home.

[*He gestures to Reverend Martin who goes up to the front of the little chapel and lifts his hands in prayer. Governor White, Captain Dare and all the soldiers pull off their caps and fall on their knees.*]

REVEREND MARTIN:

Almighty God, our Father, we thank thee for thy mercy and compassion upon us.

Yea, in thy great wisdom thou hast seen fit to bring us safely to this haven—

Here thou hast commanded us to build our homes and a temple to thy name—

Thou hast given us this land to have and to hold forever to thy great honor.

We have it not by our own sword, neither was it our arm that gat it—

But thy right hand, and thy arm, and the grace of thy favor

That vouchsafed it unto us.

[*John Borden and the three soldiers come quietly in and bow down with the others.*]

And in the thanksgiving of this hour

Let us remember in sorrow these thy servants

Who perished here before, a sacrifice

That we the living

Might continue in their stead.

Above their ruined and scattered bones

We swear devotion to our cause.

And not unto us, O Lord, not unto us

But unto thy name be given the glory.

Amen.

[*They all bend and kiss the earth, then rise to their feet.*]

WHITE: And in the spirit of this prayer I command you to go in peace amongst our enemies. Let there be no efforts for revenge against the Indians. At Sir Walter's express charge we are to foster friendship with them. I counsel ye, make no untoward move against them on pain of grievous punishment.

[*Borden and his three companions turn around and then begin moving backward across the scene, holding their muskets at the ready. The other soldiers move over to the left and stand with their weapons ready, for Wanchese, accompanied by Uppowoc and three warriors with spears and bows, comes out of the woods at the right front. He carries a long-handled flint-headed spear. The medicine man shakes his rattle menacingly and warningly again. The soldiers are on the alert at seeing Wanchese.*]

DARE: [*somewhat excitedly*] See ye—it's Wanchese! Wanchese!
WHITE: We greet you again, Chief Wanchese. What do you wish?
WANCHESE: [*in a hard cold voice*] White men must go—leave land now.
DARE: [*with sudden authority*] Disperse at once. We order it in the queen's name and Sir Walter Raleigh's.
OLD TOM: [*emboldened as he holds his musket before him*] Get out of here, ye knavish rogues! Scat!

[*Wanchese suddenly makes a guttural growl and a move at him, and Old Tom springs back with a squeal of terror.*]

WANCHESE: [*in the same dull hard voice*] White men must go—leave our land.
WHITE: Come now, come. This is our land. Captains Philip Amadas and Arthur Barlowe made treaty for it, and in England we swore eternal friendship to her majesty the queen—Chief Manteo here and you.
WANCHESE: Chief Manteo is snake.

[*Manteo starts forward, and the warriors around Wanchese lift their bows. The soldiers raise their muskets likewise. Manteo stops and stands looking at the ground, his whole form trembling.*]

WHITE: [*shouting*] Ground arms!
DARE: Ground arms, men, ground 'em!

[*The men slowly lower their guns.*]

WHITE: [*to Wanchese*] Put down your weapons. We come as brothers.
WANCHESE: Wanchese have no brother. Wanchese brother Wingina—white men kill. Wanchese never forget. When moon come big, white men be gone. Not?—then—[*He draws his hand across his throat, then hurls his*

*spear before him. It sticks quivering in the earth a few feet in front of Manteo. Wanchese turns and strides back into the forest, Uppowoc and the warriors accompanying him.*]

OLD TOM: Mary in heaven, I feel the knife at me throat!

WHITE: [*after a pause*] An idle threat. What say you, Chief Manteo?

MANTEO: My people make great fight with Wanchese! We kill him! Kill him!
  [*He jerks the spear from the ground and breaks it across his lifted thigh, then flings the pieces from him.*]

WHITE: With Manteo as our ally we have no fear. His tribe is powerful.
  [*looking at Fernandes*] What do you advise, Simon Fernandes?

FERNANDES: [*still sarcastically*] I am a pilot. I brought you safe across the sea. Unload my ships and I will sail again to England.

WHITE: Sir Walter advised we settle farther north if we found conditions bad here. What do you advise to that?

FERNANDES: I advise nothing.

WHITE: [*turning to the men*] Soldiers, men, it is set down in our articles of government that we hear opinions from you all. And 'tis right, for in the building of a country, men must act together or that country will fail. You have marked the tragedy here, you have seen this sudden threat of Wanchese. You know the report of Master Lane. Shall we abide here or sail on and plant a new colony on the Chesapeake? What say you, Master Dare?

DARE: [*looking about him*] There are arguments on both sides.

WHITE: [*grimacing*] Good. [*to George Howe*] Sergeant Howe?

HOWE: I like not this place.

WHITE: Soldier Borden?

BORDEN: First I do stand ready to maintain as ever that Simon Fernandes is no friend of this colony.

WHITE: [*as always, anxious for peace*] Now, now, John Borden—

[*Eleanor Dare comes in at the right rear, accompanied by Dame Colman, the midwife, and two colony soldiers. She is very pregnant.*]

BORDEN: [*not perceiving her*] Did he not lewdly forsake our flyboat in the Bay of Portugal?

FERNANDES: Proof—proof, I challenge you. The boat was but a hindrance.

ELEANOR: [*calling out*] Proof or not, it's true.

[*At her words they all wheel around and Governor White hurries over to her.*]

WHITE: [*in alarm*] My child, we left you resting in the boat!

ELEANOR: [*smiling*] Think you I'd remain there quietly waiting—waiting? See, I am well attended. [*to Borden*] What is this quarrel with Fernandes?

BORDEN: [*bowing, and with a touch of coldness*] Fernandes refuses to carry us farther north. [*addressing White and the others again*] And why? Because it is his desire that we remain here to be destroyed as others have been before us. He fears the new settlement on the deep waters of the Chesapeake as a threat to Spain. Let him fear. But I say this is the better site even so. For there we needs must start a new settlement, shelter and fields to be made. Here we have them already. There we would be at the mercy of the Spanish pirates in their big ships. Here the shallow sounds protect us. There the winters are fierce, here they are mild. Let us dare Simon Fernandes' advice and remain here.

VOICES: [*from the soldiers*] Aye, we agree.

ELEANOR: Well spoken, John Borden.

WHITE: That it is well spoken. Mount the guard!

HOWE: Mount the guard.

DARE: Sergeant Howe, keep a watchful eye. But no display of firearms, we command you.

[*The men scatter around, some of them take their places at the right and left, and others go up on the walkway at the left and stand on watch. Borden takes the flag from the bearer and mounts aloft behind the little chapel. Old Tom steps savagely out into the center of the stage and aims his musket in the direction Wanchese has gone.*]

OLD TOM: Old Beelzebub Wanchese, show but a horn and I'll shoot it off for ye. Oh, but I will, Mistress Eleanor. [*shaking his fist toward the right*] This is our country now, and we be ready to defend it till Gabriel blows his judgment horn. Did not another man slay his thousand with the jawbone of an ass? Eigh, then what a mighty destruction of lives I could manage with this weapon of terror! I am good for a whole army of Indians.

ELEANOR: [*pointing toward the rear*] The flag, the flag!

[*A cheer bursts from the men, and they twirl their caps in the air as Borden fastens the flag above the stockade. The music begins playing a dynamic martial air — the powerful notes pouring across the scene and echoing through the dark forest. The cheering of the men dies out, and Borden speaks above the swelling music, his voice fresh and triumphant.*]

BORDEN: Three cheers for our new home — Virginia!

WHITE: Three cheers!

MEN: Hooray! 'Ray! 'Ray!

ELEANOR: And may this flag never fall except as we fall first. Long live Virginia!

MEN: [*cheering*] Virgini-ay! Virgini-ay!

[*The music makes a strong salute and dies. White calls out loudly through the scene.*]

WHITE: Unload the ships!
DARE: Unload the ships!

[*Dame Colman and the two soldiers solicitously attend Eleanor back the way she came. Borden hurries out at the right rear to assist in the unloading. The music strikes up in the dynamic old ballad of "Sir Walter Raleigh's Ship," and the colonists, men and women, now begin entering from the right and right rear, fetching household belongings—bundles, bags, hampers, etc. One man carries a spinning wheel and another a cradle. Here follows a choreographed action of getting settled—cleaning up the debris of the fort's wreckage and setting things to rights. White and Dare participate in the action somewhat as overseers, pointing and helping. All sing as they work, the pantomime fitting the rhythm of the song.*]

COLONISTS:
Sir Walter Raleigh's ship went a-sailing on the sea,
And her name it was the name of the Golden Trin-i-tee,
As she sailed upon the lone and the lonesome low,
    As she sailed upon the lonesome sea.
[*Some of the women are now busy in the chapel, pushing the pulpit back into place and the little baptismal fount likewise. Others are cleaning out the cabins. The historian stands at the left front observing the work.*]
There was another ship went a-sailing on the sea,
And her name it was the name of the Spanish Rob-ber-ee,
And she sailed upon the lone and the lonesome sea,
    As she sailed upon the lonesome sea.
[*Still other colonists have entered, Borden and Old Tom among them. They join in the action.*]
Up stepped a little lad, Great Sir Walter, Lord, he said,
What will you give to me if I sink her down like lead,
If I sink her in the lone and the lonesome low,
    If I sink her in the lonesome sea?

Ten thousand pounds in gold shall be given unto thee,
And unto my daughter fair likewise wedded you shall be,
If you sink her in the lone and the lonesome sea,
    If you sink her in the lonesome sea.

[*The scene fades out, and the light holds on the historian. The music reprises a bit of the ballad and dies.*]

HISTORIAN: The colonists settled in and around the fort. The chapel was restored, buildings were repaired, fields chopped and ploughed, and roads cleared. A smithy and weaving room were soon set up, and in a few days Fort Raleigh looked like a thriving permanent settlement.

[*The light fades from the historian and comes up on the center stage.*]


SCENE 2


[*At the downstage center several of the colony women have spread a great fish net on the ground and are beginning to mend it. Two sentinels pace back and forth along the high parapet built across the palisades. The flag still flies in its place as before. The women are singing as they work.*]

WOMEN:
Adam lay ybounden,
    Bounden in a bond;
Four thousand winter
    Thought he not too long.

And all was for an apple,
    An apple that he took,
As clerkes finden written
    In their book.

[*Dame Colman, the midwife, comes hurriedly in from the right and crosses the scene over toward the cabin at the left front. She is a spry peppery little woman of about fifty, with a kerchief tied over her graying hair. Joyce Archard, a plump youthful woman of about thirty, calls out to her.*]

JOYCE: How fares it with Mistress Dare, Dame Colman? [*But the midwife has already gone into the cabin.*]

ELIZABETH GLANE: [*another of the group, about twenty-five*] I hope it will be a boy.

ALICE CHAPMAN: [*about twenty, slow of speech and with a bit of a stutter*] And I — I would a — they — they named him Walter Raleigh Dare.

MARGERY HARVIE: [*about thirty, a motherly sweet woman*] Aye, it would please Sir Walter, proud and great though he be in England.

JANE JONES: [*a thin tired looking young woman of about twenty-five*] And how would he be hearing of it across the great water? [*murmuring and staring off*] The great water.

JOYCE: [*with firm energy*] Now none of that, Jane Jones. This is Virginia.

MARGARET LAWRENCE: [*a vivacious girl, about seventeen or eighteen*] Governor White will carry news when he sails.

JANE: When he sails.

MARGERY: Every day draws nearer toward the time of storms. And we need supplies.

JOYCE: This is no time to talk of supplies and we on Roanoke Island only two weeks.

JANE: [*as the midwife comes out of the cabin at the left with some linen and a basin*] I dreamed last night Simon Fernandes weighed anchor and fled away to England leaving us to die.

JOYCE: Whist on your dream.

DAME: [*locking the cabin door with a great key and coming forward*] And I wish he might sail away and the governor with him. Here they sit around waiting — waiting in a clutter. I have delivered a hundred strapping Devon girls in my time, yea, and more, and I don't need their help here.

JOYCE: Is everything well?

DAME: Is everything well? You'd think never had a babe been born into the world before. Lah, but then it's Mistress Dare who is the mother and sure she is greater than the Virgin Mary.

JANE: Oh, you shouldn't talk so.

DAME: No? Wait till you hear me railly talk. And if they don't get some of the crowd away from my door I'll begin. There sits Master Dare and the Reverend Master Martin on a cushion of pins. And the blessed governor, anxious grandfather, with his brushes ready to paint the portrait the minute the wee girl comes into the world.

JOYCE: [*laughing*] Girl? — But we are praying it will be a boy.

DAME: Well, it won't be, for I can't abide men.

JOYCE: But without men your job would be lost.

DAME: Then I would mend fish nets with you. And now won't you tell me why these same men don't catch any fish with all them mighty nets you're fixing?

JOYCE: Because Wanchese's tribe has got possession of the fishing grounds, that's why.

DAME: And why haven't we got possession of the fishing grounds?

JOYCE: There's to be no bloodshed. The governor's orders — and wise ones too.

DAME: They're all cowards. Only one man is among them — John Borden. Without him and the help of Manteo, God bless that savage, this colony would not last a six month. [*Old Tom comes in at the left with two buckets of water hung from a yoke over his shoulder.*] Oh, there you are!

[*She darts over to him, dips out a basin of water and hurries away at the right. Old Tom starts on heavily. A middle-aged pudgy Indian squaw comes in, following along close behind him.*]

OLD TOM: [*as the women begin to laugh*] Laugh! Laugh! Here I am a beast of burden and all me valor perished in me feet. [*turning angrily around on the squaw*] Leave me in peace, will you? Be scarce and get gone. Phewt! [*But the Indian woman only smiles at him, and the women laugh again.*] Funny, ain't it? But there's scripture for me condition. Didn't they set Sampson to grind in a mill? Yea, and what did Sampson do? Wham, and down came the great pillars!

JOYCE: It's your lady-love we're laughing at, Tom, not you. Oh, but she's faithful.

OLD TOM: Aye, since the day she heard me singing down by the creek, I won her savage heart away. [*yelling*] Scat, you old — old sow! Whew, she's all anointed with bear grease again! Love ointment it is, people.

JOYCE: You should be proud to be so sought for.

OLD TOM: Ah, Lord, what a wonder is this? Here I went sixty-odd years in England without so much as a glimpse of a woman's sweet favor, and now I'm favored to undoing! [*yelling*] Get out! Trot, run, march! [*but the Indian woman only smiles the more blissfully at him*] Verily this is a new land of opportunity, as Mistress Dare maintains. Oohm, me a ladies' man and nothing but a water-carrier to the fields.

JOYCE: How is the work going there?

OLD TOM: Worse and worse, which is to say more and more. John Borden is a demon for labor. The men all grumble and growl, but he laughs and sings. And water — water — water. Well, well, well, when the springs of the world run dry I shall rest. [*Far in the distance a faint call of "Water, water" is heard. Old Tom starts hurriedly off up the walkway at the left, calling as he goes.*] Coming, coming, Master Borden!

[*He waddles on and out, the Indian squaw padding softly after him. The women watch them go, and then Joyce begins to hum in a rich contralto voice. They all start singing again.*]

WOMEN:
Ne had the apple taken been,
 The apple taken been,
Ne had never our lady
 A-been heavene queen.

Blessed be the time
 That apple taken was.
Therefore we moun singen
 Deo gracias!

[*A group of little boys, some five or six, of different ages, ranging from six to fourteen, come scurrying in down the walkway at the left front. They variously carry rude fishing poles, a string of fish or two, bundles of sassafras roots, and flowers. Two men with muskets accompany them to the center stage and leave when the boys are safely with the women. The little boys show the women their possessions.*]

THOMAS ARCHARD: [*about eight years old*] Look, Mother, the fish we ketched. Manteo showed us where to find them .

GEORGE HOWE, JR.: [*about ten years old*] And see the sassafras roots. They will make good tea for father's fever.

THOMAS SMART: [*about nine*] I got some flowers for the baby. Has God sent it yet?

JOYCE: God is sending the baby now.

THOMAS SMART: But he is so slow.

JOYCE: You boys run along. Master Bennett is waiting with the catechism.

WILLIAM WYTHERS: [*about thirteen, scowling*] I thought we wouldn't have school today.

JOYCE: Run along — And give the fish to the cooks.

[*The boys go out at the right. Manteo enters at the left. At the same time John Borden comes rapidly down the walkway at the left front. He is stained with sweat and dust from laboring in the fields. Behind him are three or four young men, likewise toil-worn and begrimed. They carry shovels and a mattock.*]

BORDEN: Is the net finished?

JOYCE: It will do.

BORDEN: Good. Greetings to you, Manteo. [*Manteo bows, and Borden turns to the women again.*] Take the net down to the boat. Tony Cage swears to a great run of fish around the point. [*The women rise, fold the net and carry it out at the right. Borden now speaks strongly to the men.*] There is yet two hours of sun for working in the fields, men. I will come later. [*The men go out at the left.*] Is there still no news of Wanchese?

MANTEO: [*shaking his head*] He hides in the forest.

BORDEN: He may, but his men don't. Again last night they raided our fields, tore up our nets and tried to fire Master Dutton's house.

MANTEO: I speak with Governor White.

BORDEN: He is with his daughter. What is it?

MANTEO: Too many your men go out alone — must go together.

BORDEN: That is the order, but some of them won't obey. George Howe is down the shore fishing now. I warned him.

MANTEO: Great danger. You tell Governor White Manteo say.

BORDEN: I've told him.

[*Manteo bows and goes back the way he came. Two artisans enter at the right, one rolling a wheelbarrow and the other carrying a grubbing hoe. They stop by Borden.*]

FIRST ARTISAN: [*as Borden examines the wheelbarrow*] A monstrous fine piece of handiwork — if I did construct it.

BORDEN: But you should've made the wheel out of gum. It's tougher.

FIRST ARTISAN: There ain't no pleasing you, Sergeant.

BORDEN: Not till it's done right.

[*The man rolls the wheelbarrow off.*]

SECOND ARTISAN: Sergeant, us have the medicine now to cure them grass and roots. [*with a proud chopping motion*] — Hah —

BORDEN: [*examining the hoe*] Good — good. We want a score of them, come Monday a week. Forks too.

SECOND ARTISAN: You'll have 'em, sir, trust me.

[*He goes out. Old Tom comes tearing in from the right and runs to the farm bell by the little chapel and begins ringing it violently.*]

OLD TOM: [*calling out above his loud ringing*] Hear ye — hear one and all!

[*Borden turns quickly around, hurries to the right and looks off and then comes back into the scene.*]

BORDEN: How is she — Mistress Dare? [*loudly*] Speak, man.

OLD TOM: [*as the colonists begin to enter from the right and left*] Oyez! Oyez! Hear ye! Hear ye! This the eighteenth day of August, fifteen hundred and eighty-seven, a daughter is born to our beloved Mistress Eleanor Dare! Oh yes! Oh yes!

[*John White, Captain Dare and Reverend Martin come in from the right. By this time a crowd has gathered jubilantly in front of the chapel. Reverend Martin enters there and stands above the people. The troops of little boys rush in pell-mell, and behind them the Indian squaw. She sees Old Tom and pushes her way through to be near him. He looks at her, suddenly stops ringing the bell, throws up his hands and stands near Reverend Martin as if for protection. Manteo and a few of his warriors enter from the left and stand on the outer edge of the crowd.*]

REVEREND MARTIN: [*as the people bow down on their knees, Manteo and his family doing likewise*] O Lord, save this woman thy servant.
PEOPLE: [*in a chanted response*] Which putteth her trust in thee.
REVEREND MARTIN: Be thou to her a strong tower.
PEOPLE: From the face of her enemy.
REVEREND MARTIN: Lord, hear our prayer.
PEOPLE: And let our cry come unto thee.
REVEREND MARTIN: O Almighty God, which hast delivered our beloved Eleanor Dare and thy servant from the great pain and peril of childbirth, grant, we beseech thee —

[*Suddenly the sentinel on the high outlook at the left rear lets out a great cry.*]

SENTINEL: Indians! They're killing Master Howe!

[*He lifts his gun and fires. Manteo springs away to the right, followed by his men. Borden runs with them. In the distance the wild yelling of savages is heard. The women and children begin to wail and cry as they gather beseechingly around their minister. The light blacks out on the center stage and rises on the historian at the left front.*]

HISTORIAN: A day later three other settlers were ambushed and killed — Tony Cage, William Clement, and Thomas Ellis — as they were cutting reeds to thatch their cabins. The colonists buried their dead and went determinedly on. Manteo met the savages in a pitched battle and drove them over to the mainland. Governor White set a price on the head of Wanchese and made Manteo lord of Dasamongueponke and all the surrounding country and subject under him to Sir Walter and the queen. On August the thirteenth Manteo had been baptized as a Christian and on Sunday the twenty-fourth the new baby was christened.

# SCENE 3

[*The light fades from the historian and rises on the center stage. The colonists are gathered in and before the chapel. Near the altar and rude font within are Reverend Martin, Dame Colman, Joyce Archard, John White, Ananias Dare and John Borden. On the rear wall above the altar is a large framed painting of the Virgin Mary. At the right front of the crowd outside are Old Tom and near him the Indian woman. Over at the left front the end of a table projects into the scene. It is loaded with a keg of ale, fruits and provisions. And to the rear of it are Manteo, his wife and son and a group of his warriors. Simon Fernandes and two or three of his sailors are near them looking on. As the lights go up, the music begins playing a traditional hymn tune, and the colonists sing.*]

COLONISTS:
    With thankful hearts, O gentle Lord,
    We bow to thee in one accord,
    Obedient to thy kind decree,
    "Let little children come to me."

    Once long ago our Saviour's word
    The children of Judea heard,
    Soft answer to their lowly plea —
    "Come, little children, come to me."
    Amen.
    [*The song ends, the light comes up more brightly within the little chapel, and Reverend Martin begins the baptismal ceremony.*]

REVEREND MARTIN: [*holding the new baby aloft, a little bundle of white*]
Dearly beloved, in as much as our Heavenly Father has seen fit to bless us with
    this child, thereby sending us a token of his favor and marking this
    settlement with the sign of permanence, we do return thanks for his
    bounty and mercy. [*Some of the little boys inside pop up for a better view of
    the baby but are pulled down instantly by their elders beside them.*]
    Conscious we are of this great event — to be marked and set down in
    history for all time to come. [*his voice strong and sonorous*] This the first
    English child to be born in the new world! [*He turns to Borden and Joyce.*]
    And now the godparents, John Borden and Joyce Archard, chosen of the
    church — [*pausing*] — name this child.
JOYCE: Virginia.
BORDEN: In honor of this our country.
REVEREND MARTIN: [*dipping his hand into the font and sprinkling Virginia's*

*forehead*] I baptize thee, Virginia, in the name of the Father and of the Son and of the Holy Ghost, Amen. [*He makes the sign of the cross on her brow.*]

PEOPLE: Amen.

REVEREND MARTIN: The Lord be with you.

PEOPLE: And with thy spirit.

[*The music sounds a salute, and the people all come out of the chapel. Old Tom begins to ring the bell, and the four musicians who have been standing among the crowd with their lutes, viol and tabor seat themselves on some boxes at the right and fall to tuning their instruments. Two or three others begin drawing ale from the keg and passing it out in mugs, first to Governor White and those near him. The Indian woman gets hold of a mug and takes it over to Old Tom. He drops his bell-rope, gives her a wink and a smile and takes it. Dame Colman, the midwife, comes down out of the chapel with little Virginia Dare, and immediately there is a great pushing and crowding around to get a look at the baby. The dame allows them this favor a brief moment and then takes her precious charge away at the right, some of the little boys tagging along behind and pulling at her apron.*

*And now the musicians strike up an English country dance. The men and women pair off, and the governor dances with Joyce Archard. Finally Old Tom and the Indian woman are going it along with the rest, and even Manteo gets out into the scene for a few turns with his wife. As the dance continues, Fernandes lifts his head and is seen scanning the heavens. He speaks to the sailors and they go out at the right. The dance ends, the dancers applaud, and then Governor White climbs up on a box. With a mug of ale he gestures to those around him.*]

VOICES: Speech! Speech!

[*The crowd grows silent.*]

GOVERNOR WHITE: Friends, this is a happy day for us. It marks the permanent beginning of English colonization in the new world. Blest of God and his holy church, our colony will from this day forth go on to a greater destiny. The hour has come at last when I must sail again to England. But I go happily in the knowledge that I leave behind me here a contented settlement. [*There are murmurings of agreement from the people.*] And now I do declare that by your vote duly recorded in the book of colony affairs—this Citie of Raleigh in Virginia and the lands adjacent thereto are placed under the joint rule of Captain Dare, Eleanor Dare and John Borden, Captain!

[*There is applause. Voices break out.*]

VOICES: 'Ray!

OTHER VOICES: Borden! Borden! Captain Borden!

STILL OTHER VOICES: Speech! Speech!

BORDEN: [*Embarrassed, he speaks simply.*] Till you return, sir, we shall be true
to our trust.

VOICES: Yea! 'Ray for Captain Borden!

[*Borden steps back.*]

GOVERNOR WHITE: And now farewell. Before the coming of Christmas you
shall see us again with several shiploads of provisions, other men and
women and children, our neighbors, to add to our number. Mayhap this
time the Queen will relent and Sir Walter himself will accompany me back.
[*The crowd applauds.*] God be with you.

PEOPLE: [*fervently*] God be with you, Governor White!

[*White starts away at the right, Captains Dare and Borden following him.
The music begins softly playing, and the crowd goes solemnly after them. Old
Tom comes along with his yoke and buckets as the last of the people leave. The
faithful squaw is still behind him. She taps him gently on the shoulder
indicating that she will willingly carry the burden. He stares at her in joyful
astonishment and gleefully puts the yoke on her shoulders. Then he skips
joyously behind her as she moves off to the left. He bursts into happy song, the
music accompanying.*]

OLD TOM: [*singing*]
O once I was courted by a lady of color,
I loved her I vow and protest,
I loved her so well and so very well
That I built me a bow'r in her breast, in her breast,
That I built me a bow'r in her breast.
[*He gives her plump rear end a slap.*] Lead on, me honey, you have won me
manly heart away. [*She goes on out at the left, Old Tom following behind.*]
Oh, up on the mountain and down in the valley,
I tell the glad news all around —

[*Now the people, standing along the ramparts at the rear and off scene, burst
into cheers for the departing Governor White. The great shaft of light comes
up once more behind the palisaded fort at the extreme right, and the masts of
White's ship can be seen, moving back to the left, headed home. The men and
women cheer and wave their kerchiefs, and the music builds toward a climax*]

*of salutation. The illuminated masts of the ships disappear at the left, the shaft of light dies, the music sinks down to silence, and the light comes up once more on the historian now at the right front.*]

HISTORIAN: But John White's voyage home was beset with violent storms, and only after great hardship and suffering did he finally reach England — November 5. In the meantime all thought of colony or empire across the sea had dropped from the queen's intent. For now Philip of Spain was preparing his great armada against her, and all resources were called upon for defense.

## SCENE 4

[*The light dies from the historian and comes up in a strong concentration at the left front, revealing a corner of the queen's council chamber. Queen Elizabeth is revealed sitting in a lofty throne-like chair, the members of her privy council behind her, and Sir Walter Raleigh standing to the right and before her. Just behind Raleigh is John White, leaning on a stick, his head bowed. Lord Essex, a proud and dominant man, is standing behind the queen. The queen is talking violently and angrily.*]

ELIZABETH: How many times do I have to tell you no! No, no, I say again! [*reaching her arms up pleadingly in the air*] This Raleigh will have the very heart out of me with his colony. [*wagging her head*] Night and day he pursues me, sends messages to my door, haunts me in my dreams with "Roanoke, Roanoke! My people are perishing in yonder world!" 'Fore God in heaven, I should clap him in a dungeon and hush his clamor. And that I will — I will if he persists. O Essex!

ESSEX: [*touching her shoulder comfortingly*] Patience, dear queen, you fret yourself for naught.

ELIZABETH: "Dear queen" — ah, that it might ever be so with you all. — And he knows I cannot spare him for a prison, not while Philip threatens me. No, that I cannot. And so he presumes upon me. [*Her voice dies out and she stares at Raleigh.*] Speak — speak, will you?

RALEIGH: [*bowing*] If I may.

ELIZABETH: "If I may" — always that knife of courtesy to cut my kindness in two — you — you — [*half-breaking down*] I shall never understand you.

RALEIGH: It is but a simple thing I request, your majesty, to save my colony in Virginia.

ELIZABETH: Too simple and too brief—hah? Like the breaking of a neck. And do you think I'll risk my country's neck by allowing you to leave England? [*rising quickly*] Did I not warn you! [*clapping her hands and calling loudly*] The guard!

ESSEX: Pray, your majesty—

ELIZABETH: [*bitterly*] Queen, queen—majesty—majesty! [*almost glaring at Raleigh*] You'd think I'm but a scullery maid to cleanse the kitchens of my people for all you hearken to me. [*She sinks down in her chair and buries her face in her hands.*]

RALEIGH: [*quietly*] Your majesty, I must give over to your wish. I do not go to Roanoke, so be it. But pray listen to this my pleading.

ELIZABETH: Once more—and yet once more. Then speak—there was a phrase I used once—aye, you strange and proud and dreaming man.

RALEIGH: [*bowing again*] Out of your great right, pray call me what you will. But no one less than a queen would doubt my loyalty to England.

ELIZABETH: Nor does your queen doubt it, Sir Walter.

RALEIGH: Then count me brave and let them write me down brave fool in ages yet to be.

ELIZABETH: Leave that to history to decide between us two. Your request?

RALEIGH: I have through several devious ways arranged for funds—to purchase two small ships.

ELIZABETH: And you would send them to your colony.

RALEIGH: At once—with provisions. God knows how stands it with them there!

ELIZABETH: You know my orders of these several months?

RALEIGH: I do—no ships may leave these shores.

ELIZABETH: [*trying to control her anger*] Yes.

RALEIGH: But then I begged a fleet of ships before. And these are only two and small at that. They could be spared, with Master White.

WHITE: [*coming forward and bowing down on his knees*] Your majesty, I beg you. My daughter—her baby—day and night they call to me. [*brokenly*] I cannot endure it. Let me go to them.

ELIZABETH: [*loudly*] Rise, Master White. [*He climbs tremblingly to his feet.*] There is an old saying taught me by my nurse—a little thread can often save the rope from breaking. Perhaps these tiny ships might be the holding strand against the King of Spain. [*after a dramatic pause*] But I consent.

WHITE: [*bowing up and down abjectly*] Your gracious majesty and queen beyond compare—your holy grace—they will be saved—be saved!

ELIZABETH: Yet if Philip attacks us and we lose—[*looking sternly at Raleigh*]—then for this tiny thread, these little ships that might have turned the tide, Sir Walter shall pay forfeit with his head. [*A trumpet sounds in the music and the queen rises quickly as a messenger enters. Falling on his knees, the messenger presents a letter which Elizabeth takes and tears open. She reads it and then smiles strangely at Sir Walter.*] It seems that destiny doth make the choice. Between my England and your Virginia, it favors me. Would God it did not in such a tragic way as this. [*loudly*] In this hour no ships shall leave England, large or small. For by the sea we live. To lose it is to perish. Gentlemen, a Spanish armada is set to sail against us. And now to arms — God save us!

[*Again a flourish, deeper-toned and more ominous this time, sounds in the music. Consternation runs among the group. Essex grabs the queen's hand, kisses it and strides away at the left. The queen and the others hurry out. Raleigh and White are left behind.*]

WHITE: [*in a low agonized voice*] This means the end of the colony. It will die.
RALEIGH: [*staring before him*] As many of us shall — that England may live.

[*He goes slowly away at the rear, White following like a broken man. Far in the distance a high, strident and summoning trumpet is blown. The scene fades out and the light rises once more on the historian now standing in the walkway.*]

HISTORIAN: And so all resources of England were kept for defense against Spain. And on Roanoke Island the colonists waited with sickened hearts for the help that never came. Day after day, night after night, month after month, they watched and worked and waited. But never the white sail of a ship was seen, never the mariner's cheer was heard to tell that help was nigh. Only the murmur of the vast and sheeted waters or the sad whispering of the dark forest broke upon their uneasy dreams.


SCENE 5


[*The light fades away from the historian. The music begins a slow dead march, and a dim glow rises on the center stage and suffuses the scene. A funeral cortege is seen entering from the right led by Eleanor Dare with a book held before her. She is reading a funeral service. John Borden walks by her side. Four men carrying a rude coffin follow behind, accompanied by Joyce Archard and several women and children who are weeping silently.*]

ELEANOR: [*The music softly accompanying.*]
I know that my redeemer liveth,
And that I shall rise out of the earth in the last day,
And shall be covered again with my skin,
And shall see God in my flesh,
Yea, and I myself shall behold him,
Not with other but with these same eyes.
The Lord giveth and the Lord taketh away,
Even as it pleaseth the Lord
So cometh things to pass.
Blessed be the name of the Lord.
MOURNERS: Blessed be the name of the Lord.

[*The funeral procession passes on out at the left. Eleanor's voice fades away in the distance, and the light dies. The music holds a long and apprehensive note and then is suddenly shocked with an anguished cry of its own, a cry of warning. Somewhere in the darkness a single woman's scream is heard, and then another from the sleeping stockade around. Yells go up in the night. A surging spotlight hits the right front of the stage. The figure of Wanchese is seen creeping forward there, followed by several of his warriors. Colonist women, led by Eleanor Dare, are now fleeing across the scene and taking refuge in the chapel. Wanchese and his men spring forward to attack the frightened women. John Borden and several of the colonist men rush in from the left rear and meet them in the center. A hand-to-hand struggle follows. Shots and screams fill the air. The fury of the music increases. The light surges in and out on the fight. We hear old Tom yell on his parapet walk aloft. The spotlight illuminates him briefly there as he clubs at the head of an Indian who is trying to scale the palisades from the back. Dame Colman has scurried up the ladder at the right rear and she and Joyce Archard with brooms and clubs are seen fighting at the climbing Indians as the spotlight hits them for an instant. The light surges in at the left front and Manteo comes flying in with a few of his warriors.*]

DAME COLMAN: [*crying out from the parapet*] Manteo's come!
VOICES: Manteo! Manteo!

[*A fire breaks out by the cabin at the left front. Several of the colonists— women and children—spring forward, beat at the fire, throw sand on it and put it out. The spotlight now hits Captain Dare hurrying in with his men from the left front—as if arriving from an outpost.*]

Captain Dare!

OTHER VOICES: Captain Dare! 'Ray! 'Ray!

[*A few of the fighters have fallen wounded and dead in the background. Captain Dare and Manteo drive Wanchese and his few remaining warriors out at the right front, pursuing them off. Smoke is now rolling across the scene, the flashes of musket fire have continued and the battle score has thundered its way in the music. The battle dies down. The music holds its long lengthened note again. The women huddle moaning in the chapel. We see Captain Dare in the spotlight at the right front now staggering back into the scene, an arrow in his back. He wavers along by the right front cabin clutching at the logs for support.*]

A WOMAN'S VOICE: [*crying out*] Captain Dare!

[*He plunges to the ground, face downward. Eleanor runs forward and kneels by him with a cry. She stares in horror at the arrow and holds the dying man to her. Borden hurries forward out of the shadows at the left.*]

BORDEN: Captain Dare. Captain Dare! [*He kneels down.*]
ELEANOR: [*after a pause*] He is dead.

[*The light fades from the scene and comes up on the historian at the left.*]

HISTORIAN: The Indians were driven off in defeat, but at a heavy loss. Wanchese was slain as Manteo had sworn. Manteo himself was badly wounded. And along with Captain Dare several colonists were killed, among them Henry Johnson, Humphrey Newton, John Starte, Martin Sutton, Clement Taylor and Ambrose Viccars. The government of the colony now devolved upon Eleanor Dare and John Borden. With unflagging spirits they strove to supply food, keep up the morale of the settlers and take care of the ailing. And every day the whisper ran — "Food will come before the summer ends. Surely before the season of storms Sir Walter will send his ships." But summer came and went — then autumn. And the specter of starvation faced them on their second Christmas.

## SCENE 6

[*The light dies on the historian and comes up inside the cabin at the right of the chapel revealing Eleanor Dare sitting by a cradle in which Virginia Dare is sleeping. She is singing a lullaby, and her fingers fly back and forth weaving a rush basket as she sings. In the center of the scene at the front is a large iron pot with a*] *circle of dull red coals under it. On the parapet at the back the dim figure of the sentinel can be seen as he keeps his watch. It is early evening of a winter day.*]

ELEANOR:
When Jesus came from heaven
To be a little child,
He chose a lowly maiden,
His mother, Mary mild.
To warm him were the oxen,
His bed a manger bare,
And for our needs he suffered
Great want and cold and care.
[*Somewhere in the distance at the rear the muffled sobs of a woman are heard. Eleanor listens a moment with strained attention and then resumes her singing.*]
Lord Jesus, now from heaven
Where thou art Lord of all,
O send thy blessed angels
To guard this baby small.
For peace in dark and danger
Thy loving-kindness brings.
O bend above, enfolding,
The shadow of thy wings.
[*A low call of "Eleanor" is heard in the cabin at the left of the chapel. Eleanor rises, takes up a mug and comes out to the pot. She dips the mug in and goes to the cabin at the left. As she enters, the light comes up on the interior revealing the wasted form of the Reverend Martin as he lies propped up in his rude bed. At the same time the light dies away in the cabin at the right.*]

ELEANOR: [*putting the cup to the sick man's lips*] Drink, Father Martin, you will feel better.
REVEREND MARTIN: [*He makes an effort to drink and then pushes the mug away and smiles weakly at her. In a tired desolate voice which he tries to make cheery:*] Thank you, my child.
ELEANOR: [*tidying the bed a bit*] Now you sleep and rest. We'll have some good potato soup in a little while.
REVEREND MARTIN: Any news from John Borden?
ELEANOR: It's a long way from Hatorask, but he will be here soon now — soon.
REVEREND MARTIN: Aye, that he will. [*The woman's low sobs are heard again*

*in the distance.*] And God grant that he bring you good news. [*listening*] Is that Sister Margery?

ELEANOR: Yes.

REVEREND MARTIN: She loved her baby. The Lord giveth and the Lord taketh away.

ELEANOR: [*recitingly*] Blessed be the name of the Lord.

REVEREND MARTIN: [*after a moment*] Eleanor, I have had a strange dream. I saw a great swan — white and with wings like a ship and it was flying south. [*sighing and closing his eyes*] Flying south it was, through the still blue sky, and I could feel the breath of air from its wings against my cheeks, and the air was warm — it was warm. And out of its mouth came melodious words sweet as an angel in paradise and it was saying, "Follow me, follow me." I wonder was it a sign?

ELEANOR: What sign, Father?

REVEREND MARTIN: To leave this spot. [*as she stares at him*] Evil has been wrought here, the spilling of blood, the murder of innocent ones. Shall we ever thrive here? Mayhap that was a voice sent from God to warn us to leave this place.

ELEANOR: No! No! [*dropping down on a rough stool and gazing before her*] But sometimes I think — [*then shaking her head firmly*] No, we must bide here. [*rising in a sudden show of cheerfulness*] This is the better place. The Indians no longer molest us. Sixty of us still remain alive and spring will soon be coming. We have our houses, and in April we will plant crops. It was only a dream.

REVEREND MARTIN: It is ninety days till April.

ELEANOR: John Borden will never desert the fort.

REVEREND MARTIN: And you will stay with John Borden.

ELEANOR: I will.

REVEREND MARTIN: And in the spring you will be wed.

ELEANOR: Aye, Father, in the spring.

REVEREND MARTIN: God's blessings on you two and on us all, my child.

ELEANOR: Amen.

REVEREND MARTIN: And how does little Virginia?

ELEANOR: [*sitting down again*] She is so pitiful and so thin. But in her sleep she smiles so — so — she does — [*She suddenly bows, gripping her knees.*]

REVEREND MARTIN: [*lifting his hand to rest on her head*] Grieve not, my child. Somehow we shall win. I have God's promise — in my heart I have it.

[*The light fades down in the cabin and comes up on the center stage emphasizing the pot. The Indian woman comes in at the right front, bowed under a great bundle of firewood. Old Tom follows behind carrying a tow-like bag in his hand.*]

OLD TOM: Sweet my love, unload. [*He helps her lift off the wood.*] Whew, but an ox could carry no more. Eigh, I am the most fortunate of men. [*Eleanor comes out of the cabin.*] How fares it with his reverence, Mistress Dare?

ELEANOR: He is sleeping now.

OLD TOM: [*as the Indian woman squats down and begins to tend the fire*] I have a bit of business with him when he mends — [*gesturing*] — her and me. Brr-rr, but it's cold. Stir up, Agona, stir up.

ELEANOR: Agona?

OLD TOM: I have lately christened her Agona — which is to say in the Indian tongue — "Agony." Brr-rr — but I've been sleeping cold of nights. [*He bends over, sniffs the pot, and puts his hand affectionately on Agona's head.*] Hmm, I never knew a stew of leaves and stale corn to smell so good.

ELEANOR: Drink Tom. The children have eaten. But save something for Master Borden.

[*She hands him the mug and he dips it into the pot. He starts to raise it to his lips, then hands it to the Indian woman. She gives an appreciative high-pitched little giggle, drinks, and hands it back to him. Eleanor pulls her shawl about her and goes up into the little chapel.*]

OLD TOM: [*calling out*] I have four more berry candles for the altar. Agona made 'em.

[*He takes the candles from the bag and goes up into the chapel. The music begins a Christmas carol. The candles are now lighted inside the chapel, revealing the snow-white altar around which Eleanor and old Tom are working. Bits of holly and mistletoe hang from the beams above, and the picture of the Virgin looks sweetly down upon the scene. Now in the distance at the left front the sound of singing is heard — a mixture of children's, women's and men's voices.*]

ELEANOR: They're coming — with the yule log!

OLD TOM: And may our hearts keep as warm as the fire it makes.

[*He and Eleanor come out of the chapel and move over toward the left to meet the oncoming singers. Two small sickly boys enter from the left, down the walkway, carrying tapers and leading the yule log procession. Immediately behind them a group of ragged young men come carrying a large log about six or eight feet long, and behind them the rest of the colonists — men, women and children. Some of them carry tapers, others little bunches of holly or bits of ground ivy. They all are dressed in nondescript clothes, old capes, shawls, and pieces of blankets, skins and woven stuffs. They are singing a Christmas carol as they enter. Eleanor moves down and steps between the two little boys, taking them by the hand and leading the procession with them. As the log-bearers reach the pot they place the log next to the fire, and the procession moves on in a circle around the pot. At the right some of the more elderly and feeble of the colonists creep in to join as best they can in the pitiful festivities—among them Margery Harvie supported by the almost tottering Dame Colman. The song continues as the procession moves on in the circle.*]

PEOPLE: [*singing, the music accompanying*]
Nowell, Nowell, Nowell,
Nowell, Nowell, Nowell, Nowell.
This is the salutation of the Angel Gabriel.
Tidings true there be come new,
Sent from the Trinity
By Gabriel to Nazareth,
City of Galilee.
A clean maiden and pure virgin,
Through her humility,
Hath conceived the person
Second in Deity.

OLD TOM: [*shouting above the singing*] Hurrah for old yule!

PEOPLE: [*still singing*]
Hail, virgin celestial,
The meekest that ever was!
Hail, temple of the Deity!
Hail, mirror of all grace!

[*As the procession passes around the pot again, Eleanor moves up into the chapel. The people crowd toward her and stand looking into the chapel, singing. The candles are now extinguished, and the light widens on the scene.*]

PEOPLE:
Hail, virgin pure! I thee insure,
Within a little space,
Thou shalt conceive, and Him receive
That shall bring great solace.

[*The song and music die, and they all kneel down on the ground for a moment of silent prayer. Eleanor then rises and goes up to the altar. The people still kneel beggingly and piteously where they are. She opens her prayer book and reads strongly and comfortingly.*]

ELEANOR:
The Lord is my light and my salvation —
Whom shall I fear?
The Lord is the strength of my life —
Of whom shall I be afraid?

[*Low moans of pain and hunger and grief begin to break among the people.*]
For in the time of trouble
He shall hide me in his pavilion,
Yea, in the secret places of his dwelling
Shall he hide me,
He shall set me up upon a rock.

[*The little bleating cries and calls grow more insistent and louder among the people.*]
Hearken unto my voice, Oh Lord,
When I cry unto thee.
Have mercy upon me and hear me!
Oh, hide not thy face from me,
Nor cast thy servant away in displeasure.
Have mercy upon us,
Oh Lord, have mercy!

A CHILD'S VOICE: [*plaintive and high*] I'm hungry, mommee!

[*The low lamentation of the people now seems stimulated by the child's call, and the pleadings grow louder. A woman breaks into sudden and shrill hysterical sobs. Another woman's voice rises in a dolorous lament.*]

WOMAN'S VOICE:
O Death!
O Death rock me asleep!
Bring me to quiet rest,
Let pass my weary guiltless life
Out of my careful breast.
[*Other voices are added in a hoarse muffled harmony.*]
Toll on the passing bell,
Ring out my doleful knell,
Let fly sound, my death tell.
Death doth draw near me.

There is no remedy, no remedy,
There is no remedy.

[*The sentinel on the parapet lets out a high wild cry.*]

SENTINEL: Merciful God! Merciful God, save us! Save us! [*He flings up his arms and lets his gun fall. Then he jumps headlong down into the scene and bobs his head about in prayer. The cry runs among the people.*]
VOICES: Save us! Save us or we perish! O God have mercy upon us!

[*A few more of the women grow hysterical, the children begin to cry, and three or four men outside the chapel fall to beating their breasts in a paroxysm of woe. Eleanor springs up and moves among the women trying to quiet them. Joyce Archard does likewise. The men continue to moan and pray. Eleanor comes down out of the chapel.*]

ELEANOR: For shame — shame! You frighten these little children. Are ye men or cowards? [*She seizes the sentinel by the collar and tries to shake him.*] Stop it! Stop it!

[*John Borden, accompanied by three raggle-taggle soldiers, comes suddenly down the walkway at the left.*]

BORDEN: [*his words cutting across the scene in a loud command*] Silence! [*Snatching a gun from the nearest soldier, he fires it into the air. The hysteria subsides. The colonists hurry toward Borden, some still jerking and shivering and others emitting low moans. Borden strides over to the sentinel and pulls him to his feet.*] Back to your post!
SENTINEL: [*beating his hands together*] I cannot, I cannot. Ten hours I have stood the watch — ten hours and I am perished with cold! [*He staggers and falls.*]
BORDEN: Take him to his bed. [*Two soldiers come over and lift the sentinel up. Borden takes a mug from Old Tom, dips it into the pot and gives it to one of the soldiers.*] Make him drink of it. [*They bear the sentinel away.*]
A VOICE: What news, Master Borden?
OTHER VOICES: [*rising in vehemence*] Yes — tell us! What news?
BORDEN: Friends, there is news, but it must wait.

[*A growling murmur goes up from the colonists.*]

VOICES: [*bitter and jeering*] Wait! Wait!
OTHER VOICES: Tell us now!
BORDEN: I command you to your cabins. Get yourselves rest, and tomorrow the council will be called.

VOICES: Tomorrow! Down with John Borden! Aye, down with him!

[*The Reverend Martin comes creeping in from the left rear. He stops and stands holding to the corner of the chapel for support.*]

REVEREND MARTIN: Blessings, my children.

[*Jubilation breaks out among the colonists, and some of them run to him and kiss his hands.*]

VOICES: Father Martin! He is well again. Thank God, thank God!

REVEREND MARTIN: Yes, yes—I have had a sign from God—His words came to me—a voice speaking—saying fear not, all will be well. Go now and sleep. Go. [*with benign authority*] Go to your beds!

[*Quieted by his gentle voice, they all gradually move out of the scene at the right and left. Old Tom stops by the Indian woman who has already stretched herself out on the ground.*]

OLD TOM: [*pulling her up*] Come to your bed, old lady.

[*He goes out with her at the left. Eleanor moves over to Reverend Martin.*]

ELEANOR: You must lie down now.

BORDEN: Good night, Father.

REVEREND MARTIN: Bless thee, my lad. On thee we rest. [*He takes Borden's hand and joins it with Eleanor's, then lifts his own in blessing over them.*] In you two—united—the symbol of our strength shall remain secure. God bless you. Good night.

[*Eleanor goes with Reverend Martin into the shadow at the left rear. Borden stands by the pot, his head bowed in thought. Then looking about him, he spies the sentinel's gun, picks it up and returns with it to the fire. He satisfies himself that it is primed, lays it aside and begins holding first one foot to the coals and then the other, his shaggy stern face lighted by the dull glow from below. Eleanor comes quietly back and stands by the fire opposite him. He looks at her, smiles, and then brings a box forward for her to sit on.*]

BORDEN: He is very ill.

ELEANOR: Yes.

BORDEN: And in his fever—dreams of signs and wonders and hears the voice of God.

ELEANOR: Would that the others could hear the same if it gave them peace. And you? Sit down and rest.

BORDEN: Even if I would, my feet keep on walking from habit — and my arms, rowing, rowing.

ELEANOR: And now tell me — the news is bad.

BORDEN: Yes. [*Eleanor bows her head.*] Manteo is dead.

ELEANOR: I feared it.

BORDEN: [*speaking swiftly*] The tribe — what is left of them — is in despair. Tomorrow they begin moving south back to their home in Croatoan. The game has fled away from these islands, food is scarce. A few pitiful bushels of corn they had, no more. They could spare none, nor potatoes. On Croatoan there will be game. [*He begins pacing back and forth by the fire.*]

ELEANOR: If the ships do not come soon — tomorrow —

BORDEN: They will not come — neither tomorrow nor the next day. I know it now.

ELEANOR: [*quietly*] And how do you know it?

BORDEN: Rowing the sounds and tramping those endless bogs and wilderness of salt sea grass, my mind worked in a turmoil of fever and fret. Why? Why? Why? I kept asking myself — why has no sign, no word come from the governor and Sir Walter? What could keep them back? Suddenly I saw the answer. How, I know not, but the answer came. England is at war with Spain.

ELEANOR: [*springing up*] It's true. We should have thought of that.

BORDEN: And the queen keeps back all ships for her defense.

ELEANOR: And may for months to come. Now we must act. Thank God for that. We have supplies in the storehouse to last us but two days at most.

BORDEN: And what would you do?

ELEANOR: If there is game farther south, then we must find it.

BORDEN: And desert the fort?

ELEANOR: [*sitting quietly down again*] My mind runs fast ahead. [*looking up at him*] Only if you wish it.

BORDEN: If I wish it. [*smiling down at her, the hardness of his face softening away*] Thus we agree — we two, standing here tonight upon the outpost of the world, the last survivors — keepers of a dream.

ELEANOR: [*murmuring*] A dream!

BORDEN: And we'll keep that dream — keep it to the end!

ELEANOR: Yes, we will — together we will.

BORDEN: Together — aye, that's it — together — we two. [*Eleanor bows her head. His voice rises with a touch of fervor.*] All this hardship, this desolation and death sit lightly upon me when I think of you. To fight for you, to work for you till I fall in my tracks — that is enough. [*He lays his hand on her shoulder.*]

ELEANOR: [*reaching up and taking his hand*] Think not of me but of the others. [*She puts his hand against her cheek.*]

BORDEN: That too — [*looking up into the night*] And by that great spirit that guards this world and holds our little lives in the hollow of his hand I swear we will fight on and on here until this wilderness is won.

ELEANOR: [*murmuring*] And you will win.

BORDEN: Even if we die, we win. For — [*vehemently*] Ah, Eleanor, tonight I feel — somehow it was meant to be this way. Somehow a destiny, a purpose moving deeper than we know has brought us both together here upon this lonely land — to prove our love, to test our strength — aye, to make us worthy of the heritage we hold for those that shall come after us. For as we hold true — [*He bends and kisses her on the forehead and then stands up straight, his voice filling with a firmer strength and certainty as she rises and clings desperately to him.*] And if in the wisdom of God we should be forced to live out our days here forgot and deserted of the world, I should have no regret — none.

ELEANOR: [*after a moment — lifting her head bravely*] Nor I.

BORDEN: [*staring ahead of him, his voice running on as if in communion with some listener in the dark*] No regret — none. Yea, once Sir Walter said — the victory lieth in the struggle, not the city won. To all free men it standeth so, he said. Out of his suffering he knew. [*He kisses her and holds her close to him.*] And so we know — tonight we know. And down the centuries that wait ahead there'll be some whisper of our name — some mention and devotion to the dream that brought us here. Ah —

[*His voice dies out. For an instant they cling together. Off at the right rear a woman's voice is heard singing. Margery Harvie enters half-clothed and walking like one in a dream.*]

MARGERY: [*her hands held before her as she sings*]
Sir Walter Raleigh's ship went a-sailing on the sea,
And her name it was the name of the Golden Trinitee,
As she sailed upon the lone and the lonesome low —

BORDEN: [*Hurrying over to her, he tries to lead her back the way she came.*]
Come, Margery, you must bide in your bed.

MARGERY: The ship — Sir Walter's ship. Look, there it goes.

[*She breaks away from him. Eleanor goes to her and puts her arm around her.*]

ELEANOR: This is Eleanor, Margery.

MARGERY:
> There was another ship went a-sailing on the sea,
> And her name it was the name—

JOYCE: [*Running in from the rear with a blanket, she wraps it around Margery.*]
> I dozed a bit, and then she was gone.

MARGERY: [*crying out*] My baby! My baby! Oh, Queen Elizabeth!

JOYCE: [*leading her off*] Darling, we'll find him, yes—yes, we will.

[*They go out at the rear. Borden stands a moment watching them, then turns and takes Eleanor by the arm.*]

BORDEN: And you must rest too. Come.

ELEANOR: [*her body shaken as if with an ague*] Take them away from here, John! Take them away! [*moaning*] They can stand no more! They are dying—all of us are dying here.

BORDEN: [*after a moment of silence*] I know—I know—you must sleep now. Tomorrow—tomorrow—we shall—

ELEANOR: Yesterday—today, all day they kept coming to me, begging me to let them leave this place. Let them go. Promise me. [*She suddenly pulls his head down and kisses him vehemently.*]

BORDEN: [*with sudden hardness*] Tomorrow we will all decide. [*loudly*] But the Citie of Raleigh shall not die!

ELEANOR: [*leaning heavily on him*] Not while we live.

[*He leads her into the shadow toward the cabin at the right rear. Old Tom enters at the left with his musket. Looking about him, he clambers up the ladder at the rear and places himself on watch on the parapet, taking the place of the sentinel. Borden reenters.*]

BORDEN: [*hoarsely*] Come down from there, Tom. It's my watch.

OLD TOM: You're dead on your feet, John Borden, and here I am all in the prime of a great fervor. [*Borden who is staggering with weakness, turns toward the fire and sinks down on the box.*] Agona snores like a hundred horns in bedlam. I can't sleep.

BORDEN: [*groggily*] Can't sleep—say you can't sleep? Hah-hah-hah.

OLD TOM: But you can. And while I walk this post with me instrument of vengeance you'll all be safe as Peter's rock. [*authoritatively*] Lie down, lie down, young man, and ease your weary bones.

BORDEN: With men like you, Tom, we'll win this fight.

OLD TOM: I am your man, Captain Borden, small and pitiful-like though I be.

[*Borden leans over from the box, topples down on the ground and lies sprawled out by the fire.*]

BORDEN: [*calling drowsily*] Thank 'ee, Tom, thank'ee. You will be remembered.

[*He sleeps. Old Tom begins walking his post, the light emphasizing him a bit.*]

OLD TOM: [*talking to himself*] I will be remembered. I hope not. [*stopping and staring through the night*] There in England all remembered me — aye, with kicks and curses and a terrible usage of tongues they did. Hah-hah-hah. And deep I drowned me sorrows in the mug. But here where there is no remembrance I who was lately nothing am become somebody. For, item — have I not now the keeping of some sixty souls in me care — I who could never care for me own? Verily, Tom, I hardly know thee in thy greatness. [*saluting the air*] Roanoke, thou hast made a man of me!

[*He draws himself up and marches proudly back and forth a few times. But gradually his steps slow, and finally he leans against the palisade and remains motionless as he gazes off into the darkness. The music begins to play a low requiem as if addressed to the scene. Borden stirs restlessly in his sleep, and Old Tom's head is seen sagging over on his breast as if, for all his great endeavor, weariness were overcoming him. The light dims slowly down. For a moment the music continues. Suddenly off at the left a man's voice is heard in a high halloo. Old Tom jerks his head up, looks about him, and hurries over to the extreme left of the parapet. Then he lets out a loud challenge.*]

OLD TOM: Who comes there! Halt in the queen's name!

[*He raises his musket as one of the colonist runners comes flying in at the left, his gun dragging in his hand and his clothes in tatters.*]

RUNNER: [*calling*] Captain Borden!
OLD TOM: Stop your yowling. Let him sleep.
RUNNER: Captain Borden!
BORDEN: [*raising his head as the light brightens on him and the center stage*] Who calls? [*springing to his feet as the runner hurries over to him*] What is it?
RUNNER: Rouse the people. To arms! A Spanish ship has anchored in the inlet.
BORDEN: [*seizing him by the arm*] Are ye certain?
RUNNER: Aye, sir, by their flags and colors — a ship of war. They bespoke me in their broken tongue.

BORDEN: I fear Fernandes has betrayed us.

RUNNER: Nay, I know not. A party came ashore. They send us terms. Surrender peaceful, we will be protected — and fed.

OLD TOM: [*from above*] We'll not surrender! We'll fight to the last man, Captain Borden!

RUNNER: If we resist we are to be killed — to the last man — [*gasping*] — and woman and child. [*beseechingly*] Oh, Captain Borden, they will murder us! They will!

[*He falls exhausted on the ground. Borden springs away to the bell and begins to ring it loudly.*]

OLD TOM: [*shouting down from his walkway*] Assemble, assemble! Everybody assemble!

[*Eleanor Dare comes out of her cabin. Borden is seen gesturing and speaking to her. She hurries away at the right. The colonists begin to run into the scene from the right and left — men, women and children — in their pitiful clothing. A medley of excited voices breaks around Borden.*]

VOICES: What is it? Have the ships come? They've come! They've come! Sir Walter's ships! Oh, thanks unto God!

[*Some of the men and women begin to embrace one another in trembling jubilancy. Borden stops ringing the bell and stands on the steps of the little chapel. By this time other colonists have assembled. They all grow silent waiting for him to speak.*]

BORDEN: Friends, I fear the hour has come when we must leave the fort. But you shall decide — whether we stay or whether we go —

VOICES: [*bursting out in a high pleading*] What is it, John Borden? Speak, speak.

BORDEN: We must decide — the fate of this colony.

BENNETT: [*a stalwart, lean-faced young man*] The fate of the colony? What do you mean?

BORDEN: Decide — whether we leave this fort, or whether we stay.

VOICES: [*bursting out in a high agonized pleading*] Speak, Captain Borden, tell us!

PEOPLE: Yes, what is it?

BORDEN: [*lifting his hand as the colonists keep crowding around*] Manteo's people are moving south where there is game. They offer us haven with them.

A WOMAN'S VOICE: But why wake us from our sleep to tell us that?

OTHER VOICES: Aye—and ring the bell—like the murdering Indians were on us again. Yea, and all hell screaming in our ears.

PEOPLE: [*wildly*] Yes, why?

BORDEN: [*with a shout*] Because the time is urgent!

[*The runner staggers to his feet.*]

RUNNER: [*loudly*] Friends, a Spanish ship has anchored off the bar.

[*A pall of horror falls upon the assemblage and they stare at one another with stark faces.*]

VOICES: [*whispering*] The Spaniards! The Spaniards!

[*Bennett throws out his hands in a great gesture.*]

BENNETT: The treason of Simon Fernandes has borne its fruit.

BORDEN: Mayhap, Mark Bennett, it is so.

RUNNER: They have a man-of-war to destroy us. Tomorrow or the next day they will reach here and attack us. We are too weak to stand against them. Too weak.

[*He moves over to one side, and a number of the colonists immediately begin gathering around him.*]

ELIZABETH GLANE: [*in a high frightened whimper*] Let us leave this cursed place.

JOYCE ARCHARD: [*wrapping her arms around the hysterical girl, hugging her to her*] Shame on ye, Elizabeth, shame!

[*Dame Colman and Eleanor move among the women and ragged children, trying to quiet them.*]

RUNNER: [*to the group around him, fiercely*] I tell ye the Spanish offer us terms. [*gesturing off at the left*] A party awaits our surrender there. We have but to show a white flag. They will spare our lives.

VOICES: Surrender, surrender!

[*At a push from the runner, a youth darts into one of the cabins.*]

OTHER VOICES: Stay here and we shall be slaughtered in cold blood. Leave! Leave! Leave!

BENNETT: Silence!

[*The runner lifts his hands to cry out again. Bennett rushes toward him as if to knock him down and silence him, but a number of colonists surround the runner to protect him.*]

VOICES: Let him speak!

[*Hysteria is beginning to run among the people.*]

BORDEN: [*above the turmoil*] Let us behave ourselves like soldiers!
OLD TOM: [*from the parapet*] Aye, that we will, Captain Borden!

[*But still others gather around the runner, some of them defiantly, some hopelessly and despairingly. Old Tom clambers down from his post.*]

ONE OR TWO OTHERS: We'll follow ye. We'll follow, Captain Borden!
BORDEN: Good. On Croatoan we'll start a new settlement.
OLD TOM: [*with loud buoyancy*] A new settlement!
VOICES: We'll begin there again.
RUNNER: [*fiercely*] The Spaniards offer us food, I tell ye!
BORDEN: [*yelling*] We'll never yield. We'll carry on the fight — on Croatoan — in the wilderness — wherever God sends us — and to the last man!
VOICES: [*in a great husky groan*] Food! The Spaniards will feed us.
OTHER VOICES: Food, food, give us food.

[*Led by the runner, the group with him now moves swiftly and suddenly toward the left to go to the Spaniards. But Old Tom steps in front of them, lifting his musket menacingly.*]

OLD TOM: [*yelling*] Back, back! I'll kill the first man tries to pass me! [*He cuts at them with his musket. Before his bloodthirsty manner they hesitate.*]
A WOMAN'S VOICE: Feed us.

[*This sets the mutineers off again and they move forward. Old Tom fires his musket across in front of them. Two soldiers rush down from the colonists' houses at the rear with muskets and join Old Tom. The runner and his mutineers are stopped.*]

BENNETT: [*yelling at them*] And it would be the food of slaves!

[*The youth who had gone off reappears with a huge white sheet held aloft on a halberd. The mutineers rally solidly around it and the runner.*]

MUTINEERS: Surrender! Surrender!

[*The youth waves the white cloth aloft, and the mutineers start off again to the left in a body. Led by Dame Colman, several of the women fling themselves on the youth and tear the white cloth from him.*]

DAME COLMAN: [*fiercely as they overpower the youth*] Use my sheet would ye, ye cowardly knave! [*She kicks at the now groveling youth and clutches her precious sheet to her.*] The times John Borden held your fevered hand and nursed ye back from death! [*She kicks at him again and then turns with fury on the mutineers.*] God in heaven witness me, ye shall all burn in hellfire if ye desert us now!

[*The mutineers glare at her. Bennett lifts a flag from near the chapel and stands by Borden. Borden begins to speak with fervent earnestness.*]

BORDEN: You shall know all and make your choice. True, the Spaniards ask us to surrender. True, they will spare our lives, they will feed us. [*Lifting his hands high and continuing, his voice deepening with fervor.*] The question is clear — shall it be dishonor and life, or a brave struggle onward — [*gesturing off to the right*] — out there — even to an end no man knows.

OLD TOM: We'll fight!

A GROUP: [*led by the runner*] No, no!

BORDEN: I know what it means to make this choice. And I know you will make it and you will not fail. You will stand firm for the colony.

[*As Borden continues his pleading, some of the mutineers begin to move back from the runner's group to him and to the flag.*]

JOYCE ARCHARD: [*as she brings forward the citie's coat of arms and holds it up*] Aye, aye, John Borden.

BORDEN: [*with suddenly loud and crushing convincingness*] As for me, I will die before I surrender. [*more loudly*] Here in this new world we have planted the emblem of our race — [*with a gesture toward the flag held by Bennett*] — of free men!

[*A few more mutineers turn back toward Borden.*]

VOICES: And we'll be men.

[*Father Martin enters waveringly from the rear.*]

BORDEN: And in Sir Walter's name, and in the name of her who stands beside me — [*He reaches out and takes Eleanor's hand.*] — let us swear to be true to ourselves and the trust reposed in us.

SEVERAL VOICES: [*a little stronger now*] Yea, Captain Borden! God bless you! Bless you, Mistress Eleanor.

BORDEN: [*with more certainty, a touch of exultation creeping into his voice*] By the death of our friends and companions — [*He gently removes his hat and some of the men do likewise.*] — and those who lie buried in this ground, let us swear our consecration to the best that is in us.

OLD TOM AND ELEANOR: We swear!

JOYCE ARCHARD, DAME COLMAN AND OTHERS: We swear!

[*More of the mutineers return to Borden's group.*]

BORDEN: [*his voice soaring through the night, his eyes straining ahead as if searching to see the invisible enemy hidden in the darkness which he challenges*] Let the wilderness drive us forth as wanderers across the earth, scatter our broken bones upon these sands, it shall not kill the purpose that brought us here!

VOICES: [*still more strongly*] No, John Borden. We will stand with ye, Captain Borden. Stand with ye.

[*By this time the group around the runner has shrunk to some four or five people. But these are sullen and determined not to yield to Borden's persuasion.*]

BORDEN: For it shall live. [*loudly*] Shall live!

[*Bennett holds the flag triumphantly aloft. Joyce lifts the coat of arms likewise.*]

VOICES: We're not afraid. Speak, lead us!

BORDEN: And down the centuries that wait ahead there'll be some whisper of our name, some mention and devotion to the dream that brought us here. And now into the hand of God we commend us. Amen.

OTHERS: [*fervently*] Amen.

[*Led by Borden and Eleanor, they all sweep forward a step or two and kneel. After an instant Borden rises and the others also rise.*]

BORDEN: And now every man to his duty!

OLD TOM: On to Croatoan! [*He hurries out at the left.*]

BORDEN: Bennett, see to the supplies. [*He goes out at the right with Eleanor.*]

BENNETT: Aye, sir. [*calling as he goes away at the left*] Double load every musket!

VOICES: We will that, sir. Down with the Spaniards!

RUNNER: We will not go!
THE GROUP OF MUTINEERS: No! No!

[*The colonists scatter in all directions. The runner and his little group move up into the shadows at the left rear. Reverend Martin creeps slowly to the chapel and kneels in front of it, bowing his head in a last silent prayer. The light fades down somewhat on the scene as the historian speaks.*]

HISTORIAN: [*from the shadows at the left*] And so the colony made ready to leave the fort, driving themselves on with their last gasp of energy and strength. And even the rebellious ones shared in the tragedy of their going. In the cold hours before dawn they began their march into the vast unknown.

[*The light fades from the historian and comes quickly in again on the center stage. The music strikes up the hymn with which the play opened, and the colonists weakly arrange themselves in marching order. Two soldiers with muskets lead the procession, followed by Bennett with the flag, and Joyce with the coat of arms, then Eleanor with Virginia Dare in her arms and Borden with her, and after them the men, women and children of the colony. Old Tom and Agona are at the end of the line. So the march begins toward the right and up along the edge of the woods. Old Tom calls out.*]

OLD TOM: Sing, me hearties, sing. [*He leads off and the others join in.*]
COLONISTS:

O God that madest heaven
　And hedged the seas around,
Who that vast firmament on high
　With golden stars hath bound.

[*As the people move on, the rebellious ones are pulled as if against their will into the march one by one. Father Martin feebly falls. The runner, the last of the rebelling group, hurries forward and lifts him up, and the two move on. The faces of the colonists are raised now, their forms beginning to be energized as they sing. Straight ahead they stare as if looking down the long road which they must travel to the end. At the top of the rise in the edge of the woods Borden and Eleanor stop and turn, as the last of the procession passes by them. They stand looking back on the deserted fort. The light emphasizes them there and fades from the center stage. Another light comes on now, illuminating in a tight spot the flag flying gallantly from the rampart. The song has continued.*]

O God, our mighty Father,
O bright immortal one,
Secure within thy mercy,
We walk this way alone.

[*Borden swings his hand toward the fort in a final farewell. Then putting his arm around Eleanor as if to protect her from whatever lies ahead, he turns, and the two of them plunge into the darkness, following the others. The music continues as the light fades from the scene. The illumination holds on the flag. After an instant the music dies out, and now from the strangely luminous air high above the chapel the echo voices of the colonists are heard in the final words of the hymn, coming as it were from the very deep of heaven—"We walk this way alone." The light fades out.*]

*The End*

# II

# Stories

# The Cornshucking

She was the sweetest thing under the sun. Not an apple in old Squire Johnson's orchard could equal her, none was as red as her cheeks. And that boy loved her better than anything before or since. He would plough in the fields all day with her nestling in his mind, sweeter than honey in the comb. But she didn't know it, didn't know that he was crazy about her. Such a fool he was in those days, timid and scary as a fly. He would go to church and sit at the back listening to her play the organ. There she'd be with her head lifted up, singing and playing, her face alight like an angel. What for him then was the preacher's thundering, what did he care about fire and damnation?

Sometimes she'd pass along the lane, visiting a girl down the road. He would be out in the fields spreading the stinking compost or cutting cornstalks. The sight of her red dress coming around the bend sent his heart up in his throat with a sharp ache. And if someone casually mentioned her name, a sweet thrill would shoot along his spine and down painfully into his toes.

He thought about her, dreamed about her, and the year he was eighteen he began to make plans. Breaking that old stiff land with a heavy two-horse plough, he would ponder in his mind some things he'd do. Before long he'd get up courage and maybe ask her to go riding Sunday. And then before long, you watch him, his mule would be tied at her yard fence at least one night a week.

That spring went by, the summer came, and he hadn't had a single date with her. Once or twice—choked in a high collar of those days, his new bow tie crossed pretty nice and his glass scarf-pin shining like the sun—he had spoken to her at church and commented upon the weather. The merry quick look out of her dark eyes and the tilt of her brown head crucified him with joy. He could never come near such a wonder.

Along with his loving that summer he took up reading, for he knew she liked reading. She had been the brightest scholar in the school. By josh, he'd up and do something, he would. And some of these days—well,—some of these days. He read a poetry book, E. P. Roe and Mrs. Southworth. And through the last named amorous lady his feelings ran amuck. Fool, fool, why couldn't he get up courage to ask her for a date? She was sixteen and old enough.

Then, lo and behold, on a Sunday following his mournful musings, she went by in the lane, swift as an arrow, sitting with Judd Hockaday behind his fast race-horse. Misery, misery. That long lonesome Sunday afternoon he sat in the woods on a log with a stub of pencil and a sheet of paper, pouring out his soul in poetry. The red bugs and seed ticks did their work on his crotch and thighs, but he paid little mind.

*If the high mountains and the deep sea*
*Loosed their power and wrath on me,*
*'Twould not be like the pain I feel*
*Bring me your balm, love, my heart heal.*

There were fifteen verses as good as that. Then in the grey of the twilight he went home somewhat eased. Art hath its compensations. Why couldn't he be a poet? He might. A great writer. He straightened up. Another thought came to him—he might send this poem to her. Why not?

"By josh, she might like that. She would. I bet she didn't know I had it in me." It was good, if he did say it himself. He pulled it out and read it again, walking along the road.

*I looked at the birds and looked at the sky,*
*And hated to think my love would die,*
*I looked at the moon and looked at the sun*
*And thought of my love till day was done.*

Out of his misery came the poem and out of that the decision to act. He put it in an envelope and mailed it to her, no letter or anything, just the poem. Then he waited. Part of his emotion was transferred to the mailman. The sound of his buggy in the lane thrilled him like the sight of her dress. But the days went by and nothing came. Lord, he'd ruined things. Of course she was mad. Anybody would get mad at such brass as that.

For weeks he suffered burning remorse and embarrassment. That poem! He wouldn't have her know who wrote it for anything. But too late now. In the days that followed, even a thought of it and his goose-foolishness would redden his face and cause beads of sweat to pop out on his forehead.

He was out in the lot one afternoon in October when her little brother came by riding their black mule.

"Heigh," said the brother.

"Heigh," said he.

"Gonna shuck corn tomorrow night and want you all to come," the ruffian said, letting loose a squirt of tobacco juice at the gate and eyeing him sternly. Lightning like visions and plans raced through his mind as he stood in his tracks.

"Kin you come?"

"Some of us'll be there," he answered gravely.

With a mocking look below his stubby hair the boy soused his heels in the flanks of the old mule and sent her grunting down the road. He'd be there if torment — if hell didn't freeze over.

He watched his time, and the next afternoon when everybody was out of the house he slipped in and got Pa's razor and took his first shave. Uhp, there's a cut. Nothing much though. Other boys with cuts on their chin — he'd heard them say so casual-like, "My razor slipped this morning." He slicked down his hair and put on his suit and stood ready to ride. As a last measure he sprayed himself plentifully with his sister's perfume. Then he hitched up his mule and drove through the country, feeling fit and ready as a man of God.

The cornshucking was in full swing when he got there. Young men, old men and boys were sitting and squatting round the horse-shoe pile. In the dusk the ears were pouring over the barn like a thick swarm of dancing bats.

"Heigh, you, bring your shucking-peg?" called Laughing Gus Brown.

"Got ten of 'em," he answered.

"Well, come over here, Sunday Clothes, and fall to it."

He took his place among the sweaty overalls and ragged hats. Out of his vest pocket he fished his shucking-peg, made of the hardest dogwood, seasoned by sun and fires, and coming to a fine point at the end. In a few minutes he was ripping the shucks open and shooting the ears over with the best of them. On and on they shucked, ear by ear, nubbin after nubbin, throwing the shuck behind with one hand and reaching forward with the other. And all the while there was a low drumming of the corn falling always towards the crib.

Evening was coming on. Presently Gus let out a whoop.

"The man who gets through the pile first finds a silver dollar. How 'bout it, Mr. Mac?"

"Dunno," Mr. McLaughlin answered from up the line. He was a dour old farmer and not so free with his money.

"Uh-uh!" said Laughing Gus, winking at the boy. "That got him where the hair's short."

All the while he was thinking about the girl in the house, seeing her in his mind as she helped arrange the table, dishing up the stew and all the fine things to eat. It was almost time for supper now. The fields out by the barn were growing dim, and the open door to the hayloft above was a square of blackness, and looked lonesome. He gazed up at the sky and saw that the stars were coming out. The sky looked lonesome too. That was a trait he had — when he thought of something sweet and happy, he thought of something lonesome. One feeling seemed to bring the other.

"Le's sing some," he said timidly to Laughing Gus. "Sam and Tim's here."

"That's right, music in place of the dollar," said he. "Heigh, Tim, you and Sam come over here."

Sam and Tim and Gus and he had been singing as a country quartet now for some time — round at cornshuckings, ice-cream suppers and parties and the like. They sure could make music, as everybody said. Presently Tim and Sam left their places and came around. They made room for them.

"How're you?" queried Tim.

"What shell it be?" said Sam, dumping his tobacco in his hand and throwing it behind him.

The boy was a sort of leader and knew more tunes than they.

"Oh, anything," he answered. "What would you like?"

"Sing about the mourning bride," old Yen Yarborough spoke up in his chair a few paces away. Old Yen liked music, and he specially liked that mournful piece. He'd seen a lot of trouble in his time and now was dying from a bad sore on his nose. Try doctors, herbs, plasters, all that he might — nothing did him any good. But he still kept cheerful.

"The Mourning Bride it shell be," said Sam.

Thereupon they cleared their throats and settled their knees more firmly in the bed of shucks.

"Ta-la-la-la," said Tim, setting the chord. He was the first tenor and a good one.

"Do, sol, mi, do," growled Sam.

Then they let loose a harmony that shattered the twilight air, and trembled the cobwebs in the hayloft. Out, around, and upward they sent the lady's plaintive story.

*She sot alone by the river-bank,*
*And sadly her beads did tell.*
*A year and a day he's been away,*
*A fighting the infh-idel.*

How they did make it chord! And when they'd reached the end where the poor lady's body, by desperate deed foredone, floats down the river to meet the home-coming warrior, there were grunts of approval and desultory clapping of hands on all sides.

"That sure is a piece," mused Laughing Gus.

Then through the cool October evening he heard a voice that thrilled him to the bone.

"Come on in to supper, you-all." She was outside the lot fence with some other girls.

"Come on to supper."

The fellows around the corn-pile craned their necks around, snickered and stirred with enlivement. The old men would eat first, and seven or eight of them soon rose, dusted the corn-silks from their clothes and went on towards the gate.

"We need four more," old Yen called back.

"Go on to supper, Tom."

"No, you go, Dave."

"Why I ain't hongry a bit in the world."

"Charlie, you go."

"No, you go. The old come first. Hee-hee!"

"Pshaw! Looks before age!"

"Since you ain't got 'em, you need sump'n t'eat!"

"Allen, you go."

And finally four middle-aged fellows followed the old ones to supper. The young girls in their white dresses and ribbons clustered around like beautiful butterflies beyond the fence.

"There she is," and Laughing Gus punched the boy in the side.

But he went on with his shucking as cold and indifferent as the old dummy that lived by the creek.

"You gals come over here and help us shuck this corn," three or four voices called.

The group of girls beyond the fence were suddenly animated and there were giggles and whispers among them. Finally little Cissy Tatam, who had a tongue like a scorpion's tail, shrilled out:

"Who's that all dressed up there in his wedding garments?"

A great shout went up around the corn-pile and the boy felt his face grow hot as fire.

"Come here, little Black-Eyes, and hold her hand," cried Gus who seemed to have gone crazy in his head. "Bring your handkerchief and an'int it, fer she smells like the Queen of Sheby."

Sam, who had covered many a bar of balladry with him, suddenly rolled over on his back and wallowed among the shucks with joy. He let out little puffing squeals of merriment.

If only the ground would open and swallow him up, or if he might but burrow his way deep under the corn and hide himself from all human eyes. He remembered foolishly that Enos walked with God and was not, for God took him. He looked up at the sky and wished, as the Negroes sang—wisht he had-a wings for to fly. Then the girls went away, and she called back over her shoulder,

"We'll all come and help you after supper."

"Do," shouted Gus, "and a kiss for every red yur."

"How about the Sourwood Mountain piece?" the boy stammered out to Tim — Tim who never laughed at anybody or anything. He was a solemn soul, he was. As long as he lived he had never known him to laugh. But he had fun, plenty of it, till he died in France.

"All right," he muttered.

And he lifted up his voice.

*In Sourwood Mountain there did dwell*
*A handsome youth, I knew him well.*

Ah, that was a piece! — And Tim's high tenor was as clear and sweet as a bell.

*One Monday morning he did go*
*Out in the fields some hay to mow*
*He scarce had mowed half o'er the field*
*When a venomous blacksnake bit him on the heel.*
*— Sing umble bumble skiddy and a bumble,*
*A mozi linkum too.*

Soon the old men came back and it was the turn of the young fellows to go to supper. Sam and Gus had just made a bet about who could eat the most, and there was much arguing as to the powers of each as they went out of the lot.

"Sam'll do it."

"No, Gus will. He's got more room 'twixt his ribs and his waist."

They shuffled on through the darkness and crowded around the pump outside the dining-room. There they washed up with strong home-made soap and dried their hands and faces on towels hanging from the limbs of a pecan tree. The young girls hovered about in the gloom and waited upon them as if they had been lords.

"Here's some soap, Charlie," one said shyly to her husky sweetheart.

"And here's a towel," said another.

"Hurry up there," the sharp voice of the old lady called from the kitchen.

Through the lighted window of the parlor he could see other girls playing the organ and singing, two or three were sitting on the lounge looking through the family albums. Time would hang heavy on their hands until the boys were through at the corn-pile. Like a herd of goats the fellows trampled in through the dining-room and seated themselves at the table. Old man McLaughlin was noted for his closeness, but he hadn't failed to provide on this occasion. No farmer does. The table was loaded down with chicken stew, ham, collards, early pork, potato pie and custards and cakes, and goodness knows what all. Two or three stolid Negro women moved about the room, handing the dishes on. And over it all the old woman, with face as dried as a bean-root, watched with hawklike eye. She was a stingy one, no doubt, but she did urge everybody to help himself. If she cared for her rations, as it was said, she was due to suffer this night. And so they began. The boy being so timid, and with his mind on something else, like a fool got a whole plateful of collards from the first Negro woman. He hated "greens" above all things, and in a few minutes his appetite was gone. It looked like a grimace of pleasure on the old woman's face when he soon had to say "no" to a proffered dish of stew.

After a few minutes the girl came in and shyly spoke to Sam.

"Are you going to play for us?" she said.

"We are if we can tote our vittles," he answered.

A bit longer she stayed in the room and then went off along the porch towards the parlor. Not once had the boy looked up at her, but sat bent over his plate shovelling in the hated greens.

"Come on there, Samuel, my son, how many cups of coffee does that make you?" queried Gus.

"Six."

"I'm two ahead of you. Undo your belt. Heigh, Aunt Sally," he called to the old woman, "fire up the b'ilers and put on more coffee."

"You boys'll kill yourselves," she murmured.

"Huhp, not hardly," said Gus, "I ain't had a bite all day. Been laying up for these here vittles."

"Put on another pot of coffee, Ellen," she said resignedly. The Negro woman went out into the kitchen.

"Now for the 'tater custard," Gus chuckled.

By this time several of the boys had returned to the lot. But he waited around to see the fun and maybe to see her when she came in again. It was touch and go with Sam and Gus as to who would win. Sam was short and thick, Gus was long and stringy. While they devoured plate after plate of the good things, Tim Messer, who had long ago finished, sat with a stub of pencil and an old envelope keeping tally.

"You boys'll eat me out'n house and home," the old woman laughed mournfully.

"Not hardly," Gus chortled. "Lord, your smoke-house is a-running over."

"How do they stand now?" she sighed presently.

Tim pored over his envelope.

"Purty nigh even," he answered, eyeing his scrawls with the air of the book-keeper in the bank. "Sam has sunk away ten coffees, two plates of collards, three plates of stew, two pieces of ham, fourteen biscuits and nine whole custards."

"How's Gus?"

"Two biscuits ahead."

A couple of custards later, Sam laid his knife down and sat looking at Gus with his mouth open.

"I got about enough," he murmured.

"Land a'mighty!" Gus cried in astonishment. "Where's your appetite? Pore fellow, he's on the puny list."

"Bring on your custards," wheezed Sam. He took three in his hand, staggered out into the middle of the room and lay down on the floor. He lay there flat on his back, devouring them. Several of the girls came in and laughed at him, and Maisie, his shamed sweetheart, begged him to get up.

"I can't do no more," he finally said. "Open the door there—I'm a-coming out." He crawled to his feet and stumbled from the room, his upper lip wrinkled back most sickeningly.

When Gus had emptied another pot of coffee and gone three biscuits and a custard beyond, he pushed back his chair and stood up.

"Now that's what I call a sort of a supper," he said. He pushed back his shoulders and strode from the room, never caring for the old woman's sharp look that went after him. And the rest of them followed. They passed Sam leaning over the yard fence.

"G'won, leave me alone," he spluttered.

Back at the corn-pile they shucked and shucked. Presently the cold moon came up behind the barn and peered in their faces. Gus suggested another song, but the boy, who had grown mournful, said he didn't feel like it.

"And Sam's not here, anyhow," he said.

He was waiting and hoping she would come. Well, if she did she'd go and sit with somebody, not him, of course. The corn was dwindling away under their onslaught, they'd be through in a few minutes. Then he heard the knock of the latch in the gate and the shout that went up around the pile told him the girls were there. Through the corner of his eye he saw them come in. His heart pounded in his ribs and nearly stifled him, but he kept at his task, erect and with the gravity of an Indian. He saw them settle themselves here and there along the pile with their different sweethearts. Ah, it was all so foolish anyhow. He didn't care, he didn't. Why'n thunder had he dressed up like a fool? Then a cool voice spoke up behind him.

"Let me set with you," she said.

He gripped the ear he was shucking. "There's some room here," he answered casually, making a place for her.

"Uh-uh," Gus snorted, "red yurs, where are you hiding?" And he went on making funny remarks, but the boy heard nothing now. Here she was, right here beside him, and she chose him before the rest. His head was swimming and all the fine speeches he had planned were lost in a hazy dreaminess. Bless the Lord if a sort of sleepiness didn't soon come over him. What ailed him anyway? Then he felt her soft hand against his among the shucks. She was reaching for an ear maybe, sure that was all. They shucked away in silence. She would say nothing either. Once Gus stuck a red ear at him.

"Now's your chance," he said. But the boy made no reply and Gus threw the ear scornfully towards the barn.

"How's everything at your house?" she finally said.

"All right." He wanted to talk out and laugh and cut up like the others, but something weighed him down like lead. He was happy, but something weighed him down. Once or twice she looked at him intently and then presently stood up. "It's cold here and I better get my fascinator," she said. She went out through the gate, and Laughing Gus lay back and roared with glee.

"What's all the fun?" a neighbor queried.

"The cat's got the bridegroom's tongue," he cackled.

Now if he but had a sledge-hammer or something he'd kill that Laughing Gus Brown. He wouldn't mind caving his head in, not a bit in this world. A flood of wretchedness came over him. He was the biggest fool that ever wore shoes, no doubt of it.

Well, out he would go. And he did. He stumbled up and went towards the lot gate. He would go home and go to bed where he belonged. Cat-calls and merry gibes followed him out and cut him to the quick. With a sob in his throat he went towards the fence where his mule was tied. He began hitching him to the buggy. As he was ready to drive off, she came out of the gloom with her shawl around her.

"Where you going?" she asked.

"They're about through now and I'd better go on."

"Don't go, we're going to play and have some music in a little bit."

"I better go," he muttered, but he stood making no move.

She came closer and laid her hand on his arm. "That was the sweetest poem you sent me."

"Oh, Lord," he gasped.

She looked at him with great admiring eyes. "You're smart as you can be," she stammered and looked down. "You know, I wrote several letters about it, but I was afraid to send 'em. You're so — proud and stand-offish."

"Good gracious alive!" he said. Mechanically he tied the mule again and stood by her silent. There were no words to be had now, fool.

"The moon's so purty," she murmured, "le's go walking down the lane. We'll come right back."

They went along and soon she put her hand in his arm the way he'd read in books. The wheel ruts made hard walking — so.

"I'll write you some more," he said with some confidence now.

"Oh, do, and I'll try to send you a letter some of these days," she added.

"Oh, do," he whispered.

The moon looked down with smiling face and the fields lay wide and peaceful on either side. There in the hedgerow the flowers stood dead and sere from the early frost. The yarrow that Achilles knew held up its blistered hands, and the proud old mullein nodded at them from the shadowy fence-jambs.

"It's a purty night," she murmured again. "Look at the man in the moon!"

"And everything all around us," he answered in a choking voice. At the turn of the lane they stopped and leaned against the fence. Presently she laid her hand on his and he caught it in a tight convulsive clutch.

"What's the matter?" she whispered. He looked up at her with shining eyes. "Oh, me," she cried. And he put his arms gently around her then.

"That's all right, that's all right," he kept saying. For a long while he held her so. Then a few words came stammering through his lips. "I been thinking a whole lot. I'm gonna do something in this world, gonna be something somehow. I'll do it, do it for you, you wait and see. They can laugh at me—I don't care—I'll—"

"They don't laugh at you." She leaned her head timidly against his shoulder and he kissed her hair once.

"Le's go back," she said as if afraid.

For a while they stood there and then hand in hand they went up the lane towards the house. The music had already begun, the fiddle and banjo ringing out through the night. Boys and girls could be seen having fun on the porch. Near the barn he stopped and gestured around with a quick sweep of his arm.

"You know, I'm gonna do something."

"Yes, you will."

"I'm gonna write about all these things, make poems and such—tell 'em how purty it is—"

He let go her hand and they went on towards the house.

# Salvation on a String

1.

There's hardly any doubt of it at all, my father said, a man's fate is a curious thing, and a little matter can sink or save him. Sometimes it may be a leaf blowing across the road in front of his horse, the bark of a dog, a hesitation, sudden thought and turning back, a kind word, an unkind word—a thousand things. And so it was with the soul of laughing Zack Broadhurst and a rotten piece of string.

Back in the old days sinfulness and wickedness were rampant in our Little Bethel neighborhood. They're still rampant here today for that matter, but back then they were especially bad. And the devil had come out of the mountains to the west and was promenading up and down along the river, trying his muscle power with the weak and erring ones and seeking whom he could devour.

The valley was a great turpentine country then, and vast thundering forests stretched from here to the foothills farther west. The longleaf pines stood a hundred feet high, and night and day the sound of the boxing blade and the hanh-hanh of the scraper were heard. And every few miles the smoke of a turpentine still showed itself like a swirling fog among the underbrush. The slaves, fat and greasy as butterballs, were working like bees around the boiling vats, hacking and making staves for barrels, gashing the trees, and rolling the barrels of rosin and spirits down to the landing on the river there. And the river itself was a great watery highway of trade. Steamboats and flatboats came up as far as Fayetteville from Wilmington, and some of them even as far as Smiley's Falls. And schooners and square-riggers from the North and from the South, from the West Indies and even from Europe itself came pushing up the river to anchor at Wilmington, waiting for their loads from the smaller boats above.

The turpentine farmers were rich in those days, and just as wasteful as they were rich. So it was throughout this broad land clean to the Pacific Ocean when the first great American robbers gouged and tore and cut and burnt the virgin vitals of our nation. We've learned a little better now, they say, but back then nobody seemed to give a whoop about the future. And there was plenty of liquor, peach brandy, cider, cherry bounce and scuppernong wine in Little

Bethel. They flowed like the old milk and honey of the Bible. And because the people were thriving so well in a worldly way, sinfulness and wickedness were rampant in the land.

And of all the sin-struck souls up and down the valley which the devil had in his keeping, Zack Broadhurst was the worst. Not that he ever murdered anybody or stole people's cattle or burnt a neighbor down, britches, bed and all, but that he was profane and godless, and had no respect for heaven or earth or hell, including women. And never a preacher came into Little Bethel to hold the yearly August revivals that prayer after prayer wasn't sent up for Zack. And many a tear was shed for him, and many a sob was sounded by the kind sisters of the congregation over his lost and desolated state. But it never made a hair's difference to him. He kept on with his drink and his profanity and shooting at stray cattle that happened to break into his green fields—roaring and laughing and spouting his jokes under the sun.

Zack was mainly a corn and barley farmer, though like most of his neighbors he had some dealings in turpentine. He was not what you might call one of the rich men of the neighborhood, not at all. He drank and horsed around too much for that. But he made a good living, and everybody said he paid his debts and was honest enough, but in a completely worldly way.

His name was Broadhurst, but everybody called him Broadhuss just the way you might say cornhuss for husk. But there was no "huss" about him. He was all might, fiery blood and muscle, and every ounce a man to his six-feet-three and two hundred and forty pounds. He wasn't really one of the Little Bethel people. His father had come into this section as a sort of traveling preacher from Virginia, holding brush meetings here and there among the forest settlements. This elder Broadhurst was a great laborer for the Lord and one day overexerted himself at a meeting on the bank of Duncan's Creek. In the heat of the hot sun and under the power of the spirit he fell dead right in the midst of exhorting sinners. They buried him there in Little Bethel churchyard, and in appreciation the congregation marked his grave with a little tombstone. You can see it there to this day.

The preacher had brought his little son Zack with him. And after he died the deacons didn't know what to do with the boy, for they were never able to stir up any Broadhuss relatives. So the neighbors took turns keeping Zack in their homes. And a terror and a trial he proved to all of them. There's an old saying that a preacher's children are the worst children of all. Well, it was certainly the truth with Zack. But somehow in the mercy of the Lord they endured him. Maybe they got their pay out of him, for it was said even as a child he was a tremendous worker. By the time he was eighteen he could pull more fodder and roll more logs than anybody for miles around. And as for strength no man was his match. He could pick up a barrel of turpentine like a keg of cider and fling it into the wagon with one hand. So his name soon spread far and wide as the strong man in Little Bethel.

And in keeping with his strength Zack grew up to be a roistering, snorting rounder. And as most always happens, raising or no raising, such dashing folks as that usually make their way to the hearts of women and more times than not walk off with the belle prize of the neighborhood. Now old man Ransome Oliver was one of the great turpentine men of the valley hereabouts and had a darling daughter named Polly Oliver—her name was the same as in the song about pretty Polly Oliver, though not the same girl. So what should happen but that Zack Broadhuss caught her fancy. And one night after a shindig down toward Averysboro he stole her away in his sulky and married her. They say old man Oliver's anger was enough to scorch the sky. He charged up and down and swore many a violent oath. By Arthur's Seat and the blood of Culloden, and by the paps of Jura he swore that she was none of his and not a red penny—not a brownie you understand, should go to her. But as fathers do, he finally relented and the two of them were settled at last on a corner of the old man's land.

Only a corner though, for by that time old Ransome was running into hard luck and the time for his accounting had drawn nigh. Some sort of disease broke out among his trees and thousands of acres of his forests died. He was head over heels in commitments to the bankers in the North just the way the Little Bethel farmers are mortgaged to the fertilizer kings and machinery makers today. So when they cracked down on him he lost everything he had except the little parcel of land he had already willed to Polly. And going into his big house one day he laid himself down on his bed and died and slept with his fathers there on the riverbank. Some other man on the way up and luckier than old Ransome bought in his mansion, his wide sweep of land and holdings, and put tenants to handle them. Then like most of the great homes that used to stand lordly along the river from Summerville to Southport, the Oliver mansion fell before their carelessness and fire, and nothing but a cotton patch covers the old place now. Zack and Polly went on living in their little framework house.

Now you might expect that in a few years such a wildish fellow as Zack would have run through with even that, but he didn't. In fact he added a few acres to the place now and then. But hard worker that he was and married to such a sweet woman, he didn't quiet down in his wildness any. And there used to be a tale told from old to young that one day at the Court of Common Pleas and Quarter Sessions seven scattered women swore children on him—swore seven children on him all in the same day. And the strangest thing under the sun was that they were all girl children. Of course, it might have been a tale, just a tale. But wild he was, no doubt. As for him and little Polly, they never had any children of their own except a baby boy that lived only a few weeks after it was born.

So there must have been right good reason for his bad reputation. And one of the reasons that added to its badness was the way he treated his wife. Nobody ever accused him of beating her, but he was loud and rough and overbearing. And people passing on the road could hear him shouting at her in the fields, she who had been the pampered child of pride, saying "where is that hoe?" or "when you going to bring me my jug of water, woman?" And when Zack Broadhurst shouted, his voice carried for miles and carried everything with it.

There were plenty of other outlandish tales told about him and his powers too. They say that one day he ordered Polly to cook him up a snack, for he had to go down to Fayetteville with a load of staves and turpentine. In those days Fayetteville was the main head of river navigation and a big market place for all Little Bethel. So that morning he was up before light loading his wagon. And Polly was up the same, cooking the grub he was to take with him. She put it in a tow sack, and when he was ready to ride she dragged it timidly out to the wagon to him. He reached over and lifted the bag from the ground, shook it, and roared out at her —

"You don't call this a snack, do you?"

"Yes, Mr. Broadhuss," she piped up all trembling and afraid. "I thought it would be enough." She always called him Mr. Broadhuss.

"And me hungry enough to eat the Lamb of God!" he yelled.

And sitting there in his wagon seat what did he do but open the bag and devour half a bushel of cornbread and the eleven hog jowls she had cooked for him. Then he threw the bones at the house, smashing a hole in the weatherboarding, and drove off. Of course, that might have been a tale made up too, but it just goes to show how big and powerful a man he grew to be in people's minds.

In those days most every settlement had its bully. And beyond Upper Little River near the town of Sanford lived one by the name of Bud Ragland. He had heard about the strength and power of Broadhuss so he invited him to come over to his cornshucking, saying, after the work was done they'd square off and have a fight. Zack sent word that he wouldn't shuck an ear of his corn, and any time he wanted to fight he, Ragland, would know where to find him. So one morning this Ragland rode down and hallooed out in the yard in front of Zack's house. Little Polly opened the door and said who was it? And the bully

Ragland pushed out his great barrel breastbone and said, "It's me, the bull of the upper woods, and where's your pitiful husband?"

"He's gone down in the low-grounds looking for a cow and calf," said little Polly, "and I wouldn't call him pitiful."

"Well," said the bully, feeling his arms, "I hear tell he thinks he's something, and they've got a bet laid up the country as to him and me. And I say my horse against his'n I can whip him. When will he be back, little lady of the house?"

"Most any time now," said Polly. "And if it's a fight you want, Mr. Ragland, I suppose Mr. Broadhuss will accommodate you, though the Lord knows I try to keep him from such. Ah me." And with that she went back into the house and shut the door.

"Mighty glad to hear of it," Ragland called after her, as he got down off his horse. "So I'll just sit here on the steps and pass the time of day waiting for him."

Presently he looked down the road and saw a cloud of dust uprising. "What's that a-coming yonder, good woman?" he called.

"Where?" said little Polly, sticking her head through the door again.

"It's something a-coming," said Ragland, "like the world was afire or a caravan of gypsies."

"Oh," she said, "that's Mr. Broadhuss coming home." "Eck, for the name of God!" said Mr. Ragland, standing up. "What's he got with him?"

"That's just like him," said little Polly, coming out on the porch, "always in a hurry to get things done, sir. It's the cow under one arm and the calf under the other, it is."

"Well," said Ragland, jumping as if his leg had been bit from under the steps by a stinging adder, "I reckon I'll see him some other day."

"He'll be here in a second," said Polly, "don't hurry." But by that time Ragland was already on his horse and going up the road in a balling lope.

And there were other strengthful things they told of Zack. For instance when he got ready to split rails in the deep swamp he'd cut the big logs in ten foot sections, souse his ax up in them to the eye and tote them out on the high ground by the handle of it. And there he'd maul and rive them where he had his elbowroom.

2.

So Zack Broadhuss worked and sang and drank and cursed and laughed his big laugh through the world. And just as lumbermen eye a great tree that stands big in the forest, bigger than all the surrounding trees, figuring harder how to cut it down and use it than all the others put together, so it was with the preachers that came through the country working for their Lord. Year by year they came, visited him, pleaded with him, and went their way stultified and stopped by his great spout of profane and blasphemous words. There was young Brother O'Neill, one of the fiercest of all evangels. He could make no impression. Then the righteous Brother Avery, the Pentecost man, and old Neil Hodge, that great hairy preacher from up in the Piedmont Hills. None of them could touch him, none of them could reach him where it hurt. Threaten him with the terrors of the afterworld, the boiling fiery lake, the tearing of burning irons, the awful maledictions of Revelations and the prophets, including the beast and the seals—all combined—caused him only to joke and laugh and bellow out the louder. And when he got tired of Brother Hodge's persistence one day he picked him up like a baby, the whole six feet of him, carried him across the yard and flung him far out into the road. And the preacher's feet hit the ground like a dog running.

Under the power of such a man as Zack, what woman could have stood up long? And little Polly Oliver was a woman. Everybody though said she loved him to the last, and in his rough and ready way he might have loved her. Within a few years after she married him she weakened and died and they buried her there in the family graveyard on the riverbank close by her baby's side. And you'll have to give the devil credit where credit is due. Zack put up a fine tombstone to her and the baby, with angel wings sprouting from the sides and two doves on top with their bills cooing close together. That artist fellow George Lauder, there in Fayetteville, chiseled it for him, and Zack had said spare no expense. There was never a woman as good as Polly was, he said. And I guess he was right, though what good it profited her nobody knows.

After her death he lived alone in his little house, tending his field, minding his few hogs and cows, and selling his crop in the autumn at Dunston or Fayetteville. But his sinfulness increased the while, maybe because he was lonesome. And in a drunken brawl over at Thornton's Crossroads during election time he beat up half a dozen men and crippled one of them—old Thad Maples—pretty much for life. The sheriff came, served papers on him, and the county magistrates fined him. While the trial was going on he had his horse tied in front of the Summerville courthouse to one of the elm trees. The horse gnawed the tree pretty bad and they fined him five dollars for that. The next day he was back with a grubbing hoe and dug up the tree. "Hell," he said, "it's my tree. I paid for it." And he dragged it off and threw it in the gully behind the courthouse, where they later hanged the Negro Purvis, with none to stop him.

About this time the greatest preacher the valley country ever knew showed up for the summer meeting at Little Bethel. His fame went ahead of him like a wave in front of a big ship, and wherever he appeared the sinners fell before him like dry pine masts before a heavy wind—if you know what I mean—or the way birds and animals flee before a heavy beating in the bush. His name was Brother Sandy King, and as everybody said, he was the king of preachers, even more terrible than the later Brother Baxter himself and that's going some. He had come from somewhere over the mountains in Tennessee where they raise so many good men of God. And as he made his way down from the hills towards the lowlands, he scattered the enemies of the Lord the way the old Assyrian king did the Hebrew children.

And along with him he brought something new to this section—a little golden-haired boy preacher. And some said the reason Brother King got as far east as Little Bethel was that he had heard of the great and notorious sinner, Zack Broadhuss. Anyway he preached there for two weeks in August, the little holy boy helping him out in his special way. And I've heard old people tell something of the wonders of these two. So powerful was their effect upon the congregation that not only did they clean up the sinners in a week, but practically all the brothers and sisters professed sanctification and affirmed the holy perfect life for the balance of their days, saying they felt the seal made manifest in their worthless foreheads, blessed be the Name. The unknown tongues and Pentecostal fires seized upon all and sundry, and it was told that even balking and cantankerous mules changed their ways for better and pulled at the wagon and the plow where they'd never budged before.

So it was that everybody was waiting for Brother King to try the evangelical powerhouse of his strength with Zack. And it was the proper time too, for during this big revival Zack had met that Upper Little River bully, Bud Ragland, over at Johnson's store and nearly ruined him for life. That was the most famous fist and skull fight ever known in the valley. And a ballad was written on it. It began something about—

*Oh come everybody and listen to my song*
*Of the great fight that happened 'twixt the powerful and the strong.*
*'Twas one Zack Broadhuss on a bright summer's day*
*Met old Bud Ragland in a bloody killing fray—*
*Fol de rolla—dollicum do—*

By this time Zack was about sixty years old, but full of juice and jump as many a man half his age. He still went to dances, he led the crowd at cornshuckings, both in feats of labor and eating, and at barn-raisings he stuck logs up in the sky as fast as two men could lay them down. Old man Ted Carraway made a list once of what Zack put away at his cornshucking, including among the items eleven pots of coffee.

Now naturally you might say the people must have liked old Zack even as mean and gluttonous as he was, and so they did. For he was a freehearted, generous fellow, with all his rough and ungodly ways, and he was always buying candy and stuff for little boys he'd meet on the streets of Summerville. And it was partly because people liked him that they sorrowed over the lost condition of his soul. Many a one of his God-fearing neighbors, shocked by his loose living and profanity but tickled by his wit and fun, had pleaded with him to come into the fold and be one of them, but Zack had always replied that if God and the church would take care of themselves, he'd take care of himself and die the same. Yes. But year by year they had labored with him so.

It's a little hard maybe for us to realize in this day of automobiles and airplanes and hurrying about, along with these sissy educated young preachers talking quiet in the pulpit with their hair slicked down and their hands as soft and white as a woman's, that back then the church was a matter of life and death with the people. Now any time you want to you can hear plenty of fiddling and hillbilly music over the radio, and in the big cities and everywhere round and about the people cut up and charge and carry on pretty much the way they please. So it seems. But back then it was all different. In fact when Zack was alive about the only kind of music not frowned on was church music. The fiddle was an ungodly instrument, and a banjo was worse than a strumpet's laugh.

As I said, there had never been such an August revival as the one that year. Brother Sandy King proved to be everything that rumor had announced. He was a short, sandy-haired man, not more than half the size of Zack, but with a bass voice that outdid any of the big bullfrogs along the Cape Fear River. And as for the little boy, he was a miracle, a holy miracle and angel all in one, as the flowing tears of old Marilly Clement and the other women testified — there where they sat in their seats listening to his clear voice going up to heaven in song. He'd sing —

*"From the low bending cloud above*
*Whence radiant brightness shone —"*
and every heart would be melted down. And in the eyes of the hardest men the tears would stand like dewdrops in a cotton bloom. Ah, there'd never been anything like him, and between the fire and thunder of Brother King and the sweet lamenting of the little boy, it was no wonder that the countryside was soon washed clean as a young girl's white Sunday frock. That is, except for old Zack Broadhuss. Brother King had sent word and a special invitation several times to Zack to come and drink of the waters of life freely. Zack laughed there where he plowed among his corn, and sent word back that he had a goodly well of water of his own. Then the preacher sent a committee of the sisters who prayed and wept and pleaded, but old Zack only stopped his work long

enough to laugh his roaring laugh and compliment them on their good looks which they didn't have, and they had to retire in confusion. And the same thing happened when the elderly brethren, led by old Ike Clement the sexton, came, except that Zack shouted and cursed and told them to leave him alone. And they did. They were slow doing it though, and he ran them out of the field, even chasing poor old timid Ike into a bed of briars. But he seemed to feel sorry for that fumbling old fellow with his string belt breaking and his trousers falling down, and so he helped him out again and offered him a chew of tobacco as well as a new string. But Ike refused them both—with what results no one could then foresee.

All these things were reported to Brother King as the meeting progressed into the second week, and at last he had told the congregation to fear not, that he would personally bring the old scandalous ram into the fold. And so one night just as Zack was finishing his peck of food, prepared by his Negro farm boy, lo and behold, there was a knock on the door and Brother King-himself with the little boy preacher entered.

Nobody knows just exactly what happened that night, but old Ike Clement who was standing out in the road listening and praying, later—much later—said there was a mighty turmoil that went on within. He could hear Brother King threatening and warning and then Zack shouting and swearing back. And then he said he heard the voice of the little boy talking sweetly and singing some of his tender songs. And when near midnight the preacher and the little fellow came away from the house and all was silent within, Ike still waiting in the road asked anxiously as to the outcome. But Brother King answered only that the fullness of time would show, and for him and everybody else to continue their prayers unceasingly until tomorrow.

The next day the little church was packed with the expectant congregation. The services were opened as usual with prayer and then a song in which they all joined, then another prayer. And then a song by the little boy. This time it was more of brimstone and the breaking of worlds, to fit the occasion—

"Yea though the earth's foundations fail
And mountains down the gulf be hurled—"
he sang, all in his piping, reedy voice.

After this Brother King read a snatch of scripture beginning, "Every knee shall bow and every tongue confess him," and then all of a sudden he slammed his Bible shut and sat down behind the pulpit, finished. He looked out over the congregation with his quick-darting little goat eyes, and the congregation looked questioningly back at him. Maudie Avery, the organist, wondered if she was supposed to play, and gazed inquiringly at the little boy, but there he sat by the preacher's side looking out toward the front door as if expecting someone to enter. A moment or two passed. The audience began to grow restless, and following the little boy's eyes, they turned one by one and looked back at the entrance. When they could hardly endure it any longer, for already old Marilly Clement had begun to moan under her breath and get ready to start a little confession meeting of her own, there was a dreadful thumping and stamping on the steps outside, and the huge form of Zack Broadhuss stood in the door. A sudden and gusty murmur swept up the church and old Marilly shouted "Hallelujah!" Ike, her husband, echoed softly after her. Then a few other women joined in, and some of the old men murmured "Amen." Now the congregation looked toward Brother King, but that great preacher sat silent and smiling in his seat. Old Marilly hopped up and, clasping her hands, went skipping down the aisle to Zack.

"Praise the Lord, praise the Lord," she squealed. And old Ike hitched up his waist string again and stood beside his wife to catch her if, as was her usual way, she should fall into a sudden trance. Zack stood surveying the people before him. His eyes were bloodshotten and his face haggard as if he had been on a drunk, or in the throes of some terrible upheaval of his heart. And then his great voice sounded through the church, "I'm here, just like I promised the boy I'd be," he roared.

"Praise the Lord," cried old Marilly hysterically again. And then as helpless as a falling tree she sagged down with a little moan, and old Ike took her in his kindly arms and propped her up against a bench like a wooden doll, where the sisters began to chirrup and twitter over her, fanning away with their bonnets. But Zack paid no attention to anything about him, for now his gaze rested upon the little boy coming along the aisle toward him. And that little fellow with his golden curls and as beautiful as an angel, his blue eyes full of waterdrops like a dewy violet, came up and taking Zack by the hand led him down the aisle to the pulpit and sat with him on the mercy seat. The sisters forgot all about old Marilly and left her lying stiff as a post there with her lips blue like a huckleberry, while they trooped forward and bowed down around the great sinner. And the old men moved out of their seats and fell upon their knees too, and the middle-aged men and women and the young men and women all bowed down likewise. All the while Brother King sat in his chair saying never a word, stroking the loose turkey gobbler skin under his throat. And now the little boy stood up and began babbling in the air about the mercy of the sweet Lord Jesus.

According to what they say, never in the valley before or since had such words been spoken as that little boy spoke that day—at least not until the later dispensation of Brother Baxter. And Zack kept looking at him like a man in a daze as he told of the little children and the mothers and sisters and brothers that now lived in the light of heaven. And then he began talking about his own mother who had died when he was three and loved him so, just the way Mr. Zack's mother had loved him, and who now waited beyond the pearly gates for his coming. And then he talked about his father who died before he was born, a godless man, a drunkard who had perished with his foul sins rank upon him. And standing close by Zack he put his little hand on his shoulder and begged him for his sake to come to Jesus. "For I love you so," he murmured, "more than my own poor father. My heart aches for you. And at this very minute I can see your little baby son Ransome looking out over the walls of heaven, his beautiful face sad like a pale lily flower wilted down, his eyes full of scalding tears, pleading with you to make your peace right now. And he would be so happy, he would laugh and sing with joy. He would play wonderful music on his golden harp, there with the angels all in that jeweled circle bending. Oh, but believe in Christ and trust in him!" And now the little fellow broke down and began to sob, holding tight to Zack. And Zack reached out and put his great grub pole arm around him.

"No, son, you musn't cry about me," and his voice was so broken and low you could hardly hear it.

"But I do," the little boy blubbered, "it hurts me, hurts me bad here in my heart to think of you being lost in the fires of eternal torment. Please, Mr. Zack, won't you decide to give your precious soul to God and we will all be happy in heaven together. I love you so, I love you so, and heaven will all be empty dead without you." And he hugged Zack tight about the neck.

"Don't, son, don't," Zack gasped. And then finally tears began to slide down across his rough weather-tough cheeks. And upon seeing this, the old women who thought that Zack had been broken down and was now penitent, let out a wild screeching and began to go off in paroxysms of shouting. Old Marilly suddenly recovered from her fainting, scrambled to her feet, and added her voice to the turmoil, and Ike tightened his old string belt and watched over her. The little boy knelt down as if saying his prayers, his forehead resting on Zack's lap, and that mighty sinner kept touching his golden hair with his great hand and gazing at him, his face full of pain and stricken love.

By this time several of the old men had joined in the tumult and were talking in unknown tongues. And Sister Carrington and Miss Rebecca Ogburn hopped up and down and spouted forth their Pentecostal language — "Menny-wy-flue-di-sooza" they jibbered. And Brother King, seeing that Zack had once or twice let his eyes, however empty, stray in their direction, and fearing that they were like to ruin things by overdoing it, rose and pounded on the Bible. With the thunder of his voice he gradually quieted the upheaval. When the panting congregation had returned to their seats, he briefly announced that the service was over for the time being, and they'd gather again at the church in the evening. In the meantime everybody must appoint himself a committee of one to segregate himself in silent prayer for the contrite soul now on the rack. Stepping down from the pulpit he came over to Zack and shaking him by the hands blessed him for having taken the first step of humility. The second step of conversion would come easy, close to follow. God's power was working in him now, and nothing would stop it.

"That's right, that's right," muttered Zack, looking down at the boy again.

"And we aim to eat with you at your house, Mr. Zack," said the little boy preacher, raising his tear-stained face blissfully on him.

"Yes, we'll stay close to you and pray," said Brother King. "The Lord has commanded us to give you a little more time to ponder and sweeten your soul." Brother King was smart, smart as you find them.

And then while everybody stood around and watched, the preacher and the little boy drove away with Zack in his buggy. But a great many of the congregation had no thought of going home that afternoon. They remained at the church and had separate little prayer meetings and praise gatherings around the yard and in the bushes, even young maids and youths holding secret sessions in the shrubbery, for Zack's salvation. And that evening they were all back in the church and waiting, long before the preacher and the boy and Zack returned. Everyone fully expected the announcement that Zack was already saved and that he determined from this day forth, so help him God, to live the life of Christ. Old Ike Clement, the sexton, full of prayer and workings of the spirit, had paid special care to have plenty of light in the church. A big lamp was on the pulpit stand and two others burned bright above the audience, where they hung by their stout chains from the ceiling.

And here we might say a word more about Ike. He was a silent shriveled old fellow whose mind, like his wife's, was not supposed to be too clear. The couple had had six children born dead one by one to them, and no doubt that had added to their darkening. For years now old Ike had looked after the chores at church. And even on occasions when religious fervor was at its highest, he usually went about tending to his duties, fixing the stove, if the weather was cold, or the lights in evening service. Everybody sort of took him for granted and paid no attention even if while prayer was being said he found it necessary to take his tall stepladder and climb up to fix a smoking lamp. He always wore the same old shirt and homemade jeans held up by a string, as mentioned before. He was what you might call a fixture, and it was generally understood that he, like his wife, was sanctified. And because of this maybe, and because of his quiet catlike ways of creeping about to look after his job, he was especially privileged.

3.

The church was full to the brim in the evening, with a lot of folks sitting down on the floor of the aisles and standing in the little vestibule at the back. For the news had gone around the neighborhood that Zack was in the throes of conviction.

One of the first things the deacons did was take up a collection. And pretty soon here came Brother King, the boy, and Zack down the aisle with a couple of hundred pairs of eyes on them. The preacher mounted the pulpit and Zack and the boy sat again on the mercy seat. The people eyed the sinner's countenance carefully and appraisingly, but there was nothing there to show whether he was yet saved or not. But they noticed that he held the little boy's hand and that was a mighty good sign. Brother King stood before the open Bible and read about where it said there'd be more joy in heaven over one soul that repents than over the ninety and nine that are saved. The congregation took this as almost a certain announcement and a deep "Amen" answered the preacher. And then after a song or two as was the custom, Brother King began preaching. He told about how the rich man piled up his goods and went on in his own might and how that the spirit of the Lord strove with him. There was no doubt about it, he must have been talking of old Zack, though Zack was by no means rich. Perhaps he was trying to slip up on Zack's blind side by softening him with flattery, and too, he might have been hoping to collect a haul of his own later. Who knows?

The preacher took plenty of time and did himself proud that night, they say. He beat a powerful drumming bum-bum on the Bible and the pulpit stand, stretched his great gobbler's throat and unrolled terrible pictures about the woe that awaited the rich man and the pleasures and joys that waited for that same man when he had given up his worldly goods, taken his cross, and gone following the Lord—as Brother Broadhuss himself was going to do this blessed night.

"Amen, amen!" the congregation answered with loud jubilancy. For now in a few minutes Zack must stand up, make a confession of all his secret sins, including the seven bastards, that so many people had been wondering about and accept the right hand of fellowship—the token that would bind him to their Lord.

The lamp on the pulpit had begun to gulp slightly before Brother King's poundings and the already rhythmic beat of many patted feet. Old Ike, always on the job, moved up silently and turned the wick a bit. Then, taking his little ladder out of the corner, he set it under one of the lamps in the center of the church and climbed up and began to tend it, for it too had begun to flicker. And now with sudden and dramatic vehemence, Brother King announced the great conclusion of their prayers and years of labor. The last stronghold of the devil was destroyed, and during the evening Brother Broadhuss had declared he wanted to taste of Jesus and him crucified and was determined to live a better life. Cries of joy began to break out more loudly among the congregation. And when he shouted out that he was now ready to welcome Brother Broadhuss into the fold and would accept the full confession of his sins and shake his hand, a sudden clamor broke from the audience. Old Ike up there on his ladder was caught by surprise and almost fell off in the jostling and stir of people around him. He reached up and grabbed hold of the lamp frame and steadied himself. Just at that minute Zack rose to testify to his wickedness and the change in his nature, and old Marilly, who could keep herself down no longer, jumped up and let out a wild scream. And as she did so, she bumped into old Ike's ladder and kalam-bam down it fell!

But old Ike was pretty quick and saved himself by hanging onto the lamp, and there he clung, high up in the air, wriggling like a worm on a hook. But his wife paid no attention to what had happened as she ran over and flung herself down in front of Zack.

"Brethren and sisters," Zack started off to say, "you all know I been a terrible wicked man — " And then he stopped sudden as lightning. Every word froze in his mouth, and everybody in the church froze in their seat likewise, for the tightened string that held old Ike's britches had broken loose and his jeans had dropped down clear to his ankles, leaving him hanging there naked as a yard dog fast in the face of his neighbors. For a minute everything was still as death.

"Ah-ha, ah-ha," grunted old Ike as he tried to hold to the iron frame with one hand and reach for his trousers with the other. And nobody had sense enough to set the ladder up under him again. So there he was in mid-air, a living shame and total disgrace to humankind. The sisters and brethren who a minute before had been so full of the Lord's power, now hid their faces in their bonnets or behind their hands. Then back in the church somewhere a young girl suddenly giggled. There was another giggle and then another. And that undammed the springs of fun. Brother Sandy rushed down from the pulpit and grabbed up the ladder. In his hurry to help old Ike he got tangled up in it himself and fell full into Sister Carrington's lap. And for a moment there he lay, she looking fondly down at his hot scraggly face and beginning to fan him. Then a loud ripsnorting laugh broke through the church. And every eye was turned upon Zack who stood bowing up and down and roaring with merriment. And even the little Jesus boy, they say, had begun to smile.

Pretty shortly the deacons and the preacher had got old Ike down, pulled up his britches and put him in decent shape again. But something had happened past mending. Zack, who laughed as easy as water running and loved a joke better than anybody in the whole world, kept convulsing himself and hallooing where he stood. It was just as if the spell over him had been broken and he had come to his normal senses again. And so with his wide shoulders shaken with chuckles and his great hands pushing people aside before him, he made his way out of the church. And they could hear his whickering laughter going outside, and the sound of buggy wheels and the thunder of his horse's hoofs as he rode out of the grove and down the road. Brother King and some of the brethren rushed out after him, crying, "Come back, come back! Think of your immortal soul! Think of it!" But all in vain.

They never got Zack back into the church after that. So far as he was concerned the work of Brother King and the little boy was confounded forever. "Why, I was about to make a plumb fool of myself, sure enough," Zack declared afterwards. "That little fellow had me hypnotized." And later too he said—the thing that disgusted him most about the whole business was that while the pandemonium over old Ike and his britches was going on he had caught sight of the little Jesus boy stealing money from the collection plate. That really put the clincher on matters.

And so Zack went back to his drinking and lewd living and gluttony again. And nobody was surprised at all when after lying out several cold winter nights drunk with loose women and gypsies along the river he caught double pneumonia and died in a week. Such damnation and taking off was to be expected, and his soul had sped straight to hell there to burn in a lake of fire till the Judgment Day....

Yes, as my father used to say, a man's fate is a curious thing and it may hang by a whisker, a leaf or a thread—except in this case it was a rotten piece of string, and no man knows what may come upon him in this world.

And to this day the story of laughing Zack Broadhurst and how he lost his soul by a rotten piece of string continues to be told from Little Bethel firesides and from the church pulpit as a fearful warning to others. And many an erring sinner has been brought to see the light because of it—thus proving again that ancient adage which was spoken about a better and a wiser man—that though he could save others, himself he could not save.

And Zack would find that funny, yes he would. And he would laugh.

# Saturday Night

It is a rare Green story or play that does not make prominent use of music, but the purposes of the music Green includes are untypical in that they are not used to intensify feelings or to rouse an audience through rhythm. The key to understanding the music in Green's work is to realize that most of it is "real" music—that is, songs and other pieces that exist in the world outside his imaginative works and will be known by some or many readers and audience members. Almost any story or play in the *Paul Green Reader* can illustrate this point. In *The Lost Colony*, for instance, most of the songs are hymns, ballads, folk tunes, and other airs from Elizabethan times or earlier—in other words, historically authentic music that could have been known by the Roanoke colonists. Green's purpose was to convey a sense of the Elizabethan musical consciousness as a way of characterizing the colonists, of underlining their "pastness" and also their continuing ties with later-day audiences, many of whom will recognize the music as well (one of the songs, for instance, is set to the tune "Greensleeves"). A similar characterizing use of music occurs in "Saturday Night," when the vaudeville skit known as "The Arkansas Traveler" is performed for the characters' delight and for the reader's appreciation of the characters' time and way of life.

In fact, music may be more nearly central in "Saturday Night" than is usual in Green's work. Through its characters, the story conveys a sense of music's power to carry people out of themselves, to offer a moment of release from ordinary cares and concerns, to provide an experience of pleasurable transcendence. Music, indeed, is the driving force in the plot. But one song in "Saturday Night" is an exception. It is introduced at the end as a meditation, but no reader, or at best few readers, will recognize it. That is because the song is by Green (music and lyrics) and has not been published or popularized. The story includes two verses of the song "What Is the Soul of Man?" but not its music. Since the music, not in a triumphal major key but a questioning minor, should sound in the reader's mind for full enjoyment, I give the melody line here.

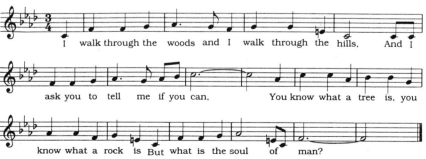

*When the hills were green, and the trees were young,*
*The flowers they bloomed and the birds they sung,*
*But none were so happy, so happy as I,*
*For my farmer lad was nigh.*

— Southern Folk Song

## 1.

If the crops are not too pushing in Little Bethel, the farmers usually end their week's work at Saturday noon. After dinner you will find them congregated in the neighboring village of Summerville buying rations, swapping news, politics, and sometimes religion, until evening comes. The boys have gathered over at the old-field baseball diamond where with run and shout and a little cussing they play their hearts out till darkness drives them home, perished for water and with the seat of their trousers dragging the ground. And if times are not too hard the old man, as the head of the house is referred to, will return with ice and vanilla flavoring to make cream for the children. And everybody will have some fun between the heat of the fields and the loneliness of Sunday coming on.

It is Saturday night at the home of John Day, a hard-working tenant farmer. Two or three men are sitting in the bare moonlit yard before the house, talking about their crops and hopes and plans for the future. And since the earth in its kindness provided them with a metaphysic as well as daily bread, they now and then vouchsafe a word concerning God and the nature of the universe. It is about nine o'clock at evening and the moon is high in the sky. Stretching around the house and away, the fields of cotton and corn cast up a silvery radiance in the air. Behind the old barn over there a whippoorwill is cutting a rust. A young woman opens the front door of the house and comes out on the low vine-clad porch. The glow from a lamp inside pours out after her, revealing morning-glories climbing the posts and varicolored flowers set in tin cans along a shelf. Through the door and across the room beyond, a little porch can be seen at the back of the house. There beside the water shelf a tall motherly woman is dishing up ice cream for a swarm of children. The young woman returns to the house — evidently the expected one has not come — and closes the door behind her to keep the bugs and gnats from streaming in.

The two men in the yard eye the night and go on with their talk, with gaps of silence between their speeches.

"Nice and cool out here, John," says Mack Lucas, turning a gleaming fiddle in his hand.

"Purty nice and cool," returns his host.

"The cream was good."

"It was that."

"Corn out there—growing fast. Hear its joints pop."

"Purty good," Day admits. "That whippoorwill's a mess too, ain't he? White bowl o' milk! White bowl o' milk. Why do they say that, you reckon?"

"Dunno. They don't say it. Just sounds like it." Lucas sighs and looks out before him, his long thin fingers tapping on the violin.

"Funny," murmurs Day.

"John Day," says Lucas suddenly after a pause, "you're a strong man, and I'm a weak one. I'm thinking of it."

"What is it, Judge?" mocks Day.

"You got crops and children," Lucas says. "And I got a fiddle." Suddenly animated, he whistles a little tune. "Like that bird, maybe, with no home but his song, and the rain pouring."

"Here's some tobacco—try it, Mack," says John Day, pulling out a golden twist, rich brown plug. "What ails that boy?" he complains, calling toward the porch. "You Joshua—hurry up with your cream and bring your banjo out!"

The two men peer hopefully toward the closed door of the house.

"Booh!" a deep voice startles them. And around the corner of the dwelling a figure looms out of the darkness. It is Allen Jones, a neighbor, a jolly man and given to tricks.

"For goodness sakes!" cries Day. "Light and cool your saddle, Allen!"

"Started the music yet, Mack?" asks Jones. "Couldn't miss that."

Day gestures toward the house. "Waiting for Joshua to get his bait of that cream."

The door opens again and the young woman comes eagerly forward onto the porch. "Heigho, Polly," calls Jones, teasingly.

The disappointed Polly replies primly, "Good evening."

"Go in and get you some cream, Allen," urges Day.

Jones spits loudly over his shoulder. "Lord," he boasts, "I et a supper would kill a bull. Eddie brought me some croakers back from Duke."

"Well, have some tobacco then," insists his host.

"Just put in a chew." And Jones sits down quickly and heavily. "How's the world with you all?" he inquires.

"All right," says Day.

"Still the world," says Lucas, drawing his bow across his fiddle in a few plaintive notes.

"And you?" asks Day.

"Moonlight and sunshine, boys," he says jollily.

"Rain?" inquires Day.

"When needed," Jones laughs. "Not moonshine," and he nods toward Polly. "He ain't come, has he?"

Day drops his voice, confidentially. "At home trying to find his collar button maybe." Then he observes wryly — "Slow — but steady."

Lucas begins to play almost inaudibly as he murmurs,

*"I been a-courting, Mother.*

*Make my bed soon, for I must lie down —"*

"Reckon he and Polly'll ever come to an understanding?" Jones persists.

"I dunno," says Day. Then he leans closer, with a glance toward Polly. "If they don't somebody'll die single."

"If he ain't been here every Saturday and Sunday night for the last three years," booms out Jones, "I'm a bull calf."

"Joshua!" shouts Day suddenly. "Call him, Polly!"

Silence falls on the group as the young woman turns and goes into the house again. Finally Lucas speaks musingly, "Sixty years is a long time to live!"

"Uh-uh, now, always thinking of something!" chortles Jones.

"Long and not so long," acknowledges Day.

"Long, measured by experience," Lucas continues, flirting out the bar of a jig.

"Well, I'm just forty-one and ain't never been sick," says Jones.

"Young," observes Day. "And Mack and me is old. We've been through a lot." He reaches over and touches Lucas on the shoulder.

"More than we'll have to again," responds the fiddler solemnly.

"That's right. Well," jokes Day, "there's some pleasure in knowing that, even." He turns to Jones. "How many miles you reckon you've plowed in your life, Allen?"

Jones thinks a bit. "Maybe a thousand or two, I don't know," he says.

"Polly and Joshua got to figgering the other day — they're always at some mess — to see how far I'd walked behind the plow in my life. Let me see. I had walked a' average of twenty miles on a plowing day, and I averaged about sixty-five plowing days to the year, and this summer I've been at it fifty years." He looks up and addresses his daughter who has come out again onto the porch. "How many miles did you say I'd walked behind the plow?"

"Over sixty-five thousand," answers Polly.

Jones gasps. "My Lord! That many miles in the plowed dirt!"

"That's just behind the plow, folkses," Day continues almost excitedly. "More than twice around the world, ain't it, Polly?"

"Yes," says Polly.

Day pokes Lucas in the ribs. "She believes the earth's round."

"It's square," says Lucas, "and flat, like a table, anh?"

"The Bible speaks of the four corners," Jones agrees.

Polly is goaded into speech. "What about them that's been around it?" she inquires loftily.

"Education!" Day almost whispers. "Listen to her. It's a powerful thing."

"Powerful," agrees Jones.

Lucas looks up at the moon. "I was putting up fence posts for the squire yesterday, and I dug up a rock." He speaks softly as before. "I thought to myself it had been there forever and ever."

"God put it there," says Day.

"He sure did," echoes Jones, taking off his hat and spitting reverently. "He sure did. God made it and put it there."

"I don't know so much about that," says Lucas.

"We've heard it said," marvels Jones, "that you're about a plumb infidel."

"I've wondered about things — some," admits Lucas.

Day speaks up, "God was always, Mack."

"Forever and ever," says Jones, even more reverently, with a touch of eagerness and awe now.

Lucas again draws the bow across the strings. "How long is that" — he asks seriously — "forever and ever?"

"All of the time," replies Jones. "Can't be imagined, except God does it."

Day speaks up with correct piety, "He holds time in the hollow of His hands."

"He's got hands?" Lucas inquires gently.

Jones speaks as if quoting, "Lifted up with His hands," and suddenly stops confused. "I heard the preacher say Sunday — "

"Say sixty-five days for plowing," Day resumes, "that leaves three hundred days. Say I walked five miles a day on them days — and I do," he begins to chuckle, "sure I do — any day."

"Every bit and grain of it!" declares Jones.

Day turns again to his daughter waiting there on the porch, "How many miles that make a year, Polly?"

"Fifteen hundred miles a year," and she speaks up quickly.

"And fifty years, not counting boyhood," Day prompts.

"Seventy-five thousand miles," says Polly.

Jones speaks admiringly to the air, "Smart, Lord! Same as them dojiggers in the bank — that add up your money."

"Ain't that a spell of a piece!" continues Day soberly.

"About as far as them stars," murmurs Lucas, adding musingly, "Wish I'd done all my walking on a path going there."

For a while the three men sit silent in their splint-bottomed chairs while Polly waits on the porch. Presently there is a sound of footsteps in the gloom, and a big hulking young farmer, all dressed up, comes into the yard from the little lane. He hesitates, looking about a moment, and then sits helplessly down in an empty chair near Lucas.

"Hy, Joe."

"Hy, Mr. Day."

"Some refreshments on the back porch," says Day cheerily, "and Polly's there on the front."

Jones snickers, and Lucas turns his face more intently toward the stars.

"Yes sir," Joe replies in confusion.

"How's your daddy?"

"Doctor says he's got to go to Richmond now, Mr. Day."

"Is?"

"To try to burn it out'n him," adds Joe heavily.

"I bet it'll hurt!" Jones blurts out. "They took out head and all that time from Aunt Minty's jaw. She said it felt like a red-hot iron being shoved through her face. Poor soul, didn't do her no good."

"Man was born to suffer," Lucas murmurs. "It was said so."

Day chimes in with gentle reverence, "Like a shadow it said, and his race is soon run."

Joe jerks his hands up spasmodically. "Ma says he'll never stand it, 'cause it's right at the base of his skull."

On the porch Polly begins whistling to herself.

"Getting lonesome?" the ebullient Jones teases.

Polly speaks up encouragingly, "There's some good vanilla ice cream, Joe."

Joe feels his high collar and heaves himself gradually out of his chair. "Believe I'll go help Josh clean out the freezer can," he mumbles apologetically to the men.

He starts into the house but gets no farther than the porch. Jones watches him go and then speaks out in a sudden loud voice, as if reciting, "And after all them millions of miles walking, what have you got, John Day? Have you got a house? No, it belongs to the squire. Have you got a horse? No. A mule? No. All belongs to the squire." Then he adds quietly, "I'm just talking like business, you know. Got little enough myself."

"I ain't made much—so," concedes Day.

"And you got your children," admits Jones. "But we all got them," he adds.

"And you got your experience," says Day.

Lucas speaks again with soft finality—"And we all got that."

"A hard-working man for you, Mack," Day observes, gesturing toward the shadowed porch where Polly and Joe are now ensconced. As Lucas says nothing, he continues, "Strong as a bull. Work, work, work. That year of the railroad building and he fifteen, he saved a hundred dollars. But pop the question?" he queries quietly — "No sir, scared."

"Can pull a stack of fodder in a day," brags Jones. "Knowed him to do it."

"And put eleven hundred dollars in the bank last year," Day continues. "But scared to death of Polly," he chuckles, "yes, goodness!"

Lucas has begun to finger his fiddle more often, now and then sticking it to his chin. "I used to play for his daddy many a time — and made something out'n it too," he says. "And Joe likes it. Too many people is against the fiddle these days, John."

"I don't see no harm in it — " Day begins.

"Still the preachers rair about it," interrupts Jones.

Lucas whiffs out a faint tune. "They think it's a' evil-spirited instrument. But it ain't."

"I believe religion's right," declares Day. "No, breakdowns is bad."

Lucas calls out in a forlorn tone, "Religion's bad as breakdowns — sometimes. Plenty of people cut up in their religion."

"Yes," says Jones, "they do." And he spits loudly again.

"Aye, but we got to have it," Day reminds them.

"Remember that preacher at Angiers?" chortles Jones. "Tried to walk on water. He had planks hid in the pond to walk on. And then one day the boys found it out and moved a plank!" He slaps his thigh with his hat in glee, rearing back and forth and roaring with laughter. "He dang nigh got drowned when — kerjook — he went under."

Lucas bounces his bow across the strings, as he speaks wryly. "And old Joel Tart announced to the world he'd been given the gift of reading from above. And a great crowd come a-Sunday to hear him do it for they knowed he couldn't spell a word. Later on they found he'd got it by heart from a preacher. Now, John, that was a come-off."

"But Joel's sister Nannie was said to have spoke real Chinaman's talk in Little Bethel church once," says Day, "and she did from what they said. It was the spirit in her tongue," he adds humbly.

3.

Joshua Day, a stout, husky lad of eighteen comes out on the porch with a lamp in one hand and a banjo in the other. He sets the lamp down on the porch, whereupon the rather sheepish Joe, now that he and his vivacious sweetheart are visible in the light, slides his chair away from her. Joshua smothers a grin in his blouse, comes out into the yard and sits down, tuning his banjo. "Lord, what a supper I've et!" he boasts. "What is it, Mr. Mack? Hee-hee! What shall it be?"

"Something short and easy," the fiddler replies, his mournful, haggard face lighted with a smile, "anything—'The Drunken Soldier'—" Rosining up and shooting his bow across the strings in a preparatory whorl of sound, he announces, " 'The Drunken Soldier,' they like that piece up in Wake County."

Mockingly and on bended knee, Joshua begs—"Lead her out'n her stall! Lead her out, Mr. Mack."

He whangs forth a flood of chords. And they begin to play. Jones rolls his tobacco back in his jaw and claps his hands in rhythm.

"Can't he play it?" Day rejoices, nodding at his young son.

Jones looks up at the moon and brays out—

*"Oh the night's a little dark,*
*And the road's a little muddy,*
*And I can't ride straight,*
*And I can't ride study—"*

"How's that, Joe?" Day calls.

Joe steals a look at Polly. "Right fine, Mr. Day," he answers, as Lucas and Joshua wind up with a flourish.

And now several little children, dressed in their nightdrawers and gowns, come to the door of the porch and peep out. "Pa, we want to hear it," they chorus.

Kindly Mrs. Day bustles out on the porch and leads them into the house again. "Well, hear it in bed then," she commands.

"I'll declare!" exclaims Jones.

In the house the children are heard clamoring—"We want to hear them play!" while Lucas and Joshua impatiently amble up and down the necks of their instruments with their fingers.

Polly, as if piqued at the interruption of her love-making, leaves her chair in the circle of lamplight and sits down on the edge of the porch. Joe looks pleadingly after her and then sits staring heavily at the floor.

"I always liked the 'Mountain Dew' piece," suggests the fiddler.

"No better made," echoes Joshua, crowding close to him in intimate fellowship. Without more ado, the two musicians are off with 'The Mountain Dew.' As they play, Jones falls in with his foot-patting, and Day leans back in his chair, a smile softening his rugged weather-stained face.

Mrs. Day comes out and sits down on the steps, dipping snuff and placidly looking off before her. From the other end of the step Polly ever and anon steals a glance back at Joe who, left alone, at first pays little attention to the music. Presently he begins beating the floor softly with his feet, in time with the dance tune.

"Lord," says Jones out in the yard, "it brings a heap of things back to me."

The music stops and Lucas leans over to his partner, who nods to his whispered direction. "That's it too." And Joshua casts up his eyes joyously and announces to those around him, running a medley of chords the while, "'The Arkansas Traveler,' folkses."

With a high tweedle-de-dee, Lucas begins his chant, "There was a traveler in Arkansas — " and he starts bowing away the while. As the monologue goes on, Joshua's whang-whang serves as a background for the presentation of a traveler and farmer in conversation —

*"Hello, stranger.*

*Hello, yourself. If you want to go to hell, then go there yourself.*

*Play the other part of that tune.*

*There ain't no other part.*

*Why don't you cover your house?*

*Can't cover it when it's raining. In dry weather it don't leak a drop.*

*What makes your corn look so yaller?*

*Fool, I planted the yaller kind.*

*How did your 'taters turn out?*

*Didn't turn out, fool, I dug 'em out."*

Here Jones cries, "Weren't never such fools!" and cracks his palms in delight. Lucas goes on.

*"How far to where the road forks?*

*Been living here fifty year. It's never forked yet.*

*Can I ford the river?*

*Reckon so, the geese can.*

*Wish you'd head that steer.*

*The devil, looks like he's got a head on him.*

*I mean stop him.*

*Ain't got no stopper."*

Mrs. Day is heard chuckling softly to herself. Joe becomes more and more absorbed in the music, now unconscious of Polly's bright eyes. Joshua lets out a loud hee-haw, and abandons himself to his banjo, while Lucas continues.

*"I mean turn him out.*

*Looks like he's got the hairy side out."*

"Worse'n the old gray mare. Hee-hee!" yells Joshua.

"Lord, Lord," exclaims Jones, "totes the rag off'n the bush!"

Lucas begins another chant, the while his bow flies across the fiddle strings:
*"I hired to a man—and he sent me to the swamp to split rails—tee-ta-ta-*

ta—told me to choose out the tall trees—the straight trees—for they would split better—and I went and hewed—and I sweated and spewed—that night when I got home—hah—he asked me how many rails I'd split—hah—and I told him when I got done of the one I was on—hah—tee-ta-ta-ta—and two more—I'd have three.—Lord God, he fired me—for I'd been trying to split—ah—them old sweet gums."

Lucas finishes with a mournful laugh, and Joshua speaks admiringly, "He won a gold piece with that at the courthouse once. I seen him do it!"

"The years come and go, Mack, but you ain't lost a bit of your power," admits Day.

Lucas gestures with his bow toward the lone figure now sitting slumped over on the porch. "Joe's pa liked it too," he challenges. Joe is silent and the fiddler turns to Jones. "And way back yonder Allen's pa used to cut a rust to that same tune."

Mrs. Day speaks up with sudden animation. "The last dance I was at Mack played it."

Jones springs suddenly up with a whoop. "Already plowed forty miles to-day," he brags, "but I feel fresh—fresh!"

"Mr. Jones!" protests Polly.

Jones throws his hat behind him and moves out in the open space, "Let her go," he calls to the fiddler.

"I don't mind," says Day mildly. "Cut up then."

"Give me a reel, real Virginia reel," Jones orders loudly, and waits as Lucas saws out a few notes. "Yeh, that's all right. Get ready!" and he claps his hands for attention as if he were on a dance floor.

"Blamed if he don't mean business," laughs Day.

Jones moves over to where Polly sits on the porch step. "Let's cake-walk a little," he says, crooking his elbow.

"I could do it some," Polly agrees, "but—"

"Aw now," says the strutting Jones, "Joe don't care."

"Go to it," encourages Day.

"Give me 'The Paul Jones,' " Jones orders.

The fiddler has grown mildly excited. "Listen folks, everybody." He plays the opening bars, as he calls loudly, "Fo-r-mation!"

As Lucas begins to fiddle Jones calls the dance, marshaling into place an imaginary crowd. "Let the figgers roll. Formation. Longways for six couples, women in one line and men in the other," he sings out. "Hurry up there if you don't want the sun to find you waiting. All right, Polly Day, here I go. Come and join me while the dew do fall." He begins to dance, bowing and scraping and turning to imaginary ladies around him. As he dances he continues to call the figures for his own partial execution. Lucas and Joshua pound on the ground, and old Day leans back and stares at the sky, his ears cocked as it were and drinking in the music. Jones shuffles, bounds, cavorts, all the while squealing out his commands. "Forward and back! — Swing with your right hand!" — From across the yard he stretches out his right hand to Polly. "How're you tonight, rosebud? Purtiest gal from here to the river. Hah! Swing with the left hand! Hah!"

He turns and fastens his eyes on Polly, then dances his way over to her. She looks directly at Joe a moment, and then tosses her head and comes out to meet Jones's reaching hands. He shouts triumphantly, "How's that, my honeysuckle queen! Swing with both hands! — How's that? — Allemande!"

"Go to it, Polly," calls her brother gleefully, as he strums away on his banjo. "Go to it, we'll feed you!"

Old Day makes a motion as if to stop his daughter, and then returns to his apparent watching of the heavens. Lucas' face seems to grow more and more haggard as the fury of the music increases — as if some grief were gnawing within him. It is a way he has of showing his deepest pleasure.

"Right hand to partner and reel!" calls Jones. He swings Polly around and around as if going down the line. Each time she turns she looks at Joe's bowed form. Jones pants and blows. "Faster! Let's get up some feeling here. Up the center!" he shouts, as with gallop steps he drags Polly across the yard.

Patting his feet in spite of his misery, Joe looks up, and Polly looks back at him as she dances. "March!" gasps Jones, holding Polly closer to him as the music flies. Joe half rises from his seat and Polly's eyes beckon him on. "Down the center!" yells her jubilant partner.

4.

"I'll do it too," cries Joe, bounding out of his chair. And he runs up and snatches Polly loose from Jones.

"What! — " explodes Jones. "Great guns!"

"I could — " stutters Joe, his face almost white with fright — "I could — almost — "

Polly leans toward Joshua. "Play as fast as you can," she begs softly.

"Let's see you dance with her, tessie boy,"[1] Jones teases gruffly, as he sits down panting in his chair — almost with a touch of anger, "Naw, you can't do it."

Polly dances up and down the yard alone, swaying as the music goes on. Joe

1. "An effeminate fellow, a weak-willed errand boy" (*Paul Green's Wordbook*).

hesitates now after his sudden outburst, makes a movement in, draws back, moves again awkwardly after his sweetheart.

Jones fans himself vigorously with his hat. "Look at him!" he jeers. "Let's see him do something!"

"I can't dance—" says Joe shyly, following Polly, "I can't dance— much— none—maybe—but I'll try, I swear I'll try it if I hurt."

"Hah-hah!" laughs Jones. "Come on now, let's see you show your raising!"

"His father was one of the steppingest men there was," pipes up Mrs. Day.

"Shoe leather couldn't hold him," Jones agrees.

"I danced through to the blood one night with him," declares Mrs. Day.

"Pshaw," protests her husband. "Listen at her."

As Polly moves by Joe, he reaches out and timidly seizes her by the hands, then around the waist.

"Let the music pour out!" Jones announces. Joshua and Lucas wrap themselves over their instruments. "Here we go."

Polly and Joe run up and down the yard, cross, bend and bow in a crude sort of rhythm. They shuffle a jig, they waltz and foxtrot together. Then, as they proceed, they seem to find a common rhythm. Old Day watches them narrowly and jubilant, significantly nodding now and then to those around him.

"Hee-hee, Lord, Lord!" cries Joshua, twanging away.

"Hooray, hooray for you, Joe! Did you ever expect it, folkses?" shouts Jones, jumping up and stamping his hat in the dirt.

Day chuckles, "I bet him and Polly pulls off something yet." And he calls to the woman on the steps, "See that, Mellie?"

Joe and Polly now whirl along in their new crude dance. Joe, with his flushed face close to hers, whispers, "Tell 'em to play faster."

"You hold me so!" breathes Polly.

"Play on, Joshua!" orders Joe suddenly and excitedly. "Tear up your banjo, I'll buy you another." Then softly to the girl in his arms, he exults, "All right then, and I'll hold you! My God A'mighty."

And they dance on.

Finally Joshua drops his banjo. "I done played the skin clean off of my fingers," he declares wearily. And Lucas gradually lets his music die down to a low moaning in the strings, and sits looking out before him as if lost to the scene of which he is a part.

"My fingers are tougher than yours," he says, "they're older."

Suddenly Joe kisses Polly with a loud smack.

"He's done it," cries the startled Jones, digging his hat up out of the dirt. "I'll swear if he ain't gone and done it! Yay-ee!"

"Yeh," declares Joe stoutly, "and I mean it."

Polly stands with downcast eyes. After an embarrassed silence her father speaks gruffly. "A fiddle's some good after all, ain't it?"

"They went to church a lot," says Jones, "but that didn't bring 'em to."

Joe speaks whisperingly in his sweetheart's ear—"Let's go out walking in the moonshine."

"Yes," says Polly.

Jones begins to sing, "Oh, when will the wedding supper be, unh-hunh?"

"Allen," warns Mrs. Day, "don't start that right off."

"Tomorrow if you say so," beams Day. "Go up to the squire's with the license—"

"Better in fall when crops are housed," states Joe, manfully.

Polly tugs shyly and wordlessly at his arm, and they go out of the yard and down the road, Polly calling back timidly, "We're going for a walk, Ma, just a piece."

"Come back in a little bit," quavers Mrs. Day. She bows her head and for no reason at all falls to weeping silently in her apron.

Jones clears his throat loudly. "You'll have a fine son-in-law," he says heartily, "and he'll own land."

Lucas still fiddles quietly as he murmurs—

*I walked through the hills, and I walked through the fields,*
*And I ask you to tell me if you can,*
*You know what a rock is, you know what a tree is,*
*But what is the soul of man?"*

In his bass voice, Joshua repeats absently, "And I ask you—tell me if you can—"

## 5.

Quiet comes over the scene, and for a while nothing is said. Finally Day makes an effort. "The young will go on and the old will go on," he says.

"It was made to be so," agrees the fiddler.

With the spell of silence broken, Jones speaks out, "Great guns, right here before us all!"

"Aye," returns Day huskily. He clears his throat. "Bad weather," he observes funnily, with lifted face.

Jones looks out toward the moon. "Yeh, rain."

"A star close to the edge there and a ring-around," continues Day appraisingly.

"Look at them little white clouds," says Joshua. "Cold like snow."

"Lonesome looking up there," sighs Jones.

The moonlight bathes their faces with its pale shine.

Presently Day speaks again. "Like a wide field. I've seen 'em so in March."

"A long ways there and back," Joshua says.

And Lucas softly repeats his plaintive song —

*"You know what the moon and the stars may be,*
*And the width of the salt sea span,*
*But where is the heart can answer me,*
*What is the soul of man?"*

"Uh-uh," says Jones. Then after a moment, he chuckles — "On a white night like this, every stump looks like an old man with a beard. I'm about a-scared to go home, hah, hah!"

"That was a come-off," reflects Joshua. "Right in the open!"

"On a night like this I rid a mule once to see Mellie there," Day begins, "and he got scared of a stump, and he throwed me. Then he run all around me, same as folks, a-laughing at me. I reached me a rail and laid down by a bush, and when he come by I whammed him in the burr of the ear and I piled him — directly he got up. . . ."

He goes on telling the story while a freshening little wind blows about the four moonlit faces and over the bowed figure on the steps. But we hear him no more.

And somewhere the lovers are abroad in the night, laying their plans for the long fat winter coming on.

# Bernie and the Britches

There are a number of roads leading to our little thriving southern agricultural town. And as you approach on any of them, you are likely to see a good splashing sign carrying the big-lettered name of Bernard Randall, dealer in real estate, horses, mules, farm equipment, and fertilizer. And then when you get inside the town you are further confronted with Bernard Randall's success as a businessman. On the corner of Main and High Streets is Randall's Drugstore. A block higher up on Main Street is Randall's Hardware Store, above which is the owner's suite of real estate offices. And farther south in the edge of the town by the railroad tracks is his livery stable.

Now to see Bernie you wouldn't think he could ever have become the go-getter he has. A rather spindly fellow he is, of medium height, sandy-haired, pale-faced and with vague blue eyes. And his manner is still as hesitant and halting as ever it was in his humbler days. And he has never yet learned to wear his clothes the way he should wear them, though he's now plenty well able to buy fine quality and fit for the wearing.

As our old local historian and philosopher, Mr. Mac, has said many a time, and as everybody knows, the ways of fate and luck in the making of a man's life are a strange and fearful thing. Just the other night I was reading a poem about how a man comes to a dividing of the road. Shall he take the right turn or the left turn? He takes the right turn, say, and in the words of the poet, that made all the difference. Sometimes a glance, a nod, a sudden whim or fancy will change the course of a man's life forever. A smudge of soot on your sweetheart's nose, the wrong word spoken and not meant, a broken tooth, the wayward laugh, the missed train — whatever it is.

Of course when accidents happen, and wayward touches and circumstances come into the course of a man's life to turn it, the man on whom destiny places her vote is the one who is able to grab the sudden chance that comes and make the most of it or skip nimbly out of the way if it is a mischance. No doubt that is true.

Now Bernie Randall happened to seize the bit of luck, or ill-luck some would be forced to call it, when it came to him one night. And from that time onward his climb to power and wealth was steady.

And Bernie seemed the last person in the world to whom good luck would come. Nobody ever expected him to amount to anything. As I've said, he was awkward, timid and uncertain with his weak friendly smile, and homely as an old shoe. His people were poor as church mice and lived down by the railroad track just a block or so from where later Bernie had his livery stables. His father was sickly and an addict to patent medicines, and early the responsibility of his mother and father fell pretty much on the thin shrinking shoulders of their only child.

Bernie grew up a drudge. From the time he was six or seven he was running errands for his parents, sweeping leaves out of people's yards, hiring out to pick cotton in some of the fields that came up to the edge of the town, even trying to shine shoes, or standing on the corner dumb and fearful on Saturday afternoons with an armful of *Grit* newspapers. But through all his twistings and turnings of odd jobs, he never developed the sharpness and quickness that one usually associates with an American boy in such situations. Rather he continued his humble and lonely browbeaten way.

Somehow he got a little schooling now and then in the winter months— enough to learn to read and write and do fairly simple sums in arithmetic. And later when he was big enough for his daddy to swear him by the child labor law, he got a job weaving in the cotton mill. And there as time went on he met up with May Eppinger who worked at one of the looms.

May was a pretty round-faced girl with a light laugh and a love for milkshakes at the corner drugstore. Bernie early fell in love with her. His devotion was dog-like and persistent. No matter with what levity or even bursts of scorn May treated him he continued his dreamings and devotions to her.

In time Bernie's mother and father died and he was left alone in the little house that had been their home. It was a rented place, and now Bernie indulged in planning for his own wide-open future.

From his earnings at the loom he was able to make a mortgage deal with young Ed Weatherford down at the bank to buy the little place. And so he started paying monthly installments on it.

Every now and then he would abstract a dollar or two from his thin savings and get a box of candy for May. And once or twice he was able to get ahead enough and persuade her to go with him on an excursion to the fair at Raleigh.

But of course come wet weather or dry, he must somehow scrape together enough each month for his house payments. And regularly he would take his few dollars down to the bank and there hand them over to Weatherford who in a swift round business hand would write out the receipt and hand it through the grill to Bernie with a cool and pleasant air.

Young Weatherford was everything that Bernie was not. He was handsome, educated at the University, and sure of a big future with the power and money he had inherited from his father. Already he was one of the key men in the bank, and as old Josh Overby, the lumberman said, was as sharp at getting interest and financing fees as ever you could find. "Yes, sir," said old Josh, "where his daddy made thousands, young Ed will make millions, watch my word."

When Bernie was twenty-five and May was near the same age, they got married. During the years she had had swarms of boy friends of her class in the mill section, but somehow time had gone by and she was no nearer married than before. Perhaps her boy friends liked the idea of courting her better than they did of marrying her. Whether from weariness of working at the mill or whatnot, she finally married Bernie, and began to take her ease in the little house down by the railroad track.

And that's just what Bernie liked. He wanted her to stay cool and comfortable. "You've already done your share of hard work, Baby," he would say. Soon after they were married he started calling her Baby. And she liked it. She liked to be treated as a baby. She liked for him to wait on her and spoil her. She would lie abed in the morning and he would be up, fixing his breakfast and off to the mill. And during the day she would loll about the house in an easy wrapper, looking at catalogues, eating bits of the candy and sweets Bernie would bring her, reading the comics and taking her ease. She could never seem to get enough of resting and sitting on the porch and rocking and looking off across the railroad tracks and drowsily daydreaming. And now and then when she could get a couple of dimes from Bernie she would go to the movies.

Weeks and months went by, one year, two years. The routine was the same. May was taking it easy, and Bernie was working like a dog in the mills. But however hard he worked, his promotion was slow. He never could learn how to deal with people, become swift and to the point, authoritative, a manager. After all the years of service in the cotton mill he was only a master beamer. Others, younger and less experienced passed him by and became floor bosses or loom inspectors or even superintendents.

But Bernie didn't worry too much. He had May. And after all, in his own humble opinion, it was quite fitting that others should become successful and he should continue in the rut he was in, though he would never think of it as a rut.

And May's little selfish demandings and spoilings continued. The neighbors saw how things were going and some of them spoke their minds about it.

"I feel so sorry for poor Bernie," said old Miz Keziah Turnage. "Thet lazy girl lies around, dolls herself up and don't turn a hand a bit and grain to help him."

"It's the truth, Ma," said Lulu Turnage, her bony-shouldered daughter who would have been glad to have behaved so differently to Bernie.

"But then men are such fools," said Miz Turnage, whose husband, a preacher, had been had up in the church for giving a choir girl a string of beads on the sly and who now was dead and buried, and another man was counting the beads.

"Yes, and Bernie's the biggest fool of 'em all," said Lulu venomously as she went on with ironing her pink blouse for Sunday.

"And he'll be drove hard and put up muddy all his life, hear me," said Miz Keziah, and she continued churning her butter energetically.

"He orter had a better wife," said Lulu.

"Hmn!" said Miz Keziah, clearing her throat angrily.

Now Bernie, the subject of the neighbors' discourse, was indeed at that very moment being driven hard. He was down at the bank in the inner office talking to young Ed Weatherford who was now an assistant cashier. He was arranging a loan of three thousand dollars on his house for remodeling it. Of recent months May had begun to wheedle him about the place they lived in. It was a shame and a disgrace and not hardly fit for dogs, she declared. And Bernie looking at her plumpish and cool and fragrant form in her loose flowered housegown knew with excruciating certainty that she was right. What a place to keep his darling, his golden honey-one in. And so after succumbing to a stiff financing fee plus the regular six per cent interest, and agreeing to a whole string of whereases, parties of the first part, parties of the second part, hereinafters and befores, he arranged with young Weatherford for the loan.

"Where'll I sign the paper?" said Bernie.

"Right here," said Ed. "You both'll have to sign it — you and your wife. And it'll have to be notarized too," he went on.

"Yes, sir," said Bernie.

"It might be more convenient to have your wife drop in here. We have a notary in the bank."

And so Bernie went off and brought Baby down. And she dressed up especially for the occasion. And there she signed the paper and Ed Weatherford looked at her as she signed. And she looked up at him and dropped her eyes and gave a little laugh, and taking Bernie by his thin and rawbony arm she went away.

Young Ed gazed after them as they went and an introspective and almost indistinct whistle pfuii-ed through his lips. He turned to his secretary and handed her the papers.

"Keep these in the current file," he said. "We'll maybe see how things go."

Then began the clattering and hammering and sawing of the carpenters as the house was remodeled, and the clanging and cracking ring of the mason's trowel building the two chimneys. The noise got on Baby's nerves and she went over to stay with her mother and father until the work was done. And when finally it was finished and Bernie had cleaned and swept the house and got the furniture arranged back, she came and took up her place there in it like the spoiled queen bee she was.

And the pinch on Bernie was harder now. It was tough, making the monthly payments on the loan. And once when he fell sick and lost a few week's time from working, the first cold grip of despair got its bite into his stolid and lightless soul. He looked at Baby propped up in bed reading a murder serial in the newspapers and for once he wrung his hands.

"What am I going to do?" he queried.

She looked at him comfortably and reached over and patted his thin long pallid hand. "My Bernie'll find a way out," she smiled. "He always does. Kiss your baby and take that frown off your face." He bent over and kissed her on the forehead with cold and colorless lips. Then he sat down by the bed and stared at the floor.

"That Ed Weatherford won't show me no mercy," he said. "I can draw ahead on the mill enough to pay the next installment. But after that—" and he shook his head.

"I seen an ad in the paper the other day," May spoke up, "where it said salesman wanted at $40.00 a week."

"Hah!" said Bernie.

"It's fifteen dollars a week more'n you're making now," she said sharply.

"Me a salesman!" said Bernie mirthlessly.

"You could get the job. I betcha Ed—Mr. Ed Weatherford would help you get it."

"Not him," said Bernie. "He'd never help anybody. It's money, money, money with him," and then he added, "and women."

"Women?" she laughed.

"Everybody knows how he is about—about that," said Bernie. "That time we were down there in the bank signing the papers, I saw him looking at you."

"Did you?" she said lightly.

"Course I couldn't blame him for that," said Bernie, patting her hand, "'cause you're the prettiest thing that ever come down the pike. But still—" His voice died out in a sigh.

"Ain't that the soup boiling over?" she said.

"Bless my life," he cried, and with that he sprang up and dashed into the kitchen.

Later when they were eating their supper she brought the subject up again.

"You could make good money at that salesman business. You don't have to talk much, just show the stuff and carry the samples around and take orders."

"But my education," he said.

"Education, the dog's foot! You write a good hand, good enough to put orders down. I'm going to Ed Weatherford myself and ask him —"

"No, you're not," he said. "If anybody's got to go, I will."

And so a few days later he did. And to his surprise Ed Weatherford recommended him and he got the job. And more than that — the young banker helped him arrange along with the agency to get him a second-hand Ford car in which to cover the territory assigned to him.

"Now all you got to do, Bernie," he said with a laugh, "is get in and go to it."

And so began Bernie's days as a vacuum cleaner salesman. He worked at it hard. Nobody could deny that. He was up early and gone to distant points, whether an outlying farm or a village or hamlet in another county. But however far he went, he was always back home sometime at night to be with his Baby. Yet, however hard he worked, he could barely make a living. Depression days were coming on now and sales resistance was growing. He intensified his efforts, he drove farther, he was up earlier, he worked later and now and then so far a-field did he go in his endeavors to sell his product that he was unable to get back at night.

The picture looked darker and darker. Sometimes when he was up and away at early dawn and the installment was coming due at the bank, he would have May go down and pay it.

Things were tightening up a bit all along the line and Weatherford's bank was retrenching some. Weatherford would go out visiting among the farmers and creditors, foreclosing here and collecting there, and often he would come humming home at night in his blue Cadillac with quite a roll in his pocket, sometimes as much as $5,000 to be deposited the next day.

That's the way it was with him. Whatever he went at, he succeeded. And all the while Bernie Randall was coming on down to bankruptcy.

One day Bernie got up early to start one of his dreary rounds. He'd heard that over at Wilson, a town some fifty or sixty miles away, there were several prospects. He told May he wouldn't be back that night and for her to get one of her sisters to come and stay with her.

"Pshaw, I'm not afraid to stay by myself," she said, putting out her pretty lips in a pout.

"You do what I say," he said.

"Go along with you," she said, "and I'll expect you back tomorrow night."

"Yes, tomorrow night," he said. And he drove off.

A half a hundred miles he drove, and then set to work in the virgin territory going from house to house. But sales resistance was a hundred per cent that day. The tobacco market had just opened and the price was bad and the papers had given the prospects as being even less encouraging for the future. And this was a tobacco country. Later in the afternoon, Bernie, completely whipped down, decided to drive around by Raleigh and talk things over with the head of the regional office.

"I'm very glad you called in," said Mr. Wayburn.

"Well," said Bernie smiling.

And that was the last time he smiled for many a day. For then the news hit him smash in the face. The regional office had decided to cancel his agency. A letter had already been written and dispatched that very day, saying so. Mr. Wayburn kindly showed him a carbon copy in which with the usual regrets and so forth the company had found it necessary to dispense with his services.

"I reckon you'll want your sample that I've got with me," said Bernie, trying to keep his voice steady.

"I'm afraid so," said Mr. Wayburn.

Bernie went out and brought it in from the car. His legs were shaking, and there was a dull nauseated feeling in his chest, sagging and going on down to his stomach. He handed over his sales pad, shook hands with Mr. Wayburn and went away.

Outside, he sat in his parked car a long while, staring ahead of him through the windshield—staring at a dull blank wall, a wall nobody else could see, but he could see as if in a blinding light. There was no hole in that wall through which he could go.

He must have sat there for hours. The darkness came down. The street lights flared on, and tap, tap went the heels of the working girls going home and the heavier solider tread of men folks passing by. Up the street was the marquee of a movie theatre advertising in shimmering letters "The Love Nest." Bernie read the sign abstractedly. He smiled wryly, quoting to himself, "The Love Nest." He remembered now that Baby had seen that picture. She had liked it.

The words "love nest" echoed in his brain. Secretly and deeply to himself he had often thought of his little house and Baby in it as his love nest. Well, it would all be different now. He had lost his nest. The bank would foreclose on him like the jaws of a steel trap. He knew Ed Weatherford well enough for that.

"He won't show me no mercy," he said to himself. "And it's a bargain he'll get. That's the way them fellows make their money. They get poor guys like me in their grip and gripe and then they squeeze 'em and take away what they got. And then they turn around and sell it to somebody else for double what it's worth."

Wait till he got home and told Baby the news of what had happened. But how could he tell her, how could he break her heart like that? And in his mind he could see her, lying up in bed, beautiful and sweet, a wonder and a joy for any man to be proud of.

"Yes, lying in bed," he said to himself. He wasn't trying to put meaning into the words. He was only reciting them to himself, and then suddenly they had a meaning and he didn't like the feeling that came over him.

For the first time in his life Bernie Randall began to feel sorry for himself. Maybe for the first time he was seeing himself as he really was, a poor plodding dull fellow, hard put on by others.

"Yeh, I work hard as I can," he said to himself as he sat there in the car and as the people flowed by. "And it says in the Bible about a helpmeet. And the preacher when he said them words over us said honor and obey and cherish and love. Well, that's what I do. I did and I do. But — "

He shook his head and cut off his thought. There was something doleful about it. He could feel it coming on, though. No, it wouldn't do to think like that. Wasn't he the luckiest man in seven counties. Wasn't he married to the sweetest, prettiest girl round and about. Didn't all kinds of other fellows want to marry her in the days gone by. They hung around her in droves, but she chose him, him, Bernie Randall. Well, he was thankful. He appreciated her, he sure did, and he could never do enough to pay back to her for what she had given him — herself.

There must be some way out. There must be. He couldn't drag her down into complete poverty and have to start living all over again in a rented two-room mill shack and he back in the mill beaming away. From morn to evening beaming away — and the lint sucking into his lungs.

Yes, she'd been right, wanting to get him out of that place, get him out into the open air, doing a job that was better, being a salesman — "My husband, he's a salesman for the National Electric Company." That sounded so much better than having to say, "My husband works at a loom in the cotton mill."

She had ambition for him, that's what. She wanted him to get ahead. He thanked her for it, and thanks was all she'd get. For now he'd failed. He'd failed her.

He bent his head over on the steering wheel, sick at heart. Thinking, thinking, planning, planning — and seeing no light, not a glimmer.

Sometime later in the night a policeman came up and rapped on the door. He woke from a cold and aching sleep.

"This is a business section," said the policeman. "You can't park here all night."

"Yes, sir," said Bernie in his spasmodic, halting way. He looked about him. The street was deserted. The neon lights on the theatre marquee had gone out.

"What time is it, sir?" he asked.

"Past twelve o'clock, son," said the cop.

"Thank you." Bernie stepped on the starter, finally got his old jaloppy shaking and choking, and then he pulled out and drove off.

Through the night he drove toward home. There ahead of him he could see the starry hunter and the dog, or the box with the handle to it as some folks called it, rising high in the sky.

"Eh, them stars," he said bitterly to himself. "Cold and no mercy in 'em. They look down on the earth, look down on man. On me. And what do they care about me, about anything. Cold, cold as Ed Weatherford's eyes!"

The words were running easy on his motionless tongue. That's the way it was with him. Inside himself he could talk and speak slick enough. He found words a-plenty when he wanted them. But when he tried to say them out, then that was another thing.

"The preachers say there's a God that lives beyond them stars," he went on. "And so they pray to him. They ask him for help. I've never prayed for anything nor asked him for anything." He glanced up and spoke in a loud vehement voice in the night, a voice that could have been heard by any passer-by above the clattering noise of his old Ford. "Well, I ask you now, God, to help me. I've come about to the end of my rope. I don't know where to turn. I'm going to lose all I've worked to earn. My wife will hate me for it. Help me, God. I'm asking you, help me this time and I won't ask you no more."

Well, believe it or not, God maybe heard Bernie, and his prayer was answered before that night was over. But it was answered in a way he would never have dreamed of and maybe wouldn't have wanted if he had.

When he got within a block of his home he cut his rattletrap motor off and let his car roll silently up to the house, as was his custom when coming in late. He was always careful not to wake Baby. He got out softly and walked along the grass up to the little front porch. When he had remodeled the house he had planted grass and flowers out in front, and he could see a few of the late roses blooming and hanging their heads in the pale starlight. And in spite of his misery there was a warm feeling in him to see the flowers. They reminded him of Baby. She was so like a flower. And in a moment he would be snuggled up against her warm soft body. And with his arms around her, he would forget for a little bit some of the black misery that was packed up killingly inside him. He took off his shoes and crept across the porch. With his key which he kept for emergency home-comings, he opened the door softly and went into the hall. He set his light pasteboard suitcase down quietly and made his way along the little hall to the bedroom.

He felt for the door, it was partly opened and he slipped on in. He took off his coat and trousers in the darkness and laid them on a chair. It was just like him, awkward as he was, to bump into a chair and make a noise.

Baby's voice cried out from the bed in sheer and sudden terror. "What's that?"

"S-s-h," he said, "nobody but me, Baby." There was a stifling shaking noise from the bed. "I didn't mean to scare you," he said. "Wait'll I turn on the light."

"No, no!" And her voice was quick and frantic. He was fumbling along the wall for the switch.

"What's the matter?"

"Don't, don't," she moaned, "don't turn on the light."

"Why, Baby?"

"Oh, I've got the most awfulest headache," she said. "I — I don't know what to do with it. It's killing of me. No, please don't turn on the light, please. My eyes would hurt so, my eyes!"

"Sure, sure," he said. "Can't I rub you? Get a hot pad?" He was feeling toward the bed.

"Don't, don't," she moaned, and he could hear her sitting up in the bed, and rocking from side to side. "Go down to the drugstore, right away, quick, and get me some aspirin. I got to have it. It come on all of a sudden, it's killing me! Oh!"

"But the drugstore's all closed up, Baby."

"Ned Sauls, the clerk, sleeps right above it, you can call him. Please, please, hurry, hurry."

So agonized, so wild was her manner that he turned quickly to do her bidding.

"Yes, yes, Baby. I'll put on my britches and my coat and I'll go right away." He bumped into another chair, then finally located his trousers, pulled them on, fumbled around some more, got his coat and made his way swiftly out of the room. He set off running toward the drugstore two blocks away, pulling on his coat as he ran. When he got there he grabbed up handfuls of gravel from a near-by walk and threw them up at the second story window and soon waked the clerk. He explained how his wife May had been taken suddenly with a pain in the head and needed something to quiet her.

"I'll be right down," said Ned Sauls.

In a moment Ned had come down, dressed in an old bathrobe, turned on the lights and let him into the store. He got the aspirin and handed it to Bernie.

"Sorry to bother you like this," said Bernie.

"That's all right," said Ned. "When was she taken?"

"Sometime during the night," said Bernie.

"Does she have 'em often, headaches, I mean?"

"No, first time I've ever knowed it. That's what scares me."

"Maybe I'd better get her up something a little stronger."

"Yeh, that'd be good," said Bernie thankfully. Ned brought forth a little pellet box.

"I'm supposed to have a prescription for this, but seeing it's you, Bernie, I'll go ahead and help you out."

"Thanky," said Bernie. "I'd a-come sooner if I'd a-knowed, but I been away on the road and — "

"That's luminol."

"How much I owe you?"

"Fifty cents. How's business on the road?"

Bernie reached into his pocket for the money. "Business? — well — " But he got no further, for his hand which had gone into his pocket for a loose bit of change, came out spasmodically and like a thing alive and of itself. And in the astounded hand which he held before him, Bernie saw a great roll of bills with a rubberband around them. He stared at the bills, a wad so big that even his own long fingers and thumb would not quite enclose it. In frozen and astounded silence, Ned the clerk looked over at the wad of bills with popping eyes a moment. "Jerusalem," he finally exploded, "business must have been good."

"Hah, hah, hah," Bernie laughed vacuously and mechanically. "Looks — er — like it," he added, stuttering.

"It does that. How much you got there? Aw, hush my big mouth."

"Hah, hah," said Bernie again, and his voice sounded high, almost shrill.

Ned the clerk was looking at him with growing admiration in his face. "Daggone my hide, you must be some salesman. I reckon that'll make folks eat their words."

"Yeah, folks, what'd they say?" he queried as his hand holding the bills was slowly lowered by his side.

Bernie let his gaze travel downward. A shock went through his spare frame though he made no outward sign.

He was wearing another man's trousers.

"You know how folks are — well, Bernie, none of us expected you to make much of a go as a salesman."

196  *Bernie and the Britches*

"Didn't?"

"Well, now, I'm afraid not."

"Reckon you'd better charge it," he said abruptly.

"Oh, sure, sure."

Bernie turned away. He slid the roll of bulging bills back into his pocket. He called back, "Much obliged to you, Ned."

"Glad to do it, Bernie, glad. And, say, anytime you want anything—anything—just call me up and I'll put it on the books—rush it right out for you."

"Thanky," Bernie called as he went through the door.

"Good night."

"Good night."

The clerk stared after him awhile, then turned off the light, and went thoughtfully back upstairs.

Bernie took his time in walking home. It was only a short distance, but a lot of things were happening in his head as he walked. Thoughts were flashing by, ideas happening, the gears inside were turning as they never had before.

As he got near the house he tried to whistle. But his lips were so dry that he had to wet them with his tongue. And after several efforts he finally got out a stave or two of about the only song he knew, called "Beulah Land" which he had learned in Sunday school years before. Baby would hear him and know that he was coming back. Then he saw that he didn't have to whistle any more, for far down the sidewalk he discerned the figure of a man rapidly disappearing into the darkness. And he knew who the man was and he knew too that he was wearing away a pair of slick-seated blue trousers with about two dollars change in the pockets.

For a moment he stood under the street light looking at a leather key case which he had pulled out and held in his hand. Stamped in gold letters on the case was the name E. F. Weatherford.

"F stands for Fitzhugh," Bernie said queerly and factually to himself.

As he got near the house a light came on in Baby's bedroom. He went into the kitchen, got a glass of cold water and took it to her. She was sitting up in bed bent over with her arms wrapped around her knees. She didn't look up when he came into the room but just sat there.

"Here you are, Baby," he said, holding out the glass. "I got you some luminol too." She said nothing. "You got the light on," he said.

"Yes," she mumbled, "I'm feeling a little better now."

"Take this," he said. He held out a couple of grains of luminol. She took them, threw them in her mouth, reached for the glass of water and drank them down. Then she lay back in the bed and pulled the covers up to her chin.

"Thanky," she said.

"That's all right, Baby," he said. He turned away, set the glass down and slowly began to undress. His back was turned toward her, but he knew she was looking at him now.

"Have a good trip?" she finally inquired.

"No, not so good. I'll tell you about it tomorrow." He hung his coat on a chair and started to slide his suspenders down over his shoulders. His hands stopped and he snapped them back up. Baby turned her soft curved body over in bed, making room for him. He went to the door and stood with his hand resting on the light switch.

"I'm sure sorry you're feeling so bad."

"Oh, I'm a lot better now. That medicine helped me."

"I thought I told you to get Minnie to come stay with you," and he looked around at her. She was staring up at the ceiling now, and as she spoke he could hear her voice tremble a little.

"Oh, pshaw, there was nobody to bother me. I wasn't afraid."

"Good," he said, "that's good. I'll turn off the light now."

"Yeh, do and come to bed."

He switched off the light and went on into the hall. He heard her body jack-knife up in bed again and she called after him. "Ain't you coming to bed?"

"I'm going to lie down out here," he said. "I got some figuring to do." He listened and she said no more. He stretched himself out on the sofa which was set against the wall in the little combination entrance hall and living room. He lay there in the darkness. Presently he heard Baby moving herself in bed again, stretching and getting fixed, and then giving a sort of easeful sigh as she pulled the cool sheet up over her soft big breasts and under her chin. He couldn't see her, but he knew that's what she was doing. She loved to pull the sheet up that way. And sometimes when they were close together they'd pull the sheet up over both their heads and look at themselves like children playing playhouse as the light shone through from the outside. He remembered the first day they were married. Ah —

A tiny noise sounded in his throat as if he were choking. He sat up and bent over, his elbows on his knees and his chin in his hand. A long while he sat there. Baby's breath was coming regularly from the next room, a little husky, animal, snuggy sound.

"Lordy mercy, she's already asleep," he said to himself incredulously.

He stood up and with his shoes in his hand slipped out through the back door and sat on the back steps looking out toward his small plot of vegetable garden. All night he sat there, and when the dawn was breaking and the chilly birds were chattering in the maples along the street, he went in and changed into his one remaining suit of clothes. Presently he came out with a little package. He went over to the incinerator in the yard which he'd built out of bricks in his spare hours so everything would be kept neat for Baby. He started a fire in the incinerator and stood there while the package burned up. Then he went back into the house and began cooking breakfast.

Later he brought her coffee and toast and eggs to her in bed as he'd done many times before. He spoke to her in his usual voice. As he set the tray down, he kissed her on the forehead and said, "How're you feeling this morning, Baby?"

For an instant she looked deep into his eyes, into his vague blue eyes, and they were the same eyes she had always looked into and they said no more or no less to her than they had always said.

"I'm all right," she said. And she sat briskly up and reached for a cup of coffee. "Uhm, it does smell good."

She sat drinking, peering over the rim of the cup with her wide lovely sleep-freshened eyes. Innocent and fresh and dewy and no blue circles or hollows there. And Bernie felt there should have been.

"Hah! Walking in blindness," he muttered to himself.

"What?" she said. And he thought he saw the cup shaking in her hand for an instant.

"Just a way I got lately," he said, "talking to myself sometimes. My daddy used to do that."

"Well, quit it," she said sharply. "You got me to talk to."

"Yeh, Baby, I have," he said. For a moment she drank her coffee in little gulps. He could see the swallowing movements of her pretty throat as the wads of fluid went down. Suddenly his knees shook and he sat weakly in his chair. She looked over at him perplexed.

"What's the—the matter?" she said.

"Nothing," he said.

A thought had struck him like a flash. A man over beyond Black River had with his two bare hands strangled his wife one night in bed. He dragged his sleeve across his forehead, then stood quickly up.

"I'll be going off today," he said.

"Where?"

"I've got some business. I'll be back later."

Bernie got in his car and headed out of town. For an hour or so he drove across the country and came to a neighboring village and went into a bank.

There he exchanged his huge roll of worn bills for newer and larger denominations — Ed Weatherford could never claim these as his money. Then he came out and drove back home.

The next day just before noon time, Bernie Randall appeared at one of the bank windows. "Morning, Miss Raeford," he said.

"Morning, Bernie," she said, without too much respect in her voice. It was the same old thing. He had come about his small payment.

"I'd like to see Mr. Weatherford," he said.

"He's busy," she said. "You can take the matter up with me as usual."

"I want to see him," said Bernie. His manner caused her to glance up. He was looking at her straight and unblinking.

"All right," she said, and she went away. In a moment the door to an inner office opened and Weatherford appeared in it. He held the knob in his hand as if ready to step back and close the door at any moment. Bernie didn't smile. His face never changed, but there was a sort of queer smile deep in his soul to see Weatherford holding on to the knob.

"What is it?" called Weatherford from the distance where he stood.

"I thought," said Bernie, "I'd like to see you a little bit about my mortgage."

"All right, what is it, Bernie."

"I'd like to pay it off."

Pierce Slocumb, a young teller over to the right, looked suddenly around in astonishment.

"Oh," said Weatherford, "you do."

"Yeh," said Bernie.

"There's no hurry," said Weatherford. "The bank's satisfied the way it is — pay it by the month."

"I'm not satisfied," said Bernie.

Young Pierce kept staring at him.

"Bring the papers out, Pierce," said Weatherford abruptly. "Are you paying by a check, Bernie?"

For a moment Bernie was silent and then said, "No, I'd rather pay cash."

"Part?"

"No, the full amount, the full three thousand." He pulled out some bills and laid them on the counter, but kept his hand on them. "I got thirty $100 bills here," he said, "new ones."

For a moment Weatherford stood looking at him.

"All right," he said abruptly. He took the papers from Pierce, went through them, stamped them, wrote across them with a flourish that they were paid, and handed the batch out to Bernie. Bernie took them with one hand and shoved the money over with the other. Pierce and Miss Raeford stood looking on wide-eyed.

"And I'd like to pay off the note on my car."

"Get that too," Weatherford said a little hoarsely. Pierce went off and brought back some papers. They were likewise stamped and marked paid and Bernie handed over four crisp $100 bills. He took his cancelled papers.

"Thanky, Ed," he said. This was the first time he'd ever addressed the banker without a handle to his name.

"You're welcome," said Weatherford coldly.

"And I reckon this sorta squares things betwixt us," Bernie concluded.

"Well, — then — all right — glad it does," Weatherford answered hastily.

"Good day," said Bernie. And with that he turned and went out of the bank. As soon as the door had closed behind him, young Pierce exploded.

"Gee whillikins," he said, "reckon that fellow must have found a gold mine. Or maybe he stole it."

"A young man working in a bank shouldn't talk too much," said Weatherford icily.

"Yes, sir." And Pierce hurried back to his work. Weatherford swept the bills into the till, turned and re-entered his inner office.


The depression came down pretty fierce after this and began to wipe out Ed Weatherford's holdings one by one. Like the fellows on Wall Street he had over-extended himself and had to pull in his horns. At the bottom of the market Bernie — with the fifteen hundred dollars he still had left — made a down payment on a farm in the edge of the town which had formerly belonged to Weatherford and the bank. He had confidence in himself now, and he held grimly on to it like a feist dog. And when the depression lifted and money was easy again he cut it up into building lots, sold them off, and made a killing. After this there was no stopping him.

As for Baby — well, she is completely changed. And as everybody knows she now idolizes Bernie and can't do enough for him. She brings him his slippers at night, she fixes his oatmeal in the morning. She mothers him and waits on him as if he were her child. And he takes it all with never a word and never a sign as far as anybody can tell as to how he feels about her.

And the dollars keep rolling in on Bernie. Everything he touches flourishes, and he has his hand into a dozen businesses. The next time you come into our town you'll like as not see a big sign by the roadside lighted up with neon lights and it will tell that Bernie is now also in the automobile business.

And in spite of all his business success, his fine new home and his better clothes, Bernie remains pretty much the same fellow he always was. He still speaks in his halting awkward way and goes with slightly bent shoulders, his face still pale and freckled and his blue eyes dull as ever they were.

But he doesn't smile any more, the way he used to do in his more humble days.

# The Ghost in the Tree

Much of "The Ghost in the Tree" is presented in the language of Lawton, an old farmer who is mostly a bootlegger, possum hunter, and storyteller. Lawton's family has lived in the Little Bethel backcountry for generations, and his speech is enriched with words and phrases to some degree peculiar to the region. Everything he says is intelligible in context, but to spare readers any momentary worry over possible typos, I will gloss a few of his expressions from *Paul Green's Wordbook*. "Layway" means to waylay. "Trojas" is the adjectival form of Trojan and means a hardworking, energetic person. "Fan it" and "light a rag" both mean to run fast, but the latter has the added connotation of fleeing in fear. You might "fan it" trying to stretch a single into a double in baseball, but if you saw a ghost you would "light a rag" out of there. And "outdacious" is what Lewis Carroll called a portmanteau word—that is, a word formed when two words are collapsed into one, in this case outrageous and audacious.

About dusk-down the old miller and I arrived at Lawton's shack of a farmhouse and hallooed him out. He was already set to go on the hunt, and little Purefoy, his Negro helper, had the two dogs Spot and Bo-peep tied with plowline, waiting in the yard. Lawton was a swarthy heavy-set man with the mark of the glutton and sot-drunkard upon him. Next to the making of liquor, 'possum-hunting was his passion.

"Better drive up the wire road a piece, Mr. Mac," he said. "Down back of the old Gregory place muscadines and 'simmons is thick as the children in the wilderness."

"Yessuh, 'possums use mighty plentiful up there," little Purefoy chirped up encouragingly.

We set off, and after driving a few miles, left the car parked in a little black-jack nook by the road and went into the forest for the hunt. And for two hours or more we tramped and waited about, but only once did Spot or Bo-peep show any signs that a 'possum had ever visited in the Gregory woods. Beyond a few uncertain yelps down in a bamboo morass, they had been as silent as the grave.

And so we kept on walking in the night, until our feet were sogged through. Finally we persuaded Lawton to stop and let us build a fire.

"Everybody tells what a good hunter you are, Lawton," said the old miller, now standing with his back to the fire of dried twigs and old broken pine rails, his palms crossed outward behind him to the blaze.

"I just hunt for the fun of it," Lawton said. "And sometimes you catch 'em and sometimes you don't." His voice was a little hard and insolent, and he seemed restless and ill at ease.

"What's the biggest 'possum you ever caught?" I asked, hoping to get him started talking. For he was well-known for his anecdotes, story-telling and drolleries as well as bootlegging.

"I ketched one that bent the scales at twenty-two pounds once—right over there on the old Barclay place, I did," he said.

"That weren't a 'possum—that was a calf," the miller scoffed. "You should a-sold it for veal."

Little Purefoy snickered, spat through his teeth and whirled over on the ground.

Lawton went on, ignoring the miller. "Yes, we ketched him—at least me and my daddy did. But that's one 'possum nobody et. Maybe the thing's children are still loose in these woods somewhere to this day—or maybe he is hisself, for they do say a 'possum lives all-fired long, like a' elevent or tairpin."

"That's news to me," said the miller.

"I'm wet as a drowned rat," I said.

We scratched up some piles of straw and sat down in a semi-circle like Indians around the fire, our feet stretched out to the drying warmth.

"Yeh—I was a shirt-tail boy then," Lawton continued slowly and musingly, looking up through the leafless twiggy trees, as if the image of his past remembrance were mirrored somehow there in the cold clear moonlit sky.

"Listen at 'em, listen at 'em!" Purefoy called as he crawled up on his knees. Far away the dogs could be heard barking now as if on a hot trail.

"And it's all for nothing," I said, "let 'em bark. We're mighty well set up here."

"Dogs never bark for nothing," the morose Lawton said.

"In that way they've got more sense than human beings," the miller said.

"You're dad-dag right," Lawton affirmed heartily. He lifted his shaggy head to send forth his hallooing call of "Go on, Man!" then stopped and sat listening with his mouth open. Presently he lowered his head, staring at the ground.

"Guess you're right. Don't 'spect there's much to that," he mumbled. Then he lifted his face and looked around at us. "And I tell you, I don't care what kind of 'possum it might be, if they tree him out there around the old Barclay place he can stay there till Gab'el toots his horn."

"What old Barclay place?" I asked. I sensed a story coming.

"Over there," he replied, with a backward jerk of his head. "'Bout a hundred yards from here you come to the edge of what was once a big field, and off in that old field you can see a tangle of cedars and honeysuckles and scrubs, and one big 'simmon tree rising high above it. That's where the old Barclay place used to stand. But it don't stand there no more. You've hearn of old Squair Barclay, Mr. Mac?"

"I have that," said the miller. "And 'twas said as a boy he served wine to LaFayette the time he passed down the valley in twenty-four. And old Peg-leg Santa Anna, the Mexican, was fed at his father's house that time they were taking him to Washington a prisoner."

"Yeh, that's him, no doubt," Lawton nodded, "though he died long before my time." And leaning out on his elbow he began digging in the ground with a stick. Presently he went on—"Well, some folks believe in ghosts and some don't, but the night me and my daddy ketched that twenty-two pound 'possum, I seen a ghost, and he was setting in a tree, and there ain't no denying it for a fact. If you want me to I'll tell you about it."

"There may be ghosts and there may not be," the old miller declared, "but if you say you saw one, then I'm ready to believe it, Lawton."

"Daggone it!" Lawton snorted, "them durn dogs is barking at the edge of that same field right now."

"Maybe that's the same 'possum," said Purefoy in a quiet voice.

"Or the same ghost," Lawton replied, and he turned and widened his eyes at the little colored boy who shook his head, shivered a bit and slid over closer to the fire.

"Anyway, they used to tell how it all got started, and after my experience out there one night it's the truth for me," Lawton declared. "And if you want to hear it, I'll tell it whilst we set here and get dried out, though I reckon everybody already knows the facts of the tale before I open my mouth."

We protested vehemently that we didn't. So he began.

"Well, you might know that a long time ago when the Yankees was fighting with us Southern folks, 'twas said old hell-fire Sherman and his soldiers marched through this Scotch country burning and destroying and seeking who-all they could layway and devour. Whe'r they did or not I dunno, but anyhow I'll tell you the tale and the facts of it as 'twas told to me—and then heel behind it with what happened to me and my daddy. Well, them soldiers come acrosst the Cape Fear River down the country there at Averysboro. You've seen that old stage road too, ain't you, Mr. Mac—that used to run from the mountains to the sea?"

"Yes, I made a sort of map of the old King's High Road once and the canals round and about," the miller said.

"Yes sir, and it was that same road that they come along. And after they'd got over the river they fou't a battle down there. And you can see the grave-yard where some of them that was killed—Yankees and Southern boys—lie buried to this day. I knowed a fellow once plowed up a skull in the field there with a bullet in it. He wore that bullet on a string around his neck to keep off the toothache—for years he done it till his teeth slam rotted out. Well, while these soldiers marched along they went all around into the highways and by-ways searching up provisions and vittles. It was Christmas time when they come up the road to Squair Barclay's grove—into that field out there. It was a lot bigger field in them days, and right where we're setting by this fire, with the hump of the furrow you can feel under these leaves, was rolling cotton land. And a power of slaves worked in it.

"Yes sir, the Squair was a big man and had a great big house in that grove and a winding drive running up to it as well as a winding staircase inside. My daddy said he'd seen the staircase when he was a boy. Made of mahogany wood it was and plumb purty. Well, the soldiers was 'specting a lot of good things out'n that mansion. Yes sir, they was gonna eat and sleep at the Squair's place. And finally old Squair come out and bowed stiff and with a shine in his eye says how sorry he was, gentlemen, we haven't got no room for you a-tall. They argued back and forth and maybe they was impressed by the old gentleman's manners. The story has come down how polite and genteel but bull-headed he was. Anyway, they say the officer man and his soldiers ended up by asking if they could petch their tents in the grove. Go right ahead, he said, and do that. Of course I reckon they would have done it nohow, 'cause I've heard tell and everybody knows soldiers is a rough bunch of folks. But manners is manners, though in these days they ain't as much of 'em as they onct was, God knows.

"Now the Squair and his wife had a little boy, and he was much took with them soldiers and all the clanking swords, the rifles and the bayonets, and the goings on down in the grove. So when there weren't nobody looking he slipped out'n the house and went down there and kept brushing about and spying at everything and asking questions and telling 'em about what old Sandy Claus was gonna bring him that night. The Squair sent one of the slave women out to get him, and he hollered and bellered when she took him in the house. When supper time come the Squair treated all the soldiers mighty fine. He had his niggers bring out the beef and ham, and there was plenty of good wine and cider there to give the soldiers some of it. It has been handed on down, as I said, what a big liver and spread-feaster old Squair Barclay was. They said once he had such a big corn-shucking that he killed seven solid beef and a hundred and ten chickens. That was the night old Lem Hockaday gorged hisself and dropped dead in the frozen road on the way home. Well, that was the kind of feed the old Squair pulled off for them soldiers out in the grove."

"I've heard tell," the miller spoke up, as he took out his tin box of sweet flagroot and bit off a chew, "that when Sherman's bummers come through Little Bethel most of the people were about to starve to death." The old man sometimes was cantankerous and zealous in his historical accuracy.

"Course I don't know all the facts the way you do," Lawton answered somewhat sourly. "You don't want to hear this old story nohow," he suddenly broke off.

"Listen to them 'ere dogs, will you!" said Purefoy, who had been sitting on his haunches with his head cocked sideways.

"Hu-m-uh," Lawton mused. "Danged if they don't sound ezzactly like that night long time ago."

"Come on, what happened that night—let's hear the story," I said.

"Yes," said Mr. Mac, as he munched his sweet flag. "And come to think of it, Lawton, it must have been after the Yankees' visit that the people starved."

"Well, as I was saying," Lawton continued presently, "before King Solomon spoke and heshed me with his wisdom—them soldiers et and drunk and felt mighty fine, and they set around the camp fire in the grove all that night, whooping and singing and all-happy, the whole slew of them. I used to know some of the words of that song they said they sung. Yeah—

*There's grapeshot and musket and the cannon's rumble loud,*
*There's many a mangled body, a blanket for their shroud,*
*There's many a mangled body left on the field alone,*
*And I'm a poor soldier far from my home!"*

"Can't you sing it all?" I urged.

"No, not without my guitar. But it's mournful-like, all right, and every verse ends with being a soldier far from his home. I learnt it from old Mis' Dela Norton. So they sung and hollered and finally one of the soldiers poking about into the cellar got a whole barrel of wine out and they all drunk some more. Purty soon they were feeling real good except a few of them maybe with weak stomachs.

"Now the Squair and his wife had done gone to bed up in the big room. Maybe they were asleep, I dunno. Maybe they were waiting for the little boy to go to sleep so they could put some Sandy Claus in his stocking, I dunno. Now the big Captain of the soldiers had done told the Squair he would see nothing was disturbed and they would take care of everything. I reckon after all the Yankees weren't so bad, though I've hearn my old man say hisself that some of 'em had horns and hoofs and a tail like the devil. Miss Betsy Gillis said she saw one with his shoes off onct and his feets were plumb forked and crotched like a hazel stick. And old Caroline McDiarmid, it was told, said she seen one with his breeches down back of her barn onct and he had a plumb sure enough tail like the devil hisself and swung it about brushing away the flies. That's what she got for her peeping."

The old miller let out a snort, gazing at the fire with half-closed eyes, his lips parted in a little teasing smile.

"Hah, hah, that's what they said. Well, that little boy he couldn't sleep for thinking about Sandy Claus and them soldiers in their blue coats and their swords and everything. And maybe the racket too sort of kept him awake. So he laid in his little bed listening to the happenings down in the grove. Finally when everybody else in the house was quiet he got up and crope out and went down there again. And there sot the soldiers all full of liquor and a-jawing with one another. — Quit listening to them dogs, Puref'y! They ain't going to tree nothing."

"Yessuh," said Purefoy humbly.

"In a minute or two it gets to the real sad part. And you can't help listening when a tale is sad — hard-hearted as ever any soul can be. Ain't it so, Mr. Mac?"

"It's so," Mr. Mac agreed gravely.

"Well, this 'ere little boy croped down there where the soldiers were. And by this time they were all drunk and some of 'em was cussing now and about to fight. When the boy come up to 'em they all stopped and looked at him, and one of 'em said, What the hell you doing out here this time of night? Maybe he's a Rebel spy, another'n spoke up. Pshaw, he ain't nothing but a little boy! another said. Yeah, but you can't tell about 'em, the talk went on. They say these Rebels starts mighty young and they suck pizen in with their mammy's milk. Like as not he'd cut your throat with a razor he's got in that nightgown. And another'n said, Sonny you'd better be in bed. Let him set up, 'twon't hurt him, one the t'others said.

"Then they all got to asking questions and bragging on him and said, Your father's a big rich man, ain't he? He must have horses hid in the swamp, and plenty of silver and things buried deep in the ground. Favver might could have some horses and silver and all hid away — I wouldn't tell, the boy said. What's that, said the big Captain of a soldier who by this time was sizzling drunk with the rest of them. I wouldn't tell you, said the boy. Well, maybe he has, said the Captain, and was lying when he told us everything had been sent to the army — all the horses and money and everything. I ain't going to tell you, said the boy, and you better quit calling my favver a liar.

"Then they got to fooling with the boy, half-joking and half-serious like. You know how it is, sometimes big boys'll pick at little boys or grown men'll bother little helpless things, especially when they're sad and maybe long ways from home and sick at their heart like them soldiers maybe was and them drunk to boot. If you don't tell us we might hang you up, said one of the soldiers. We hung a old man down the road yestiddy to make him tell. His neck stretched out long as a gander's. Another minute and he'd been flapping his wings at the pearly gates. But he give in just in time. It was the big Captain talking like that now and he looked mighty mean. Yes sir, we might hang you up high as Haman, he said.

"Of course they didn't mean all that — they was just joking and picking at him. But he begun to cry, and you know how it is sometimes when anybody cries. It's liable to make you meaner than you was, if you're set on pestering of 'em. And that's the way it was with them, they didn't give way to feeling sorry for him. Shut up, they said. And then they begun to give him some Minie balls and one of 'em give him a piece of new money with a picture on it, and he hushed his crying. Then they begun to come at him again in real dead earnest, asking him about all them horses and where that silver and money was buried, 'cause they had already got the idea from the way he was acting that that little boy knowed something. And he mought for all I know.

"Course they didn't mean no harm maybe, as I said, but they were getting drunk, good drunk by this time. And you know how it is when folks get drunk and a long ways from home — from their women folks at home — they are just as like as not to get powerful mean the way I said. And so they stood around him in a ring and kept sort of projecking at him and some of 'em now and then would h'ist up his little nightgown and laugh and try to pinch his little organ. And one or two of 'em begun to stick twigs and sticks at him. And there they was all around him, the way the wise men maybe ringed in the little Jesus child back in them olden days — where was it, Mr. Mac — Palusteen?"

"In Jerusalem, the Bible says. But maybe it was Palusteen," said the old miller.

"Jerusalem then, though it don't make no difference where. Finally the big Captain soldier said, By God, we'll hang the little rascal on that limb if he don't tell us the good news. And another said, By God, we will. But you know, that little fellow wouldn't tell 'em a word, nary 'un. He just stood there, the plumb tears pouring out'n his eyes and his little lips trembling. And one of the drunkest of the soldiers all of a sudden tied a hankcher around his little mouth so he couldn't squeal much. Lord I wish I had been off in the barn somewhere with a long deer rifle or up on a rooftop with it.

"There was that big 'simmon tree there in the grove with the limbs spread out and a little swing on it where that boy used to swing. Go there to the edge of the woods and you'll see it in the moonlight — the tree I mean — standing there right this minute, 'cepting of course it's much bigger now than it was in them days. And one of them soldiers took his sword and cut the rope in two. Then they tied the ends around the little boy under his armpits and hung him up. Now, they said, you gonna tell us about them horses and where the money's hid? And the little boy kept shaking his head. Golly, that little young'un was a stout Trojas man all right.

"Then they started swinging him back and forth, 'way here and 'way there, then higher and higher, till finally his head would almost touch the limbs of the red oaks beyond. And he couldn't make nary a sound 'cause they had his mouth covered up with that there hankcher and his hands tied. When he would swing by him, the big soldier would say, you gonna tell? and the little boy would shake his head, twisting about and the scalding tears gushing from his eyes. Then it was the big soldier got bull-mad and he shouted out so loud that he roused the Squair up in his great bed where he slept. The Squair must have missed the little boy at once, for they could hear him roaring in the house, and then a light sprung up through the window. You gonna tell me? I ask you for the last time! said the big soldier. And the little boy shook his head. And then as he swung back toward him that there soldier flew all to pieces in his mind, pulled out his swo'd and run it through the little boy's stomach and killed him — unh!"

For a moment Lawton was silent. Then he looked over at the miller. "What you think ought to be done with a man would kill a little boy like that?"

"I don't know," the miller answered, staring off into the night.

"He ought to be set in one of them 'ere electric chairs up at Raleigh where they kill the niggers — that's what — and cooked till he's done."

Little Purefoy turned suddenly over in the straw and put his face on his arm. He made such a violent and abrupt movement that I noticed him. I put my hand comfortingly on his foot, as much as to say not to be frightened, for it was only a story after all. During the rest of the tale he lay still and made no sound.

"Well," Lawton went on, "the Squair and his wife had come out on the porch 'cause they had heard the shout. And they went rushing down toward the soldiers, the two of 'em in their white nightgowns, throwing up their hands and squealing and squalling. And when they seen the little boy hanging there by the firelight, his head bent over like Jesus on the cross and the blood drip-dropping from him to the ground, they both went hog-wild and run at the soldiers clawing and scratching like cats. And what you reckon happened? Nothing 'cepting the soldiers killed both of 'em. And the big soldier stood there drunk, swinging the little boy easy with one hand, all the time swinging him back and forth like a breeze moving the swing, and looking on at the massacre. And when the old Squair kicked his last kick and lay still like a hog dead in the slaughtering pen, the big soldier give the little boy's body such a swish that it flew high up and lodged in the fork of that 'simmon tree, rope and all.

"Then when they'd done so much damage, 'cause they were all so drunk, — killed the boy, the Squair and his wife, they set fire to the big house. And the niggers run out of their cabins into the fields, hollering and wailing while the house burned down. And the soldiers shot some of the niggers just to see 'em fall. They even shot two girls that had run and hid under the corncrib, leaving 'em lying under there like dead rats, same as the way the Scotch Whigs and Tories used to do each other in this valley, so 'tis said. Then they packed up their stuff, saddled their horses and got away from there, dragfooted and quiet. And they nevermore didn't come back.

"Now ain't that a pitiful tale?" Lawton gulped when he had ended, and in his embarrassment he laid his forefinger alongside his nose and blew a fierce discharge toward the fire. His eyes were bright with the tears of his own emotion. We nodded agreement.

"Well, a day or so later they buried the dead folks there in the family graveyard, boy and all. And such a crowd! I've heard tell, I've heard tell!

"And as time passed the brambles and trees growed up over the graves and nobody went there no more. So that's how it was. Time and time later the white folks finally cleaned up that grove and they made a field of it. But they didn't touch that 'simmon tree, where the little boy had been murdered. No sir. And I don't blame 'em.

"Well, I don't hear them dogs no more. Maybe we'd better be moseying on." And he pushed a chunk toward the fire with his heel as if about to rise.

"But what about the ghost?" I asked.

"And the 'possum big as a calf?" the miller queried.

"I was coming to that," said Lawton, "though I thought as how maybe you'd forgot about it." And he grinned.

"Well, one night when I was about yearling size I went with my ol' man out coon hunting over on the hill there. And we had four dogs named Rang, Gouge, Spot and Bo-peep, — them two running out there tonight is named after some of 'em. And they were the best coon dogs that ever there was. Just as Spot and Bo-peep is about the best 'possum dogs there is — though as you might say, we ain't had no proof of it tonight. We hadn't been out hunting more'n a few minutes when we up and caught that big 'possum I told you about, and we weren't hunting for 'possums either. It's like I've heard Mr. Mac say over at the mill — sometimes when you will you don't and when you won't you will. So we put the 'possum in the sack and went on after coons.

"In an hour or so we struck a hot track and the dogs run up and down the swamp, yow-yow-yow, as hard as life would do. Then out on the hills and back again they'd come. It kept up for a long time. There was something quare about it, 'cause a coon don't usually run like that. He sticks straight in the swamp and just runs the fire out'n whatever chases him. Then they struck a trail out of the swamp again—yow-yow-yow, up the hill, across the field toward where the old Barclay house had been. And all of a sudden the racket stopped. What do you reckon's happened now? I said. The old man said they must have ketched him. Then he said no, they couldn't a-ketched him, for a coon would go up a tree, and the dogs couldn't clamb the tree to get at him, so if we'd wait they'd speak again. And he hollered to 'em, You, Man, go on! But they didn't. For whilst we stood in the edge of the fields a-talking it over, here come the dogs creeping back and saying never a sound. And they got right clost up to us and whined and whimpered. That ain't no coon, said the old man. What is it? I said. It ain't no coon, he said.

"Now it's known that a hog may run for his life, but a dog runs for his cha-reckter. And our dogs had plenty of that. They was well trained, and when the old man spoke they knowed what to do. Everybody did, when he spoke. Get on there, Rang. Get on, Gouge, you Spot and you Bo-peep. And grabbing up a brush to frail 'em, he set 'em off again—yow-yow-yow. They run the trail on across the old field and toward where the old house had been and where that 'simmon tree stood up plain in the moonlight. Purty soon here they come back lickety-lick, lickety-lick, and croped up around the old man and me and hugged close to our legs, whimpering and a-whining again. It ain't no coon, bless God, I know it now, the old man says. What is it? I says. You know what it is? he says. And I say I don't. And he says, It's a ha'nt—if what I heard is so—but I ain't never seen a ha'nt in my life, and maybe tonight's a good time to see one, he said. Of course he was half-joking-like for he didn't believe all the scary things he'd heard about the old Barclay place, and I didn't neither, little as I was. But I've believed 'em ever since.

"Now the old man he was scared of nothing dead or alive. Oh yes, he was mean, and I got scars under my britches to this day to prove it. So he says, We're going to see. Here, Rang, here Bo-peep! And we started out 'crost the fields. But you know them dogs wouldn't run nary another step. They come slipping behind, and every once in a while they'd let out a pitiful wheeah-wheeah fuss. The old man beat 'em with a stick, but they wouldn't budge a hair from behind us. Purty soon we come up to that old 'simmon tree, and there in the moonlight you could see something a-setting in the fork of it. Great God, something bigger'n a 'possum was a-setting in it. Bigger'n that big 'possum we already had in our sack he was.

"Well when we got clost to that tree the old man set the sack down. And he kept looking at whatever it was. There weren't no bears in that country then, not even no wolves, and I begun to feel funny. Come on, said the old man, and he went on up with me behind him, and Rang and Gouge and Spot and Bo-peep all in a row behind me—and everybody still as the inside of a coffin in a grave.

"Well, we come a little closer, and there, bless my Lord and wonder-working God, in that 'simmon tree shining in the moonlight was a little curly-headed boy."

"Naw, naw," the miller murmured, staring at him.

"Cross my heart to heaven, it was! There in the moonlight was a little boy with his yellow curls all hanging down and his little face pitiful and pale as death, like flour on it. And it was the Squair's little boy. And every now and then he'd reach out his little hand and pull off a ripe 'simmon, eating it, and the dark seeds kept falling to the ground like great drops of blood, one after the other falling down.

"I stood there froze in my tracks, but the old man sure had a craw full of grit and he said he was going to clamb that 'simmon tree and get that little Barclay boy, and if he was flesh and blood he'd take him home and raise him. I begged him not to try it 'cause I'd heard tales about Plat-Eye, and old Jack Muh Lan-tern and the Iron-faced Man, and how they'd put a spell on you from which you'd never wake. But he shinned on up that 'simmon tree and got right close to where that boy was sitting. And then the little fellow run out along the limb to the clean tip of it and hung there by one claw hand like a 'possum. And the old man shook the limb so hard that the little fellow fell off tumbling down to the ground.

"But he hit the dirt running, and away he went as hard as his little legs would carry him toward the graveyard back of where the old house had been. We could see him clear as day as he run, and all of a suddent he went out of sight into a hole in one of them graves. But the dogs didn't go after him, no sir. They whined and whimpered and stuck close to me. And when the old man come down out of the tree he was white as a sheet and shaking like a frosted fern plant. What's the matter, I said. Come on, he said, let's fan it. And both of us and the dogs lit a rag getting away from there. Yessir, it was legs take body away, and stay gone. And we forgot all about that 'possum in the sack. I reckon he gnawed his way out and high-tailed it like us. And later when we had hit the old stage road out there and easier going, the old man said that little boy had breathed his breath in his face and it was icy cold and stunk with the purges of death.

"And other people got so that they seen him in that 'simmon tree too, and finally nobody would go around that place at all. The brier bushes growed up about the tree and over the graveyard again, and the whole place was full of sassafras scrubs. And you can go out there now and look at it — a plumb forest of pines, sweet gums and dogwoods. And there'll never more be a plow stuck in it till the Judgment Day."

For a moment we were all silent, then Lawton rose, stretched himself and yawned. "And the dogs have quit running," he said. "Maybe they've seen that ha'nt and have gone hell-bent for home. We got to go too. Come on, Puref'y," he called, "and quit that whimpering." Little Purefoy jumped up, his shoulders shaking. He had been crying, and he kept his face turned from us ashamed.

Later when we had left Lawton and Purefoy at the bootlegger's shack and were driving home, the miller said, "Lawton never had a chance to weigh that 'possum, now did he? How could he know it weighed twenty-two pounds?"

"That's right," I said.

"I told you he was an outdacious liar. Still, it was a good story.

"And poor little Purefoy — it really frightened him."

"I doubt he was crying over the story," said the miller. "It was the talk about the electric chair done it. Remember how the boy turnt over and laid his face in the straw at the mention of it, and said never another word?"

"Yes."

"Poor fellow. He's got no home of his own. Lawton lets him sleep in the old tumbledown barn on a bed of shucks. He works and gets his board and keep and maybe a quarter now and then when his master feels in the humor to give him one."

By this time we had reached Mr. Mac's milldam, the moon had gone down, and the nebulous light of the stars illuminated the night with a vague and misty radiance. A shine was on the pond, and the shingled mossy millhouse roof glistened as if with a dewy hoarfrost. For a moment the old miller stood in front of his door looking up at the sky, his grizzled weatherbeaten face touched with a gentle melancholy.

"We older folks don't know the hearts of young people much," he murmured as if to himself. "You remember Metzanteen Watson, the Negro tenant farmer that killed his landlord? — Course you been gone from this neighborhood so long."

"Yes, I remember him."

"He was electrocuted in Raleigh last Friday."

"I know. I wrote the governor pleading for him."

"I did too, but it done no good. Well, Purefoy wasn't crying about the ghost of that little boy. No. He was crying about that electrocution. Metzanteen was his father."

"Oh," I said.

"And it's all too bad," said the miller. "Well, good night."

As I rode on back to the University I kept thinking—not of the ghost of that little boy in the tree nor of homeless Purefoy back there, but of another little boy with whom I had once climbed trees on my father's farm, played fox and the goose and studied the stars at night even—a boy with a joyous whistle in the fields at dawn and with his wide-breaking laugh in the furrow at evening time, Metzanteen Watson—and all ever before evil was.

And I looked up through the windshield at the vast night sky ahead, with its gossamer scarf of the milky way flung across it. And it was the same as always from everlasting to everlasting, graceful, careless and serene as when he and I had looked at it together and wondered.

# Fine Wagon

1.

The great forest rang as if with the clamor of iron bells from the belfries of the trees. Standing on the bank of the deep inky creek, Bobo strained with all his might at his fishing pole. Down in the depths somewhere a catfish big as a hog was hung on his hook and gradually pulling him in. Lower and lower bent the pole and inch by inch his bare feet slid in the slick mud. He felt himself jerked headlong toward the sickish black water, when there came a voice calling and a sudden soft breath blowing in his ear. Whiff! And the great forest wheeled and turned over, rushed toward him, by him. The bells were silent, and in the flash of an eye the stream was gone and so were the fishing pole and the fish.

"Wake up, sonny, wake up — it's already day." And he felt a gentle hand diddling with his shoulder. — Who — what? — Mammy. But he must sleep, sleep a little more. And that fish — that great big fish!

"Wake up, Sonny, your pa's done fed the mules."

He grunted and squirmed about under the quilts and then sat up. Rubbing his scrawny dark fists in his eyes, he blinked at the little brown woman who stood by the bed holding a wiggling lamp in her hand.

"Please, Mammy — please'm," he said. And then his eyelids drooped shut, he gaped and sank back slowly on the bed. Sweet sleepiness engulfed him instantly. Once more the edge of the great shadowy forest came moving toward him with its cool delicious shade, and once more he heard the lofty booming of the bells.

"Huh, so after all your proud bragging you done forgot you's going with your pappy?" the voice said.

He heard the words afar off. They meant nothing to him, they were empty sounds. But only for a moment. For then remembrance flooded into his mind and he sat quickly up. Today was the day and he was about to forget it. A sharp little rush of joy tickled somewhere in his chest behind his breastbone. He hopped out of bed as if a red fire coal had been dropped inside his drawers. Cramming his shirttail down in his trousers, he followed his mother into the kitchen. He hesitated before the basin of waiting chilly water, and then roaching up his shoulders, he soused his face down in his dipping cupped hands.

"Whee—oo-oo," he chattered. Already Mammy was at the stove taking the sweet fried fat back out of the pan. And now heavy brogan shoes came clomp-clomping along the porch, and Pappy entered—a tall grave black man.

"Morning, Bobo."

"Morning, Pappy," he answered, his scrubbed face coming out of the ragged bundle of towel.

"You done got that sleepy out'n them eyes—unh?"

"Yessuh, I'se all loud awake."

"That's a boy."

"When's we going, Pappy?"

"Mmn—now not too big a swivet. We got to swallow a bite of grub fust." And Pappy sat down to the table with his hat on, as he did when he had a pushing job ahead. Mammy hurried the cornbread from the stove and put it in front of him.

"Come on, Bobo," she said, but Bobo had already dived under her arm and onto his bench. She stood still at the end of the table with the dishcloth in her hand ready to get the coffee pot while Pappy bent his head over. "Make us thankful for what we're 'bout to receive," he mumbled, "and bless us all for time to come."

"Amen," Bobo whispered fervently.

Nobody in the world could cook like Mammy. How good that fat back tasted, and the molasses and the bread! And then—what's that? He couldn't believe his eyes, as she came and set a cup of steaming coffee by his plate.

"Seeing how cold it is and you going off to work same like a man," she said.

His eyes were brimming with thanks as he poured his saucer full of the dark stuff—dark as the water in that creek where the big fish stayed. Then he blew on it with a great oof the way Pappy did to cool it.

"Warm you up inside?" his father asked.

"It do that," he answered gulping it down with the noise of a small horse drinking water.

He gobbled his bread and meat, trying to keep up with Pappy, and in a few minutes breakfast was over. Mammy took Pappy's extra old coat from the wall and brought it to him.

"It'll be mighty cold riding out on that wagon, son," she said as she slipped it on him.

"Come on," said Pappy, and they hurried out of the house toward the barn. There in the gray morning light their fine wagon stood with its long tongue hanging out. It wasn't new like a white folks' wagon, but it was mighty nice just the same. He and Pappy had worked on it hard the day before, spiking up the loose spokes and driving wedges under the tires to tighten them for the heavy loads they'd have to haul. And with the new pine board seat laid across the body it stood waiting to ride.

Pappy had bought the wagon on a credit at a sale a few days before for eight dollars. It would come in handy hauling stuff for the professors up in town, and in a week or two they would make enough to pay for it. After that they'd keep on hauling. Pappy had needed a wagon. When he came home a few weeks before bringing old blind Mary to match with the other mule Suke, he had set his mind on something to hitch both of them to. He had traded a dog and gun and two or three dollars for old Mary, and it'd take a lot of hauling to get the money together to pay for the wagon. But shucks, Pappy was stepping on in the world, he was smart. Didn't Mammy say so yesterday at supper — that there weren't nobody smart like him. And she had kissed Pappy, feeling fine about how things were going.

Last night Pappy had said, "Honey, I got me a job right off the bat. 'Fessor up there in town met me on the street today and said he had some wood to haul down where he's gonna build his chillun's swimming pool and could I haul it. 'Could I do it?' I says, 'Can't nobody do it better. I got me a fine wagon and a first-class team.' That's the way it goes in this world. You get ready for the job and the job gets ready for you. I says, 'I got a boy Bobo growing like a weed, and all muscling up. Me and him both'll be back heah, suh, tomorrow.'"

These things ran through Bobo's mind as he padded along toward the barn trying to keep up with his father's long stride.

"Yessuh, put me at a stick of wood and I'll tote my end," he said out loud.

"Huh what's that?" Pappy asked, looking down at him but never slackening his pace.

"I mean — mean I'se gonna sho' work hard."

And Pappy looked out toward the glad morning star, laughed a great laugh and patted him on the shoulder.

"How much that man gonna pay me, Pappy?" he inquired as they slid open the stable door.

"I bet a whole ten cents, that's what you'd better charge him."

Ten cents! And there'd be other ten centses — nearly every day there would, for they would be so good at hauling that all the 'fessors would be asking them to do jobs. Ten cents a day! His little skinny hand slid down into his pocket as if he already expected to find a piece of hard round money there. And once more, as had happened several times during the last day and night, the bright picture of a new fishing hook and line gleamed for an instant in his mind. But he was cunning, he'd not mention that yet. But he knew where they could be got though. Up there in town in the hardware store—all with red corks and plenty of good lead sinkers.

"You try your stuff at bridling Suke," Pappy said, "this here new mule is kinder—er—mulish."

And pridefully Bobo opened the door and went in with the bridle in his hand. Old Suke stood with her head down as if expecting him, and slick as that old Syrian peddler he put the bridle on her and led her from the stall. Then the business of harnessing and getting the bellyband and the hamestring tight. It didn't matter if Pappy did come around and retie the hamestring when he'd just managed to pull it together, for the hames were fitting snug in the collar and Pappy said that was doing fine as a fiddle.

"Them's stout hamestrings too," said Pappy, "Joe Ed let me cut 'em from that bull hide of hisn."

"I bet they'll hold—hold near'bout a lion," Bobo spoke up.

"Or a' elevint," said Pappy.

"Or a steam engine," Bobo chuckled.

"Yeh, they'll hold—hold till the cows come home. And that britchin', that's a real piece of scrimptious handiwork." And Pappy surveyed the old ragged strips of bed ticking he had sewed together to help finish off the harness.

By this time the light of dawn had spread upward from the east across the sky, wide and spangled like a great peacock's tail, and Bobo wasn't afraid at all as he went into the loft and threw down two bundles of fodder for the mules' dinner. And now Mammy came out of the house bringing lunch wrapped up in a paper for her two menfolks. So everything was ready at last and not a bit too soon, for the smiling face of the sun was already peeping up over the edge of the world.

"You all be smart." Mammy called out as they climbed up into the wagon and sat down on the plank seat side by side. Pappy thudded his rope whip through the air with a great flourish, and off they went.

"We'll be home right around sundown!" he shouted back, "and me'n Bobo wants us a real bait of that fat side meat all fried and ready!"

"We'll be home at sundown!" Bobo repeated loudly, sticking his hand up out of his father's old coat sleeve in a little crooked gesture, half a wave and half a salute. He had seen the white boys stick their hands up like that at the college campus. And Mammy waved back at him, standing there by the gate with the new sun shining in her face.

2.

They drove on down the dead-weeded lane and soon came into the high road. To the right and to the left stretched the sparkly frosty fields, and yonder in the distance the sun-fired church spires of the white man's town stuck up above the wooded hill. The steel wagon tires made little harsh gritty sounds as they drove along.

"Don't this wagon run good, Bobo?"

"It sho' do, Pappy."

"It orter—I was up and give it a good greasing whilst you was snoozing."

"You'da woke me up I'da been there and holp you."

"Them tiahs cries a little, but they's tight as a drum, ain't they?"

"Tight as Dick's hatband. We sho' put the fixing on 'em, Pappy."

"Yeh, didn't we?"

"Git up there, Suke—you, Mary," Bobo chirped in his manful way. They were now mounting the hill, the air was sharp and biting, and Bobo had to clamp his jaws tight, his teeth were chattering so. But he'd never let Pappy know. They rode on in silence awhile. Bobo could see from Pappy's thoughtful face he was thinking of something. Maybe planning out the big work ahead and he didn't want to talk. A gang of robins flew across over his head going north. He watched them till they were little jumping eye specks low in the sky. It would turn warm soon—today, tomorrow. It always turned warm after a heavy frost like this one. The robins knew—they were smart like people. And they were going north.

Soon they were rolling along the asphalt streets of the town, and for the moment Bobo feared the wagon wheels made too loud a sound. Every shop was closed, every place deserted. It was too early for the white folks to be up. They were different from colored folks who had to be out to get a soon start. Already some of the women cooks were on their way to work—their arms in front of them, their elbows gripped in the palm of each enclosing hand. It was cold and they walked in a hurry. Their shoes made a clock-clock on the hard sidewalks.

"Ain't everything quiet—like somebody asleep?" Bobo half whispered.

"Yeh," Pappy replied, "sleep. That's what's the matter with people, Bobo. They all sleep too much. Now look at you and me—we's up and doing."

"That's right," Bobo agreed soberly. And Pappy continued with feeling in his voice—"By the time other folks start to work we done done half a day. That's what gets a man ahead. He that rises 'fore the sun is the man what gets the most work done."

And now they were passing by the big gray granite building that was the great bank where the white men went in and out during the day, hauling in their money and putting it away. Bushels and bushels of yellow dollars and white dollars and bales of greenbacks they kept stored away there. That was where all the money came from to buy the things that people needed. That's where the money would come from to pay him and Pappy for their hauling. And to the left there was the hardware store where they kept all kinds of blades, and knives and hooks—fishhooks. Well, when spring came again—

Next, down there by the drugstore, was the blue and white sign of the telegraph office shut up and waiting. In a few hours it would be open, and folks would go in there and write things on a slip of paper, and a man would tap on a little handle, and them taps would be words that went out along wires and 'way to New York and maybe across the world through a pipe under the sea. Lord, Lord, weren't people smart!—Smart. But he was smart too, today he was.

Bobo had always been frightened by the big buildings and goings on when he'd come up town to buy five cents worth of snuff or ten cents worth of fat back for Mammy and Pappy. But this morning he looked at the houses and stores with bolder eyes. He felt more at home among them today. He was a workingman now, and nobody ever bothered a workingman—not even big boys that liked to pick on you and throw your cap up and lodge it in a tree. He had something to do now, work for the white folks, and that made everything right. The white folks wouldn't allow no foolishness with any of their help.

In a few minutes they had gone through the village to the outer edge and came where a little alley turned off from the main street and down a hill into a new development.

"Is we 'bout got there yit, Pappy?"

"Yeh, right down yonder is where 'Fessor lives," and he pulled the heads of the mules into the alley. "He's got a lot of wood cut 'way down below his house there and he wants it hauled up to put in his cellar."

"Looks like a sort of rough place down there," Bobo said, straining his eyes ahead of him.

"Sho', but we's the men to get that wood up and out'n it, ain't we, Bobo?"

"Is that," Bobo spoke up strongly and briskly.

"And he's going to pay us a dollar a cawd to move it. He said he had ten or twelve cawds down there."

"How much is a cawd, Pappy?"

And now they were turning off to the left down a little rock path that skirted around and away from the professor's house. What a house that was, all white and pretty shining there among the bare trees. And how many chimneys did it have, and the windows with green blinds! Bobo almost caught his breath—there on the porch sat a big red bicycle. That must belong to one of the chillun, but he didn't mind how many bicycles the chillun had now 'cause some of these days he would—that too maybe—not a new one—no—no— just an old one.

"Well a cawd of wood is a pile 'bout ten feet long and as high as your head and you get a dollar for moving it," said Pappy. "Yeh, ten or twelve of 'em. I bet we near'bout will move six or eight of the cawds today, and that's six or eight dollars."

"Look out there, Pappy!"

"Sho," his father gravely replied as he pulled on the plow line reins and stopped the mules, for the wagon was going down the hill and almost pushing the collars up over their heads. "I better tighten up them britchin' strops a little bit," he said. Holding to the lines, he climbed down and scotched the wheel with a rock. In a few minutes he had tightened the straps of bed ticking and was ready to go.

"Does you think you mought drive some?"

"Lemme," Bobo answered eagerly.

Handing over the reins, Pappy got behind the wagon and held it back as the mules moved down the hill. What a strong man Pappy was there pulling on the coupling pole like as if it had been the wagon's tail, and the mules had to push a little bit against the collar now that he was holding back so sharp.

## 3.

They finally got safely down to the little wooded hollow where the firewood was piled in great heaps, and they did no damage at all other than tearing off a patch of bark from a sugar-maple tree with the wagon hub. After much backing and sliding the rear end of the wagon around, by pushing and jerking on the coupling pole, they got set near a pile of wood and began to load it. It was a fine mixture of oak and pine cut in the proper lengths for the professor's fireplace, and Bobo liked to work at it, it looked so nice. Already he could feel how it would pop and burn, making a warm blaze to keep the chillun snug at night—there with their studying and their books and playing with their toys. He heaved piece after piece up into the open body trying to match his father. Talk about being smart—huh, with a few days of this stuff he'd put a muscle on his arm like a big mice running under his skin.

"All right," Pappy called, "try the end of that thing." And Bobo took hold of the big black log of solid hickory all ready to show his strength. Then they heard a heavy voice calling down from the house above, and looking up Bobo saw a man wearing some kind of a gown standing by the porch railing with his hair all rumpled.

"Who's that?" Bobo asked, letting go of the log and stopping still as a post.

"S-sh, that's 'Fessor," Pappy said.

"Hey, what you doing down there?" the professor called. And Pappy even as far away as he was pulled off his hat quickly and bowed respectfully.

"Morning, 'Fessor," he answered in a low voice and smiled same as if 'Fessor was right in front of him.

"Morning, suh," Bobo whispered pulling off his hat likewise.

"You make enough racket to wake up the neighborhood," said the figure on the porch.

"Yessuh," Pappy began and then fumbled a bit for his words. "We thought we'd get an early start, suh."

"Well, you have that, it's just seven o'clock."

"Yessuh," and Pappy bowed again.

"Well, go on and be as quiet as possible. Haul the wood around to the cellar door. I'll come out a little later."

"Yessuh," said Pappy again, still holding his hat in his hand.

The figure on the porch looked around at the world, yawned and retired into the house. Pappy and Bobo waited a moment and then went on with their loading but this time slow and careful-like, laying each piece of wood gently in the wagon as if they were packing eggs.

"Why do he do that?" Bobo at last timidly inquired.

"Who you mean do what?" his father asked in a low stern voice.

"The man up there in that big house — 'Fessor."

Something seemed to be bothering Pappy, for he laid down his piece of wood and looked at Bobo. "Why you ask that?"

"He kept looking around at the earf and up at the sky. It ain't going to snow, is it?"

"Oh," said Pappy as if he had been thinking of something else. And then he turned back to loading the wood again, and Bobo turned back also. But they decided to leave the big hickory log until the next load.

"Must be some kinder big man, ain't he," Bobo said presently, "living in that big house with all these woods around?"

"He's a 'fessor — teaches boys and gals. That's what 'fessor means." Pappy was silent a bit and then went on as if to himself, "He a mighty big man, and plenty of things to worry his mind. I heard some folks say he a big man," and now Pappy looked carefully about him.

"Huh?" said Bobo.

"Do what?" and Pappy seized a piece of oak and lifted it aloft.

"Yeh, do what, Pappy?"

"Don't ask so many questions. 'Fessor wants his wood hauled, he going to pay for it and we going to haul it. He a big man, he stand mighty high. I hear 'em say he writes books and play pieces and makes money enough — enough to burn." And surveying the pile of wood on the wagon, he added, "Looks like we 'bout got a load."

"What do he write about, Pappy?"

"Huh?"

"'Fessor. Do he write tales like what Mammy read from a book that time?"

Pappy suddenly snickered and looked around at him in a way he didn't understand. Then he said, "Say he writes books and things about the colored folks."

"Sho'?"

"Sho'."

"And do the colored folks read 'em?"

"Shet your mouth and go 'way," Pappy answered. And snickering again, he went on, "White folks buy 'em and read 'em 'way off yonder. That's how he gets so much money to build his house and this heah swimming pool."

Now Pappy's hand went into his pocket, and Bobo watched it like a hawk. How long had he been waiting for that. This time it was true, he was going to do it. And sure enough Pappy pulled out a twist of homemade tobacco and bit off a big chew. Bobo edged up to him, waiting. For a moment the twist hesitated in Pappy's hand, and then he pinched off a big crumb and handed it to him. Bobo's skinny black paw darted out and seized it quick as a bat catching a bug. He stuck it in his mouth, rolled it around with his tongue and settled it over on one side making his jaw push out.

"Well I spec's we better start up the hill with this," and Pappy gathered up the reins. Suke and Mary who had stood drooping in their tracks suddenly woke as if a swarm of hornets had come up out of the ground at them. At Pappy's first word Suke gave a lunge forward and old blind Mary gave a lunge backward. "Get up there," he said, whopping Mary a blow on the rump with his whip. And now she sprang forward and Suke stood still. "You Suke!" he shouted. And quicker than hailing out of the sky the blows of the whip danced from one mule to the other. With a rattle and groaning of the wheels the heavy load began to move up the stony hill, and Pappy winked at Bobo as much as to say, "Ain't that pulling for you?"

As they swung around into the little road, the rear wheel hooked the sugar maple again. "Whoa," said Pappy, and just in time, for the coupling pole was bent like a sick cow's tail. The mules stopped, slumped down in their tracks and began to gnaw the dead scattering brown oak leaves that hung from a branch above their heads. Suddenly the creaky twanging of a screen door opening sounded across the hollow. Bobo looked out toward the house and saw the professor partly dressed standing on the porch again.

"There he is again, Pappy," he said, clutching his father's arm.

"Whoa," said Pappy softly to the mules.

"Heigh," said the professor, "didn't I tell you to keep quiet down there?"

Pappy's hat was already off in his hands again as he answered gently, "Yes-suh, yessuh, we's just getting started, 'Fessor, and we" — Pappy looked down at Bobo as if asking him what to say.

"Haven't you hung your wheel in that maple tree?" the professor called, and Bobo saw him sliding his suspenders on his shoulders in a quick nervous jerk.

"He's coming down here, Pappy," he whispered.

"No suh," answered Pappy, "we just giving the mules a little breathing space, suh!"

"Well, see that you don't hurt anything." And once more the professor gave that look around him and turned back into the house.

After much prying and straining, they shoved the wheel loose from the tree, but not until another great gleaming gap of bark had been torn off in the process. When they had got the load farther up the hill, they scotched the wheels and went back. Pappy grabbed up a handful of dirt, smeared it over the scars so that no one would notice them, and Bobo ran about picking up the pieces of bark which he hid under the fallen leaves. Then they returned to the wagon and rode out onto the high ground. They drove proudly around back of the house and stopped near the cellar door.

"Look a-there, Pappy," Bobo whispered, horrified, pointing to one of the rear wheels. The wedges had fallen out from under the tire and the old wheel stood all twisted and crank-sided.

"Oh, that wheel'll stand up," said Pappy lightly, eyeing it. "We'll get un-loaded and then take a rock and drive that tire back on." And climbing down, he wrapped the reins tight around a front hub so the mules couldn't get at the spirea bushes. Bobo passed the wood piece by piece to his father who took it in armfuls quietly down into the cellar. By this time the people in the house were astir, and Bobo could see into the kitchen where Miss Sally the cook, wearing some kind of fancy lace thing on her head, was preparing breakfast. The smell of coffee and bacon came out to him and he sniffed the air hungrily like a little dog. And now the professor reappeared, his face clean-shaven and his hair brushed. He came up to the wagon and looked sharply at the load. Bobo tried to keep his mind on his work handing down the wood to his father below, but he could smell the clear pine-winey stuff the professor had used for shaving. It filled the air, getting into his mouth and nostrils so wonderful and strong that he could taste it.

"You'll never move that wood with such a turnout as that," said the profes-sor a little shortly and abruptly. "Look at that wheel!"

"Yessuh," answered Pappy, as he laid his hat on the ground beside him. "We'll fix that up in a minute, suh, the wedge just fell out."

"Yes, I see it did. How are you, son?" His voice was suddenly kind.

"Fine, thanky, suh," Bobo choked, almost speechless at being addressed by the mighty man who lived in such a house and had cooks and bicycles and automobiles and a big furnace thing down there in the cellar that kept the house warm.

"What's your name?" But now Bobo had lost his tongue.

"His name's Roosevelt, suh, but we calls him Bobo," answered Pappy gravely.

"H'm," said the professor softly. "And pile the wood straight back against the coal bin, will you?"

"Yessuh, we's fixing it up fine and dandy."

"And you can turn around down there next to the garage."

"Yessuh."

"What have you got in your mouth, son?" But Bobo could only stare at the professor with wide frightened eyes. "Don't you know chewing tobacco at your age will stunt you and keep you from growing up? Why, you're nothing but a baby." And once more the professor looked inquiringly about the world and up at the sky as he turned to re-enter the house.

4.

At last the load was stored away. And after much knocking and wedging down at the garage, the old wheel was strengthened, and they returned to the woods. But now it seemed the mules had decided not to do any more work that day. They kept twisting and turning about and sticking out their heads trying to get at the dead leaves. And when after a lot of trouble the wagon was finally backed and skewed around to another pile of wood, old Mary suddenly began to kick and lunge in the harness. Pappy seesawed on the reins and spanked her with the whip, and only after she had torn the britching off and burst one of his prized hamestrings did he finally get her quieted. All the while Bobo kept looking up toward the house expecting the professor to come charging out yelling at them. His heart was in his mouth, and he breathed again when at last the britching was mended, the hamestring retied and everything ready for the loading to begin. This time Pappy pitched the wood boldly into the wagon. The white folks were up and having breakfast, and the chatter of children was heard in the house. It didn't make any difference about noise now.

"We better not put such a heavy load on this time, had we, Pappy?"

"No, we ain't going to load up furder'n to the brim," he replied. And when they were ready once more, Pappy mounted briskly to the top of the seat and gave the word for the mules to go. Bobo started following behind, but old Mary acted like Satan was in her. She lunged forward, broke the hamestring again and ran straight out of the harness. And before Pappy could do a thing she had turned herself completely around and stood facing them with her white, sightless eyes as if laughing at them. Pappy suddenly lost his temper, and leaning far over with his rope whip, struck her a knock in the face. She reared up on her hind feet, and giving a great jump, left the harness behind her.

"Look out, look out, Pappy!" Bobo squealed in fright.

Pappy sprang down from the wagon, and with a strong hold upon the reins kept old Mary from getting entirely loose and running away. And now from the porch Bobo heard the dreaded voice again.

"What is the matter down there?"

Bobo didn't dare look up, for he knew the professor was coming down the hill. And in a minute there he stood beside them. Without a word Pappy dropped his whip on the ground and began straightening out the harness, and old Mary started greedily eating the dead leaves again. Suddenly the professor broke into a low laugh, and Bobo shook in his tracks. Somehow that laugh made him feel queer and trembly.

"Why in the name of mercy did you come trying to haul wood with such a mess as this?" the professor said.

"Yessuh, yessuh, but — " Pappy began.

"But nothing," the professor replied irritably and sharply, and he took a step backward and surveyed the wagon and the team. Then his voice was kind again. "Here, son, you hold her head and let's see what we can do." The professor took off his fine coat and undid his white collar and set to work tying up the britching and rehitching the traces on old Mary.

"You sho' knows your stuff 'bout mules, 'Fessor," Pappy broke in presently, standing there pinching a dead twig in pieces between his fingers.

"I was raised on a farm."

"Do tell, suh."

"And I learned not to starve a mule to death and not to try to haul wood with the harness and wagon falling to bits," he added.

Pappy was silent.

Bobo stood looking on, every now and then spitting in noiseless excitement off to one side. He watched the deft movements of the professor as if mesmerized, and his gaze traveled to his father, who stood all shamed and humbled with his hat off. A queer lump rose up from his breast and stuck in his throat, and he swallowed quickly. Then he began sputtering, trying to get back the wad of tobacco that had gone down behind his breastbone. Gritting his teeth, he blinked and shook the tears out of his eyes, making little choking noises in his throat.

"What's the matter with you, son?" queried the professor, staring at him.

"Nothing," he answered quickly.

"You look sick. Have you had any breakfast?"

"Yessuh."

"Yessuh, we both et a big bait of good coffee and side meat 'fore we come off," Pappy said, coming over and timidly offering to help fasten the breast chains.

"You wait, I'll drive for you," said the professor. And clucking kindly to the mules, he jiggled the reins gently. The wagon slowly began to move. The professor walked along as the mules pulled on up the hill, and then blam, that old rear wheel struck a stone hidden by the leaves, and with a moaning groan it collapsed. And now once more the professor gave his queer laugh. He stood a moment looking at the reins in his hand, and then throwing them down took out some money and handed it to Pappy. "Here's a dollar, though you've not earned fifty cents," he said.

"Thanky suh, thanky suh," said Pappy, wiping his hand on his coat and humbly taking the money.

Without a word the professor turned and strode off toward the house. When he had gone a little distance, he turned and called, "Take your bundle of trash and clear out, I'll get somebody else to haul my wood! I'm sorry." With that he was gone.

Bobo stood looking at the ground. He could see the toes of his father's ragged shoes in front of him. Finally the shoes moved, and he heard his father say, "I reckon we just about as well quit and go home, son." And then he heard another voice saying—a woman's voice up on the porch—"What's the matter, Harvey?" and the professor replying, "The same old story, Nan—My God, these everlasting Negroes—poverty—trifling! Come on, let's finish our breakfast." And the door of the great house slammed shut like the jaws of a steel trap.

Pappy slowly began unloading the wood and laying it gently and heavily on the ground. All the while Bobo stood by without moving. His hands and arms hung down by his sides. He made no effort to help Pappy or do anything, but just stood there. "Come on, boy," Pappy said harshly.

## 5.

When they had finished unloading, Pappy tied a limb to the coupling pole under the axle, and the old broken wheel was loaded into the wagon body. Then they climbed up into the wagon. And the mules now, as if glad to be free of work, moved quickly up the hill and back into the main highway. Through the town they rode, the old limb dragging under the wheel-less end of the axle. People looked out from the houses as they passed, and a group of white school children playing tag on the sidewalk stopped and pointed at them. Bobo sat on the seat by Pappy looking straight ahead, and Pappy was looking straight ahead too. When they neared the business section of the village, Pappy turned off and went along a side street. And soon they came to the other edge of the town and descended the hill.

When they rode up near the yard gate, Mammy unbent from her sweeping by the door and stared at them.

"Why you back so early?" she called. "I ain't got a speck of dinner ready. Eyh, and look what's happened to your wagon wheel!"

"Shet your mouth, woman!" Pappy roared.

Jumping down from his seat, Bobo entered the yard.

"We don't want no dinner," he heard his father's rough brutal voice shout behind him.

"What's the matter, son?" Mammy said.

"Nothing, nothing," he gulped. And catching hold of her apron, he began to sob.

"Dry up!" Pappy yelled after him, but Bobo sobbed and sobbed.

"What's happened, son?" Mammy said, smoothing his woolly head with her hand.

"Nothing, nothing," he spluttered.

And then a dreadful thumping and squealing began in the edge of the yard. But Bobo didn't look up. There was no need to. For even with his face buried in his mother's apron and his eyes stuck shut with tears he could see a skinny black man there by the woodpile beating old Mary with an ax helve, and that black man was Pappy—and he was ragged and pitiful and weak.

# III

# On Race and Human Rights

# To Ward Morehouse on *In Abraham's Bosom*

Morehouse (1898–1966), drama critic for the *New York Sun*, was writing a book about American drama and had asked Green if there was anything he particularly remembered about the writing or production of *In Abraham's Bosom*.

[Greenwood Road, Chapel Hill, N.C.]
4 June 1948
Dear Ward Morehouse:

I am very glad to hear that you are writing a book on the American drama. It is bound to be good, and I am looking forward to seeing it.

You ask about an anecdote connected with my play *In Abraham's Bosom*. I remember something connected with the genesis of the play, but perhaps you wouldn't call it an anecdote. Rather it might partake of the nature of what the late philosopher Alfred Whitehead called an event. Anyway there were several people involved in the happening—and I am sure that ever since then it was remembered as an event.[1]

It was many, many years ago. I was a little boy come to the neighboring town of Angier[2] on a bright spring day to get a load of fertilizer for our farm. I wanted to see the train come in. I stood by the little shack of a station waiting along with several others, among them an old Confederate soldier leaning on his walking stick, for the train to put in its appearance. Soon it showed its round black moon of a locomotive end around the bend. It puffed and wheezed along toward us and finally drew in with a rusty squealing of its brakes. It was an old wood-burner, and the climb into town had been tough. The engineer piled out of the cab, greasemarked outside and full of spleen and frustration inside. He began to work on the old locomotive and squirting grease here and there into its aged joints. I looked down the track and spilling out of the Jim Crow car—there were only four in all, a white car,

---

1. Whitehead stressed that an event is a happening that calls to mind past happenings and presages future ones (see Alfred North Whitehead, *Science and the Modern World* [New York: Macmillan, 1925], pp. 106–7).

2. About six miles north of his father's farm.

a Negro car, a freight car and a caboose—spilling out was a swarm of little Negro school children all dressed in their pink and white and blue picnic garments and with ribbons in their hair. Also there was a sprinkling of young Negro boys all ironed and pressed and scrubbed clean by their mamas for this great day. At the head of them was a tall yellow Negro man wearing gold-rimmed glasses and with a white expanse of white slick-ironed shirt front and wing collar and big black bolster tie. The little Negro children twittered and chirped in the sunny air, looking about them, happy as only children can be happy. They were on their way to Durham, North Carolina, on what was called in springy parlance of those days "a 'skursion." The big yellow man was the teacher and he was taking the children on this jaunt as a wind up for his year's school teaching. He came strolling forward toward us and toward the irate and working engineer. He felt good. He was expansive. The world was sitting to his hand.

"Good mawning, gentlemen," he said graciously to us. The old Confederate soldier blinked up at him, continued leaning on his stick, said nothing. I a little boy naturally said nothing. But I was already in my heart admiring this gracious, this genial, this successful and respectable representative of the Negro race. (Even as I looked at him there echoed in my mind one of the Southern commandments on which I was raised, oft repeated by my father even—"A Negro is like a mule. Treat him fair, work him hard, feed him good and you get the right results." Even then that morning—as much as I loved my father—I knew he was wrong. Here was a fine Negro man that showed he was wrong. No, Negroes were not mules, nor were they animals as our old local preacher was wont to say, generating them in his mind out of the loins of Cain and the woman he married in the land of Nod—even as the Scriptures themselves do tell.)[3]

"What time do the train get to Durhams, suh?" the Negro teacher asked of the engineer.

"None of your damned business," called the engineer behind him, still bent over one of the drivers with his oil can. Then he looked around. He straightened spasmodically up and glared at the colored man.

The Negro already had taken a shocked and rebuffed step backward.

"Sorry, suh, sorry," he said, and he was beginning to bob his head up and down a bit, bending his body at the waist.

"Take off your hat," the engineer suddenly squealed. Off it came in the culprit's hand. The little children down at the other end of the train began to see

3. Genesis 4:16–17.

something was wrong, and in the blink of my eye I saw them begin to huddle together a little closer as if some fearful threat were beginning to be felt in the air.

"Take off your specs," the engineer snapped.

"But I ain't done nothing, white folks, ain't done nothing," said the colored man, and he backed away a couple of more steps.

"Don't white folks me," the engineer shouted. He flung the oil can behind him, snatched the walking stick from under the old Confederate soldier's resting hand and quick as lightning struck the Negro teacher a terrific wham across the face. Before the engineer pulled the stick away the blood had already rushed out and stained its splintered wood.

A little babble of shrieks and moanings rose from the school children, and like a gang of pursued goats they bounded up the steps of the Jim Crow car and inside to safety. The old Confederate soldier had almost fallen on his face when his support was jerked away. He righted himself with spread-out legs, the engineer handed his walking stick back to him. The old soldier took it and resumed his resting without a word. I couldn't look at the dreadful stick. I couldn't look at the colored man. I shivered as if some bitter freezing chill had overspread the world. It seemed — as I remember it now — that a darkness overspread the sky — just as I'd seen it one morning when the sun was eclipsed and the chickens began to cluck uncertainly and start strolling toward their roost down by the garden.

A low whimpering moaning sound came from the Negro school teacher. And what did he say? What was his accusation there for a moment in time and space? He simply said —

"Lawd, white folks, you done ruined my shirt."

"All aboard," yelled the engineer. He climbed hastily into his cab, pulled the whistle cord a couple of times. The Negro school teacher turned, still holding his big white handkerchief, now dyeing itself all over crimson, against his face. . . .

Yes, that was a sort of anecdote. Years later when trying to speak a word for the Negro people, the scene haunted me and I sat down and wrote the story of a school teacher who tried desperately to help his people and failed.[4] It wasn't a Confederate veteran's walking stick that laid my hero low. It was something more up-to-date and final — a shotgun.

The school teacher of that spring morning long ago still lives — now a very old man. A bad scar still shows on his face, running from his forehead down

4. *In Abraham's Bosom.*

across his chin. And there must be a scar in his heart too. There is in mine, and always will be.

Good luck to you in your venture.[5]

Cordially and sincerely yours,

5. The letter narrates its event "with such poignance," Morehouse wrote, that he reproduced it nearly verbatim in *Matinee Tomorrow: Fifty Years of Our Theater* (New York: Whittlesey House, 1949), pp. 211–14.

# To J. C. B. Ehringhaus and M. Hugh Thompson
## on the Bittings Case

The following four letters exemplify Green's involvement in capital punishment cases. During the 1920s and early 1930s he did not oppose capital punishment on principle, saying that he accepted the analogy between society and a garden that must be weeded, but he strongly opposed its practice in North Carolina and elsewhere in the country because among those convicted of capital crimes the supreme punishment was most apt to be inflicted on the poor and uneducated, especially black people. During the 1930s, however, his thinking shifted toward principled opposition as he began to argue that no absolute punishment should be based on less than absolute knowledge, given the possibility of error, and that the death penalty frustrated a major tenet of Christian faith, which held that any individual could experience redemption at any time. Over the years Green spent a great deal of time visiting inmates, pleading their cases, and looking into the circumstances of their crimes (or paying others to conduct investigations and defenses), sometimes with startling results.

The first three letters focus on the case of Emanuel Bittings and the fourth letter on the case of William Mason Wellmon. Footnotes provide information to make the situations intelligible. In the footnotes a few abbreviations are used for citing sources: *DMH* stands for the *Durham Morning Herald*, *NO* for the *Raleigh News and Observer*, and PG-SHC for the collection of Paul Green papers in the Southern Historical Collection, Wilson Library, the University of North Carolina at Chapel Hill.

### TO J. C. B. EHRINGHAUS

[Hollywood, Calif.]

20 May 1934

Dear Governor Ehringhaus:[1]

During the winter I was in North Carolina and had occasion to become acquainted with the facts in the case of one Emanuel (Spice) Biddings, or Bittings who is at present under sentence of death for the killing of his landlord, Auffy Clayton, near Roxboro, a year ago.[2]

1. J. C. B. Ehringhaus (1882–1949), a lawyer from Elizabeth City, was the governor of North Carolina from 1933 to 1937.

2. Emanuel Bittings, a black tenant farmer and former soldier in World War I, shot

A thorough study of the circumstances surrounding the killing and the subsequent trial and sentence convinced me that the defendant, Biddings, received a rather heavy sentence. I won't go into all the details for these have been prepared for submission to the Supreme Court by M. Hugh Thompson, an attorney of Durham.[3]

As a citizen, interested along with you in the welfare of the people of North Carolina, no matter of what race, color or creed, I am making a plea for clemency for the negro in case he is not granted a new trial. Unfortunately, my individual efforts for him have been handicapped by my having to return to California[;] and because I am afraid that in the show-down only public sentiment and your executive power can save Biddings from the electric chair, I am writing you this letter. Of course I realize as well as you and other leading men of the State do, that the majesty and justice of the law must not be handicapped by sentimentality and zeal of a misguided point of view. But when one considers the character and practise of Clayton with his tenants, the oppression and even brutality that Biddings endured, and when one considers the subterfuge methods indulged in by the defendant's counsel, Escoffrey, one can hardly arrive at any conclusion other than that the sentence of death was extreme.[4]

---

T. M. Clayton on the morning of 7 September 1933. According to Bittings, Clayton ordered him to move his share of the tobacco crop into Clayton's packhouse. Bittings started the job, then Clayton told him to stop and Bittings returned home. A little later, Bittings said, "My wife—she had just got up after having a baby—hollered up to me that Mr. Clayton was on the front porch knocking one of our boys up against the house. I came down and told him to leave." Clayton walked into the yard, called his wife, and "told her to listen to the last words he told that God-damned nigger before he shot him." Thinking he saw Clayton reach for a pistol in his pocket, Bittings got his shotgun from the house and shot Clayton ("Death Row Inmate Tells His Story of Life, Death," *NO*, 5 April 1934, p. 14, cols. 4–7). On 25 January 1934 in Roxboro, North Carolina, Bittings was tried, convicted, and sentenced to death, his electrocution set for late March.

3. Early in March, after spending several days in Roxboro talking with people about the murder, Paul, Elizabeth, Phillips Russell, Louis J. Spaulding (a prominent black businessman from Durham), and others formed a Bittings Defense Committee ("See Parallel in Paul Green Play: Playwright's Defense of Spice Bittings Recalls *In Abraham's Bosom*," *NO*, 5 March 1934, p. 5, col. 1). The committee dismissed Bittings's trial lawyer, who refused to appeal the conviction to the North Carolina Supreme Court, and, after unsuccessfully attempting to bring in an International Legal Defense lawyer, replaced him with M. Hugh Thompson, who filed an appeal on 18 April, thus suspending the execution ("Bittings Appeal to High Court Is Filed," *NO*, 20 April 1934, p. 11, cols. 4–5).

4. In addition to refusing to file an appeal, Phillip Escoffrey, a black lawyer in Durham, had failed to bring in witnesses who could corroborate Bittings's testimony, thus creating the impression during "the trial that Bittings killed his landlord without provocation, fol-

A few months ago I went over the facts as well as I could—talked with people around Roxboro—had a session with Escoffrey himself—talked to white and black citizens and more than a few of them said, quite openly: "Well, somebody should have killed Auffy Clayton long before Biddings did."

A former attorney of Roxboro told me that if he or any other reliable white lawyer had appeared for Biddings he could have secured a compromise on a second degree verdict. I am sure that Escoffrey was the "nigger in the wood-pile" and I hate for the fairmindedness and prestige of our State, as well as Biddings, to suffer by his connivance.

I sincerely trust that if events should warrant such action that you, by virtue of the power vested in your office, will see that Biddings gets something of a square deal.[5]

Yours very truly,


## TO M. HUGH THOMPSON[6]

[Hollywood, Calif.]
9 July 1934

I AM ASTONISHED TO HEAR OF THE TURN OF EVENTS IN THE BITTINGS CASE STOP APPARENTLY COMMISSIONER GILL HAS CO-OPERATED IN EVERY WAY POSSIBLE TO SEE THAT THE CONDEMNED MAN GOT A FAIR CHANCE AT LIFE STOP THE CASE STILL REMAINS VERY MYSTERIOUS TO ME FIRST IN THAT NO REASONABLE PROVOCATION FOR THE MURDER HAS BEEN ESTAB-LISHED AND SECOND IN THAT THE WIFE AND CHILDREN WHO HAD SUCH AFFECTIONATE FEELINGS FOR THE HUSBAND AND FATHER UNANIMOUSLY

---

lowing a dispute over a division of their crop" ("See Parallel in Paul Green Play," *NO,* 5 March 1934, p. 5, col. 1).

5. In mid-June the state supreme court denied Bittings's appeal for a new trial (Paul Green to Harriet Herring, 28 June 1934, PG-SHC).

6. Black lawyer in Durham handling the Bittings case. Following the state supreme court's refusal in June to grant Bittings a new trial, Thompson attempted to win a reprieve for Bittings from state commissioner of parole Edwin M. Gill. In a letter Green received on 9 July, Thompson outlined Gill's activity (PG-SHC). Gill interviewed Bittings's two daughters and his wife, all of whom corroborated the testimony at the trial that Bittings shot Clayton in the back following an argument over the disposition of his tobacco crop and that Clayton was unarmed and made no threats against Bittings. Gill was surprised by the testimony. He had intended to grant Bittings a reprieve but now could not, and Bittings's execution date remained Friday, 6 July ("Daughters Seal Doom of Father," *DMH,* 4 July 1934, p. 2, col. 2). Receiving this news, Green wired Thompson immediately.

SWORE TO EVIDENCE THAT SENDS HIM TO HIS DEATH THIS DEVOTION TO TRUTH AT ALL COSTS IS SO IDEAL THAT MEDALS ARE IN ORDER STOP NO THE ONLY CONCLUSION I CAN COME TO IS THAT EITHER BITTINGS WAS CRAZY OR THAT THE RELATIVES WERE INTIMIDATED STOP I SUPPOSE IT IS TOO LATE FOR ME TO DO MORE AT THIS GREAT DISTANCE AND SO THE SUBJECT IS ENDED BUT WITH THE HOPE THAT THROUGH A BETTER MUTUAL UNDERSTANDING OF US ALL SUCH TRAGEDIES WILL OCCUR LESS AND LESS OFTEN STOP WILL YOU PLEASE WIRE ME COLLECT AT ONCE WHETHER BITTINGS HAS BEEN EXECUTED OR NOT REGARDS PAUL GREEN[7]

## TO M. HUGH THOMPSON

[Hollywood, Calif.]
10 July 1934
Dear Lawyer Thompson:

Your wire yesterday afternoon also gave *me* a ray of hope, and I needed it after the queer news in your letter a few hours before.

Perhaps there is no need to enlarge upon what I said in my wire, but I will repeat as a matter of emphasis that the staunch loyalty to truth of the Bittings wife and three children at the expense of the condemned man is more than startling — it is downright suspicious. Another thing. — They all seem to agree like Happy Hooligans upon what happened. If you can get from anybody who talked with them something of their first statements, I am sure you will find a great divergence in them. Escoffrey told me that when he talked with the wife (I don't remember as to the children) soon after the murder, she told quite a different story from what she later told him when he was ready to bring her to court as a witness. Have you heard from any source that Mrs. Bittings (who was sick in bed at the time Clayton was killed) said she heard Clayton call out to his wife to "Come here and take a last took at this goddamned nigger before I blow his brains out?" I have. Will you ask Escoffrey if she didn't first tell him that?[8]

7. A few hours after sending the wire, Green received a telegram from Thompson saying that Gill had postponed the execution until September to allow more time to investigate circumstances surrounding the murder.

8. At a hearing before Gill on 24 July, Thompson presented two men from Roxboro who swore that Mrs. Bittings "told them before her husband was arrested that Clayton had struck her in the face before he was shot by Bittings and that her version of the shooting then was substantially the same as that given by Bittings on the stand" ("Bittings' Case Takes New Turn at Clemency Hearing," *DMH*, 25 July 1934, p. 3, cols. 3–4).

Another thing. — Is it certain that Clayton was shot in the back? Wasn't he shot in the side? Bittings claims that Clayton was turning toward him with his hand on his hip pocket when he pulled down a shotgun and killed him. From the report of the Coroner you no doubt already know the location of the wounds on Clayton's body, but I was rather reliably informed that he was not shot in the back. If he wasn't, then the wife and childrens' testimony that he was killed while walking away from Bittings, stands partially contradicted.

Can't something be made of the fact that Clayton's reputation as a landlord was bad and that he was a quarrelsome person when drinking?[9]

To repeat once more. — One man doesn't kill another man because he is ordered to move his tobacco. There is more to it than this, and I believe that in view of all these qualifying and uncleared-up matters, Governor Ehringhaus and Commissioner Gill have a clear right and duty to set aside the verdict of the courts and commute Bittings' sentence to life imprisonment.

Will they? — is the question.[10]

Yours very truly,

Copy to: Mr. Daniels.[11]

9. At the hearing on 24 July, Thompson presented a third witness who testified "that Clayton was extremely hot-tempered and frequently had trouble with his tenants . . . [and] that Clayton had ordered him off Clayton's farm at the point of a shotgun only a few weeks before the killing took place" (ibid.).

10. Because Bittings's family adhered to their account of the murder, Commissioner Gill did not set aside the verdict of the court, and Bittings's execution was set for Friday, 28 September. On Wednesday morning, 26 September, Elizabeth Green held a four-hour conference with Governor Ehringhaus, pleading with him to commute Bittings's sentence to life imprisonment. Ehringhaus refused, and the execution took place as scheduled ("Two Victims Face Execution Friday," *NO*, 27 September 1934, p. 1, col. 2; p. 2, col. 2.

11. Jonathan Daniels, editor of the *Raleigh News and Observer* and supporter of blacks (see Charles W. Eagles, *Jonathan Daniels and Race Relations: The Evolution of a Southern Liberal* [Knoxville: University of Tennessee Press, 1982]), had been alerted to the Bittings case by Green and had asked Green to keep him informed on it (Jonathan Daniels to Paul Green, 21 March 1934, PG-SHC).

# To E. M. Land on the Wellmon Case

Chapel Hill, N.C.
18 November 1942

Dear Mr. Land—[1]

It was kind of you to lend me your transcripts of the William Mason Wellmon case,[2] and I have read them with the closest interest. Apart from your understandable professional attitude as prosecuting attorney in the case, I believe you are as anxious to see justice done to the condemned man as I am. Your record as a citizen and civic leader shows that. So I am sure you won't object to my writing you how the evidence strikes me in these records and won't mind if I call attention to a few points that seem to me to still need clearing up before final judgment is imposed upon Wellmon. For as long as there is the vaguest shadow of doubt that he is the guilty man we ought to do what we reasonably can to get at the truth. Here are some of the questions that have risen in my mind—set down at random:[3]

1. Did anybody check as to whether Wellmon signed for his pay on the payday of Feb. 11 (the date of the crime)? Testimony shows that he was supposed to have signed the envelope in which his pay was handed over.[4] What has hap-

---

1. E. M. Land (d. 1949), a University of North Carolina at Chapel Hill graduate (1899) from Statesville, North Carolina, was prosecuting attorney in the trial of William Mason Wellmon, a black man convicted of and sentenced to death for the rape of a sixty-seven-year-old white woman, Cora Sowers, on her farm near Statesville. The rape occurred around 2:00 P.M. on 11 February 1941; Wellmon's trial took place in Statesville on 11 and 12 August 1942; and he was scheduled to die at the state's central prison in Raleigh on 2 October 1942. That date was set aside while he appealed his conviction to the state supreme court, but the court denied the appeal and fixed a new execution date of 20 November 1942. On 17 November, the day before the present letter, Green led a group to Raleigh for a clemency hearing for Wellmon before Governor J. Melville Broughton, a hearing at which Land argued against clemency.

2. Throughout, Green spells the name "Wellman."

3. But the text of the letter is marked by Green as "Revised Copy."

4. Raised near Statesville, Wellmon had moved to Washington, D.C., in 1940 and worked on a construction project at nearby Fort Belvoir, Virginia. During his trial he contended that he was at work at Fort Belvoir on the day of the crime, that his presence there

pened to the envelope? Was it thrown away? O'Neill[5] says he would have had to sign for his pay. So does Frick.[6] Obviously if he signed for it and it could be proved, his alibi as to his whereabouts would hold — that is, if Feb. 11 was the actual pay-day. And there is no proof to show it wasn't.[7]

2. Gertrude Ingram,[8] one of the chief witnesses for the prosecution, says she was sure it was the 11th day of February she saw Mason Wellmon on his way to Mrs. Sowers' place, though she acknowledged on cross examination she couldn't guess "by making three guesses what day of the month today is" even though she had been summoned to court and was a witness at that moment. Like O'Neill she appears to remember what she wants to.

3. Gertrude Ingram also says that on the same day, the 11th, she told someone about seeing the colored man (Mason Wellmon) going towards Mrs. Sowers'. Whom did she tell? And what did she tell? Did she describe the colored man she had seen? She makes a point of being afraid of strange negro men and of observing them carefully. Her talk doesn't suggest that she is afraid of strangers, least of all those of her own race.

4. What has happened to the $1,000 or $1,200 reward offered for the apprehension and so forth of the guilty party? Has it been paid and to whom?

5. Is it possible that the woman Gertrude Ingram could have been motivated by the reward (or have had any other motive) in pressing on towards her identification of the Wellmon clothes (coat and hat), an identification which came nearly three months after the crime, May after February? And why is it that she is more certain as to the matter of clothes than even Mrs. Sowers is?[9]

6. Is it reasonable to think that Gertrude Ingram could identify these

---

was proved by a receipt he signed for his pay, and that therefore he could not have committed the crime that day in North Carolina (trial transcript, Wellmon file, PG-SHC).

5. William Robert O'Neill, Wellmon's supervisor at Fort Belvoir (ibid.).

6. Elihu Frick, auditor for Wellmon's employer, the Charles H. Tompkins Construction Company (ibid.).

7. Payday was 11 February 1941, which was also the day of the crime. Although Wellmon and others spoke of the receipt during his extradition hearing in Washington, D.C., and his trial in Statesville, the receipt itself had not been located and Land assumed it was lost (E. M. Land to J. Melville Broughton, 12 December 1942, Wellmon file, PG-SHC).

8. Black woman from Statesville.

9. Following Wellmon's arrest on 27 April 1941, Cora Sowers and Gertrude Ingram, recently employed as a maid in the Sowers household, went to Washington to identify the rapist. At a jail lineup there on 6 May, Sowers could identify none of the eight prisoners as her assailant and Ingram thought the man next to Wellmon was the one she had seen. At a lineup on 7 May Sowers still could not identify anyone, but Ingram now thought Wellmon's brown coat and dark cap were those worn by the attacker (trial transcript, Wellmon file, PG-SHC).

clothes in a "bad light,"[10] having only seen the man once in passing (even though she said he was acting queerly)? You and I couldn't do it. I don't even know what kind of clothes you had on yesterday at the hearing, though I paid a lot of attention to you during your argument. All I remember is that, I think, they were dark. I'm afraid this Gertrude had been inclined towards the identification of a certain kind of hat and coat from former conversation, questions, etc., referring back to maybe Mrs. Sowers' disordered remembrance of the unknown assailant.

7. Is it reasonable to suppose that a man out to commit a crime of vengeance, as the prosecution says Wellmon's crime was,[11] would inquire along the way as to the home of his intended victim? It is claimed that the "strange negro" so did. Is Wellmon feeble-minded? Nobody has said that he is. Rather he was foreman over a group of workmen. He had at least that much sense.[12]

8. The sheriff said yesterday at the hearing that Wellmon offered at the time of his arrest to return to North Carolina to meet whatever the charge might be. Later, of course, seeing how things were setting against him, he naturally fought tooth and claw to keep away. This seems a reasonable reaction on his part.[13]

9. Again, testimony shows that after being arrested Wellmon requested permission to change from his workman's overalls into his street clothes before being taken to police headquarters. Now I ask you is it reasonable that if he had been guilty of the charge—remembering that he had been in the toils of the law before and must have been somewhat "conditioned" to trying to protect himself[14]—is it reasonable that he would go into his boarding house and put on the very clothes which would help identify him as Mrs. Sowers'

10. Reason given by Land at the clemency hearing the previous day for Sowers's inability to identify Wellmon in the lineup.

11. Land argued that the black community of Statesville, backed by the NAACP, planned the rape as revenge against the white community and the court. In January 1941, he said, a white jury had found a black man guilty of simple assault when accused of raping a black woman, and the black community was outraged at the seeming lack of seriousness with which the jury took crimes of blacks against blacks. According to Land, the black woman's lawyer had said in court that the next rape victim would be white (E. M. Land to J. Melville Broughton, 12 December 1942, Wellmon file, PG-SHC).

12. And scored "above the average for members of the colored race" in state prison mental examinations, according to a prison official (J. M. Neese to William Dunn, Commissioner of Paroles, 18 November 1942, PG-SHC).

13. Land had construed Wellmon's fight against extradition as a sign of guilt.

14. In December 1934 Wellmon had been convicted of raping a young white woman and sentenced to five years in prison.

assailant? To repeat Gertrude Ingram identified him by these clothes as being the man she had seen in the vicinity of the crime the day it was committed.

10. From the record it appears that Wellmon was formerly a good prisoner in the Central Prison at Raleigh, since in his testimony in one place he says he paid the full five years and later says the actual term of service was three years and nine months — this of course was for an old alleged crime some years ago — and I presume that his shortened time was due to good behaviour.[15] Now if he did commit the crime with which he is charged, he is or was either some sort of imbecile or a sadistic pervert. What does his former record show as to his mentality and such possible tendencies? Has anybody investigated?

11. The captain of the (Washington) prison guard testified that neither Gertrude Ingram nor Mrs. Sowers identified Wellmon at the first line-up there. Yesterday you spoke of the light in the prison as being bad. Yet Superintendent Rives of this prison says the light was good — several big windows in that room, etc., and he also says that Wellmon was not identified at this first line-up. Yet apparently Gertrude *could* identify the clothes, light or no light, even if they happened to be worn by another man. Wellmon says she first picked a man next to him, a man by the name of Young. Did she?[16] Also isn't it strange that though Gertrude Ingram had identified the face of Wellmon in the prison photograph shown her by Mr. Scott as resembling the man seen in the vicinity of the crime[17] — that when she came to Washington she first identified clothes and not the face? The more I consider this woman's testimony, Mr. Land, the more I wonder at it.

12. At the second line-up testimony tends to show that none of the men in the former line-up were included except Wellmon. Why not? Was the intent of the "law" already settling against him because it had become generally agreed that he had to be the man? This doesn't sound like scientific and fair criminology methods, does it?[18]

15. Green's spelling.

16. Wellmon testified that at the first lineup (on 6 May 1941) Ingram identified Eugene Young, the man next to him, as the one she had seen going to the Sowers house, and that at the second lineup (on 7 May 1941) she identified no one. Ingram's testimony is not known on the point, but apparently after the second lineup she identified Wellmon by his clothes and said that Young had worn those clothes in the first lineup. When cross-examined, Wellmon said he had only one set of clothes in jail and wore it at both lineups (trial transcript, Wellmon file, PG-SHC).

17. Basis of the warrant for Wellmon's arrest.

18. Making a suspect the sole common member of different lineups, an acceptable practice at the time, has tended since the late 1960s to be judged unnecessarily suggestive and

13. Yesterday you introduced copies of two "damaging" letters against the defense. Where are these originals? Why weren't they with the copies? "They have been mislaid somehow" is not sufficient answer.[19]

14. As to Wellmon's having given a false name to the officers in Washington at the time of his arrest, that is perfectly reasonable, for he was trying to save himself from whatever he was wanted for. Again it is reasonable to think that the officers might have misheard him and he gave his right name after all. "William Wellmon" could have been mistaken for "William Williams." You remember that yesterday the sheriff fumbled quite a bit and didn't seem so sure at first that "William Williams" was the name given at the time of the arrest.[20]

15. In his self-description Wellmon says he has a scar under his left eye. Is this scar noticeable? Mrs. Sowers doesn't refer to it in her testimony. Wouldn't she have noticed that scar as much as she would the teeth if it is in any way remarkable?[21] Wellmon also says he is 6 ft. 3 inches high. And Mrs. Sowers when first asked couldn't say that her assailant wasn't about five feet, six inches tall. Have you measured him? Has he grown some since his former prison measurement of years ago[22] — which measurement was introduced yesterday?

16. O'Neill testifies that Wellmon was a foreman of a smaller group of men under him, and he declares that if Wellmon had been away from work on Feb. 11 he O'Neill certainly would have known it. What is the custom with

---

thus a violation of due process (Charles H. Whitebread, *Criminal Procedure: An Analysis of Constitutional Cases and Concepts* [Mineola, N.Y.: Foundation Press, 1980], pp. 356–60).

19. The copies, dated 6 May 1941, which were unsigned but were purported to be copies of letters written by the wife of Wellmon's brother, who lived in Statesville, advised members of the family to keep Wellmon away from Statesville because "Sheriff offering reward and good description of him, woman say she'll know him if she see him again and she will and it be to bad for us all" (Wellmon file, PG-SHC).

20. Land had contended that giving a false name was a sign of Wellmon's guilt. Wellmon testified that he always gave his name as William Wellmon and never gave a false name to law officers.

21. In her original description of the assailant (reflected in the reward notice [Wellmon file, PG-SHC]), as well as in her testimony during the trial, Sowers stressed that one or two of his upper front teeth were gold. Wellmon had no gold fillings or caps (trial transcript, Wellmon file, PG-SHC).

22. In 1934, when Wellmon, age twenty-nine, first went to prison, prison records gave his height as five feet, eleven-and-a-half inches (E. M. Land to J. Melville Broughton, 13 November 1942, Wellmon file, PG-SHC). Sowers described her assailant as about five feet, ten inches tall (reward notice). Land had argued that Wellmon, in describing himself as six feet, three inches tall, was trying to deceive the jury.

other such foremen? Are any of them white men? What do they say? Has this been checked?

17. Yesterday you called the governor's attention to how cold blooded Wellmon was, illustrating it by referring to Wellmon's words to one of the deputies taking him to death row—"When they say I'm going to die?" (Then the answer.) "Why the hell they wait so long." You remember of course that Wellmon had been through a tough trial, had fought long and hard in the Washington courts, had also lain a year in jail. His words were natural and not cold blooded. I wouldn't mention this trifling point except that you and I know that in a delicate balance sometimes these trifles can take an innocent man's life away. I am sure, however, that this sort of thing won't affect the governor in his judgment, and I am sure you stuck it in "professionally."

18. It seems to me that five days is an all too short time allowed for the defense to prepare a case of this kind. The Supreme Court doesn't say so, still it seems so to me.[23]

I have great sympathy for Mrs. Sowers and her family, and for her son whom I knew as a fine fellow at Carolina.[24] It is a nightmare they have been through. We all share in their suffering and sorrow. But whatever our sympathy is, I still think the case should be further investigated. I believe Wellmon should be reprieved long enough to allow for this investigation. The cause of justice and race relations throughout the South would, I am sure, be bettered by an act of clemency on the part of the governor. As he himself so grandly put it yesterday—"Justice is not a matter of race." Let us all prove it, help to give the cause for which we are mutually working a little more time to be tested and justified. Sixty days, ninety days soon go by, they don't mean too much to you and me, but now they mean everything to William Mason Wellmon, whether he be guilty or innocent.

With cordial regards, and I hope you'll give me a ring when you're down this way and we can get together for a meal,[25]

23. Wellmon's appeal to the state supreme court had been based on the fact that his court-appointed lawyer had only five days to prepare his defense before the trial in August 1942.

24. Neil S. Sowers, University of North Carolina at Chapel Hill class of 1927 and law partner of Land.

25. At the hearing on 17 November, Green convinced Broughton to investigate Wellmon's claim that he signed a receipt for his pay on the day of the crime (point 1 of the present letter), an investigation neglected during Wellmon's trial. That night Broughton dispatched to Washington two agents of the State Bureau of Investigation, one a handwriting expert, and on 19 November stayed Wellmon's execution until 28 November. By

21 November the agents had located the pay receipt (showing wages of $32.40 for 40.5 hours worked), authenticated Wellmon's signature on it, and developed evidence showing it could have been signed only on 11 February (SBI report, Wellmon file, PG-SHC). Broughton extended the stay of execution to 18 December, then an additional sixty days, saying, "it is quite obvious that the prisoner could not have been working at Fort Belvoir and receiving and receipting for his pay there during the middle of the day on February 11th, 1941, and have committed the act of criminal assault at or about one-thirty in the afternoon of the same day in Iredell County, North Carolina." He added that he would continue the investigation but that "if my present impression of the case should be confirmed during [the period of the reprieve], I should consider it my duty as a matter of justice to release the prisoner" ("Statement of Governor Broughton," Wellmon file, PG-SHC; excerpted in NO, 16 December 1942, p. 16, cols. 6–8). On 15 April 1943 Broughton pardoned Wellmon, who thus became the first person in the state acquitted of a crime for which he had been sentenced to death (NO, 16 April 1943, p. 1, col. 1; p. 18, cols. 4–5). In 1971, under a law allowing the state "to award damages for pecuniary loss sustained by reason of wrongful imprisonment up to $500 per year," Wellmon, who had been in prison nearly two years, was awarded $986.40 (NO, 13 May 1971, sec. 1, p. 3, cols. 1–4).

# On Writing, Education, and Life

# Drama and the Weather

Edith J. R. Isaacs (1878–1956), one of the founders and longtime editor of the journal *Theatre Arts*, sent Green a list of questions about his work as a playwright, starting with the question "Why do you write plays?" (Summer 1934; PG-SHC). This essay grew out of his response to her questions and was first published in *Theatre Arts Monthly* 18 (August 1934): 631–43.

If you've ever been down in the country during a severe summer drought, you have noticed how the crops stood lifeless and how the leaves and limbs of the trees sagged under the wilting heat, and how the chickens in the barnyard sat slothfully on the ground, and the cattle in the shadow of the buildings looked out at the world with dull and inert eyes. The farmers themselves seemed testy and irritable about the house, and with reason, for day after day the sun has risen like a ball of fire, swum across the brazen empty sky and gone down beyond the rim of brown hills — a fiery curse to animal, earth, and man. The world itself is perishing for rain, but there is no rain.

Then one morning a different feeling is in the air. After breakfast you walk in the lane, and a change is over everything. The flowers and the trees have perked up their heads, the chickens step about lively, and the pigeons no longer quarrel under the eaves. Down in the pasture the cattle move briskly around biting off green willow tips, and the farmer and his sons are long ago abroad looking to their dikes and ditches. You go down to the village for the mail. More than once you hear a store loafer say, "The air feels like rain." Being a summer boarder, you read the morning papers, then an article or two in a magazine about trouble in Europe, and after lunch sit on the front porch and take a rest.

Looking off across the burning fields about two o'clock, you see low on the horizon edge a faint little wad of cloud, no larger than the cloud Elijah or Polonius saw. And as you sit there watching, another little cloud appears swimming up the sky, to be followed by another and then another. Soon the whole southwestern horizon is marked by these little upboiling racks. And in less time than it takes to tell, a low dark swollen band begins shoving itself up behind them and above the line of sycamore trees along the river. Presently there is a roll of low ominous thunder below the earth, and the windows rattle in their sockets.

The moments pass, the dark wide stretching cloud now reaches from north to south and pushes up until it touches the edge of the burning sun. Then it obscures the sun. A flash of lightning marks a sudden fiery crack from sky to earth. The elm trees around the house shiver with a strange delight. The chickens start going into the henhouse and the doves fly into their cote. And then up from the meadow the old bell-cow comes leading the other cattle, her head high, her tail arched merrily.

Another roll of thunder sounds, a gust of dust cuts a little jigging whirlwind swift down the lane, trying to keep up with the edge of the cloud which now has raced across the sky and passed over the house. The wind blows more strongly, and somewhere a door slams. You continue to sit, waiting for the rain to fall. The wind dies out, the thunder is no longer heard, nor is there any lightning. Everything is breathless, expectant, still.

Now with a sudden clatter like stones on the roof or gravel thrown, the rain begins. A fine mist of dust is beat up in the yard, and in the lane and out across the fields. Like a morning ground-fog it is. And then it too is wetted down to earth as the rain settles into a steady pour. A sheet of wetness begins to blow in on you, and the air is full of a rich sodden, loamy smell. You pick up your chair, lean it against the wall, and enter the house. There you stand by the window looking out where a world is being refreshed and where a snake of yellow water has started wriggling down the dry road ditch. The drought is over. In a few days everything will be green again.

There was once an old question as to who could chart the winds and the nature thereof, and who could foretell the weather and its whims. The question still stands today unanswered as it did in Job's time. No doubt there are laws governing all such phenomena, and maybe someday these laws will be understood—laws that have no irrational phantom dancing within them. But even so those who understand will have little power to bring either drought or rain, for the wind will still blow where it listeth, and in the universe at large it will rain when it will rain.

And as with the weather, so with writing a play—so with any work of art. It comes pretty much when it will come, is absent when it will be absent, and no man can provide its presence at his will. So if I may be personal in replying to your question, "Why do you write plays," I can on first consideration easily say, "I don't know." It is much like the weather to me—the what and why, the wherefore and results. About the only answer I would venture is that I seem to need to. If I were certain that the drama were the one means of gaining honor or wealth or mental stability, there would be some obvious sense in spending one's life trying to set down lines for people to speak on a stage. I believe I should want to write plays, though, if little or nothing came of them, but naturally I want a lot to come of them.

Of course your question goes further than any easy answer or any meteorological metaphor. It raises the whole problem of aptitude and calling. I think all people are by nature artists, that is, more or less so. The usual European designation of the American builder and business man as a money hog, for instance—a creature who takes pleasure only in dollar profit and pain only in dollar loss—seems to me obviously false. There is more to it than that—always more. Sinclair Lewis in one of his novels, *Work of Art*, tries his hand at showing that one Myron Weagle with his dream of a perfect hotel might be considered essentially an artist. There is a lot of human truth in his contention. Now if all of us have this so-called artistic urge, then why do some of us become hotel-keepers and others banjo-pickers or playwrights? That is the next question. The answer is perhaps that circumstances always play their part. One child happens to have access, say, to a piano near at hand but finds his fingers too stiff or too short ever to allow of his becoming a performer. Perhaps he turns to composing, or bricklaying. And so it goes. Each of us could make some sort of statement as to his proper calling. Take your own case—you run a drama magazine. All sorts of odds and ends of circumstances and people went into your choice of that career.

Two incidents happened to me years ago, I remember, which turned me to writing plays. Norman Foerster, who was one of the finest English teachers ever to appear at the University of North Carolina, announced in class one day that the seniors had decided to do a play at Commencement and were holding a contest for original scripts. He advised me to try my hand. I took a chance at the thing and happened to win out. The play was produced in the Forest Theatre and I was thrilled to death. After that though I didn't set my heart on playwriting, for I had always been more interested in poetry and short stories than anything else. Then in 1919 "Proff" Koch came riding in from the Dakota prairies, his arms full of plays and his head full of dreams. In no time a stage was up, and everybody near and far, little and big, black and white, realized for the first time that he, said body, was an artist of some sort—mainly a dramatic artist. Some went in for designing, some for acting, some for writing. I chose the last. And after a few productions, I was caught fast in my choice and had struck acquaintance with all the bat-like terrors that inhabit the shadows of the stage.

Your next question is easier to answer. "Why do you write the plays you do?" The answer is—that's the only kind I know how to write. Most of the plays I have written can be designated as folk plays, and I know this seems a narrow boundary. Perhaps it is, but since the "folk" are the people who seem to matter most to me, I have little interest in trying to deal with others who are more foreign and therefore less real to me. Not for a moment do I claim to have done justice to an inspiring subject matter, but the challenge is there, clearer, sharper, and more compelling every day. For there is something in the life of "the people" which seems of deeper significance so far as the nature of the universe goes than the characters who might be termed sophisticated. To examine the matter a little further, it seems to me that the folk are those living closer to a terrible and all-wise nature than their brethren of the sidewalks and opera house, and if I were seeking a philosophical statement for the matter it would be somewhat as follows:

The folk are the people whose manners, ethics, religious and philosophical ideals are more nearly derived from and controlled by the ways of the outside physical world (Cf. Synge's *Riders to the Sea*) than by the ways and institutions of men in a specialized society (Cf. Schnitzler's *Anatol* cycle). And the outside natural world is the fountain of wisdom, the home of the fruitful all-mother, the omnipotent God. The line of demarcation between the folk and sophisticated drama is not always easily contrasted; to instance once more, Ferenc Molnar's *The Guardsman* and S. Ansky's *The Dybbuk*. And between the last two I'd always choose *The Dybbuk* — even though technique should shift for itself.

I don't claim that sophisticated drama may not be great in its own right, but somehow I never thrill to it as I do to what I like to term the folk drama the Greeks wrote, the kind Shakespeare and Tolstoy and Hauptmann wrote; the kind Alexis Granowsky used to produce in Russia with its lovely burden of folk-imagery, music and song. In reading *Lear*, for example, I always feel a sudden lift when we come to the heath scene. There is something grand and universal in the naked relationship of the old king to the powers of nature and the weather around him.

And as characters available to art purposes, to repeat, those who live as it were with their feet in the earth and their heads bare to the storms, the lightning and the gale — those who labor with their hands, wrestling from cryptic nature her goods and stores of sustenance — these develop a wisdom of living which seems to me more real and beautiful than those who develop their values and ambitions from rubbing shoulders in a crowded city.

And that wisdom it is which seems important — a wisdom which is a consciousness of the great eternal Presence by which men live and move and have their being, and without which they die. And if the playwrights who tell of captains and lords, kings and queens, dolls and manikins, can open up the doors of crowded buildings, cut through the filmy arras that conceals our human instincts and hopes and fears, and go to the first principles of human identity—then they raise the hair on our heads too with their voice from the sacred grove of Colonus. And no longer do we think of man as sophisticated or folk, but man—man alone with his God and his destiny. And when this happens—and rare is Shakespeare, rarer than the Phoenix—then the matter is all one and listeners are all one.

But the present clang and confusion of wheel on iron, yelling and clamor of tickers and tellers, the secrecy of vaults and locks and braggarty monoliths of incorruptible concrete and steel—these all make it harder for us to see and hear the God who is the principle of our lives. (Not God, a supernatural personality sitting on a foolish throne in heaven. No, no! But the Principle of worship, of reverence, of awe—the primal Verity native to the soul.) Maybe I'm crazy on the idea of God, but then aren't we all? I refer to the wild pell-mell rush every evening out of the city to the country—to the country where the birds are, where the grass is, and where there is peace or should be.

Now you catch me almost carrying on into a scheme of social philosophy. And if I wanted to apply this half-surmised aesthetic theory to the control and arrangement of peoples, I should say there ought to be plenty of trees and land and outdoors for every man. For only in the outdoors can we associate with power and mystery in their most sublime manifestation. And heaven knows we ought to sense in any way we can whatever touch of sublimity there may be vouchsafed unto us in this darkness.

Now it seems that after all I'm saying for myself that folk-drama as such is or can be more significant than sophisticated drama. Not at all. I mean to repeat that in the last analysis it is a question of neither folk nor sophisticate—but of man, man in his environment, and it is in the main a matter for the poet, the creator, the seer. And I would say that indoors sooner or later man must perish and outdoors there is more of a chance for him.

To make another dogmatic statement, I would say that cruelty, scorn, and evils of all sorts are more native to the great cities than not, and therefore we should be better off without any great cities—I mean close, skyscraper, bedlam cities. (There's something other than politics behind Russia's efforts to create the ideal commune.) And all the little towns that get too large for their britches and so full of metropolital urges and apings that they cut down all the trees on their main streets and cover the grass and ground with concrete, will be better off when they tear up the concrete, reset the trees, and grow grass again. And maybe now that we have evolved wheels and telephones and radios and machinery of long-distance cooperation of all sorts, we can all begin to live more among flowers and trees again and yet keep in touch with each other enough for our sophisticated needs. Then haply now and again we may also have a word with the Great Presence where He walks by the river bank at evening.

As to your next question of "What happens when you turn your play over to the director, designer, actor, and see them add their form to yours?" — it is more than easy to say that sometimes you are pleased with what they do and sometimes disappointed. It is never possible for the image-picture of your characters to be entirely duplicated on the stage. Their habits, their actions and appearance are always different and necessarily so. But I think the production as often improves the play over the author's mind as it is likely to hurt it — that is, a good production.

Your last question as to what the playwright should be to the theatre and to the world he lives in, opens up a huge wheel-full of diverging thoughts. Briefly though, he should be, don't you think, the same to the theatre as the gardener to his garden, or the blacksmith to his smithy, and the carpenter to his house? And as for the world he lives in — his business is simply to express in dramatic form the human struggles, both evil and good, that exist in that world. In the Aristotelian phrase, he is a maker, and his business is to fashion or make his material fit the imaginative demands of his craft. But how wonderfully difficult it is and how joyful! How like the weather, like the rain!

And in these two words of material and craft all the trouble lies, of course. But the trouble is not final, however mysterious and difficult the matter is — do you think so? For in the great outside universe around us nature is always solving these dualistic antagonisms, whether it be raining or whether it be dry, and from her we may no doubt derive both the axiom and the dream.

It occurs to me that I make no place for comedy (which includes melo-drama and farce). Well, it apparently belongs to another point of view, just as the grotesque requires still a third kind of judgment. Comedy seeks to belong entirely to man's world and to have no place in nature's world. In fact one might say that it arises from man's delight in prankishness with himself and fellowman in so far as he forgets that he is a part of an all-powerful and de-manding universe. Its basic pattern is a non-harmful incongruity which man himself provides, and that would seem to justify the definition. For nature is never funny or playful, not even when she smiles, is she?

As for the grotesque (the hysterical), it disappears before definition and stands representative of nothing more than the frightful effort to combine the comic and the sublime (or the finite funny with the infinite serious) into the body of one piece.

You see, your letter has stirred up a whole hornet's nest of trouble for me. And now that I've had to take refuge in the quagmire of metaphysics, I'd better stop. So I'll conclude by—yes, I'll say it—the play's the thing after all, whether it's indoors or outdoors—but like the weather it is most outdoors.

# The University in a Nuclear Age

On October 12 each year, the University of North Carolina at Chapel Hill celebrates its founding in 1789 with an academic procession, awards bestowed on distinguished graduates, and an address before the assembled faculty and friends of the university. On University Day in 1963 Green was the speaker. His speech, "The University in a Nuclear Age," reflects its own day in several respects, starting with the title, but it focuses on education and gives Green's views on the importance of teaching, the centrality of the arts and humanities in a liberal education, and the purpose of education in a democratic society. These are social issues about which he cared deeply and which are as timely now as when the speech was delivered. Moreover, the speech, written largely in terms of personal experience and anecdote, gains the charm of autobiography.

In his speech Green had much to say about a kind of teaching that in his view diminished the experience of literature for students, a kind of teaching based on old-line historical scholarship that emphasized historical periods, literary types, and authorial influences — all based on "objective" facts. Teachers may still have difficulty conveying the direct experience of literary works, or stimulating strong responses in their students, but styles in scholarship change and the kind of scholarship Green attacks is no longer the problem. To conserve space in the *Paul Green Reader* I have deleted several paragraphs from the speech — most attacking historical scholarship, others dealing with then-current political problems or quoting extensively from literary works — and marked the point of each deletion with a row of asterisks.

It should be noted that in 1963 the University Day ceremony was held in Hill Hall on the Chapel Hill campus. At the time Hill Hall housed the Department of Music, and the main campus library was the Louis Round Wilson Library (the domed library to which Green refers). During Green's student days and early years on the faculty, however, Hill Hall had been the university library.

1.

I fear that much of what I have to say in my somewhat informal talk this morning will seem obvious to most of you. Some of it will certainly appear to be sentimental and other parts simply not true.

But I suppose each of us has to appraise the world, size it up, appreciate it from his own frame of reference or from his own point of view or stance as he goes along in life and thus set forth his findings and seeings as best he can.

258

Naturally in this scientific age, we have all been pretty much conditioned to the fact that frames of reference, points of view or stances or appraisals and findings themselves do not forever remain in a status quo fixity but are also gripped in the process of nature and the process of change, of becoming, of growing.

*   *   *

[And why shouldn't this be so?] For the essential character of change so far as it concerns man — and that is the real concern — is a matter of development, of growth. The life of man then is like a tree forever growing, and the blessed thing about it, the blessed miracle which sets him apart from all other things, is that he himself can participate enormously in this creative process. Not only can he participate in it, but that actually is his sole purpose insofar as he is man — to make himself grow and to help others to grow — to grow in excellence, human excellence, say — call it manliness, virtue, good conscience, poetic spirit, grace or what not. In this is his own true happiness and his single worthwhile victory.

And so with this brief offertory to philosophy, I beg your kind indulgence as I talk rather frankly and even personally a while on the subject of the place of The University in a Nuclear Age. And by this title I mean of course a specific reference to the University's duties, its responsibilities, its challenges, its opportunities.

*   *   *

2.

We are met here, ladies and gentlemen, on an important occasion truly, and we have cause to celebrate, to memorialize the birthday of a great institution, an institution we all love, an institution whose long length of life of a hundred and seventy years spans most of the important history, the growth and the reach of this mighty country. And it has played some part in that growth and in that reaching — played it sometimes in tragedy, sometimes in failure and waste but often in accomplishment and triumph. We honor it, we love it. I know that some of us love it beyond all places on the earth. I for one do. Again and again I have moved away — bought a house in Hollywood, lived in New York, stayed two years in Europe, traveled around in Asia — but I have always come back home. This is not only home. It is a shrine to me, a home-shrine. And I tell you whenever I feel low in my mind I can come up here on the campus from my house some two miles out, walk under these old and beautiful trees out there, think of the old days, remember the perished friendly comrades —

"I have had friends, I have had companions —
All, all are gone, the old familiar faces — "

—and feel a sweet rich sense of their nearness, their living presence, again, as I walk under these trees, feel again not only the inspiration of the past but the dynamic pressure and push of the present in the hurrying and criss-crossing figures of the students, say, and the professors. And as I watch them go by I dream and ponder on the days ahead. And my heart begins to beat right again, and my low spirits to lift.

And then to fasten gladness and certainty deep in my heart I wind up in the great library over there. I like to look at its dome, for that building is the true altar of this ancient shrine. May I say I believe that as a university library is great so a university can be great, and there can be no great university without a great library.

For — to change the figure — stored in it are the mighty witnesses to truth, the riches of wisdom gathered up in the several million books and documents — mighty summonings and commanding communing voices waiting to speak to you, to me. And all one has to do to hear them, to feel their message of daring and of glory, to take their best inspiration into his soul is to open the covers between which they wait, and then by reading and study let them leap out into him, onto him like a Pentecostal fire. And if he is a true servitor of life he will feel like dancing before his Lord. I often do.

\*   \*   \*

And not only do I get lifted up and most often get my gloom dispelled — and I have had plenty of gloom lately as we all have had over the present world-in-threat situation — but on every visit to the campus here I get some of my creative powers back. And I needn't describe these different sorts of powers. They are human enough. Sometimes, for instance, I get hung over a plot problem in a play or story and can't move on. I have faith somehow that I can solve it. I have faith that perhaps in the most difficult places the best scenes of human relations can be produced, just as in the most difficult crises the greatest characters and statesmen can be produced to solve these crises, and the finest actions result.

So in my writing difficulties I often come up here and poke about. If I am trying to do a Stephen Foster story, for instance, or write about some Negro citizen struggling to make his way to the Canaan land of equal opportunity promised to him, or write down the struggle of the Lost Colony as I hear a perishing people crying their funeral hymn, and can't make any headway, I can come up here, walk around as I say, visit the music library, go down into the practice rooms, peck out a lot of folk melodies on an old tin-panny piano, talk with some of the music faculty and students and tell them my troubles, and when I've done that I usually go away with a good workable dose of exhilarating and creative laxative. And it's the same when I wander over to the bigger library and mingle with the books there or some of the staff. I usually go away recharged.

And as I walk about, pass by and hear and see the processes of young minds and bodies at work inside the dozens of classrooms, hear the professors inside talking away—and sometimes I get in there and talk away too—then I know that a mighty miracle is at work here, the miracle of human creativity at its human almost best. I say almost best.

Yes, this is a shrine, a creative shrine. A shrine is a place where something great has happened and something great can happen and is happening, and it is a place where people come and remember, meditate, commune, memorialize, think, resolve, and go away readier for action. I am sure that many a bothered alumnus businessman, questioning alumnus politician, returns here from time to time to seek re-inspiration and help. (I wish the politicians would come more often and stay longer.) And the lawyers, farmers, engineers, doctors, druggists—alumni and friends of every sort—keep coming back here to renew their spiritual youth, to charge the batteries of their soul as it were. Many are here today. We welcome you. You too are the University. The University lives in you and it lives the more vibrantly and creatively the more you continue to live in its spirit and its soul.

3.

I remember long, long years ago when I used to yearn for this place as a ploughboy down there in Harnett County. Yes, I even then felt its pull and inspiration from afar. I determined early that someday I would come to school here. Way ahead of time I got a catalogue and studied it. Already I'd been able to get some scattering books and was enjoying and feeling the fire and fervor of the poets Wordsworth and Coleridge, Keats and Shelley, of singing Tom Hood and darkly lyrical Tom Moore. And from a peddler in Raleigh once I got a little nine-volume set of Shakespeare for fifty cents. And in the catalogue I read about the many courses given here, and my mouth watered. And I began to spread out a little bit and get hold of some philosophy—with the Republic of Plato, the ethics of Aristotle—all in preparation. You could order such books from Sears-Roebuck in those days. I read them but I couldn't understand much.

And there at the country school I attended a few months in the fall and winter I studied away as best I could, dreaming of the day when I might come up here. In the summer too when I worked on the farm I dreamed the same.

And often there as I ploughed or scattered compost with a pitchfork in the wide burning fields I could cool my soul and ease it a bit by quoting or even singing some of the beauties that I had been reading the night before and memorizing, taking a cue now and then maybe from the handwritten sweaty copies I carried in my pocket—

> "Now and I muse for why and never find the reason,
>     I pace the earth and drink the air and feel the sun.
> Be still, be still, my soul, it is but for a season.
>     Let us endure an hour and see injustice done."

This in my pathetic self-pity seemed especially to fit my case.

Many, many were the beautiful things I learned and said to myself as I worked. Though I didn't know the philosopher Schopenhauer at the time I already had proof of his theory of the healing power of art, of poetry—

> "There was a time when meadow, grove and stream,
>     The earth, and every common sight,
>         To me did seem
>     Appareled in celestial light,
> The glory and the freshness of a dream . . ."

\* \* \*

And sometimes I would get so full of emotion and inspiration, call it that, that the tears would gush out of my eyes and I would cry out toward the bending sky, yes, give a big shout, feeling I could fling a pitchfork full of manure straight toward the unseen stars above and even into the face of God himself, crying out, "You better dodge, sir! Here it comes."

\* \* \*

And sometimes I would make up poems myself, try to, ahead of the great day when I would come up here and learn the greater glowing wonders of poetry and how to make some that was good myself—

> "Look down to see the sun boil on my naked back,
> Repeat, repeat my heavy shoe, the selfsame track!
> And the dust swirls and chokes, the hot winds moan.
> Hear the riving rip, the tear of bone on bone.
> Have mercy, God, God, where mercy is due,
> So would I be merciful if I were God like you."

Well, like a bat with his antenna, you send out a call and you're likely to get response. But mine was a long time coming. And hope was mixed with disappointment.

Then there came a day when my wonderful teacher there at the little academy in Harnett County[1] put his arm around me and standing in the doorway and looking out of the old building toward the bowl of blue sky above said he had some good news for me. "I've got a scholarship for you," he said, naming a good denominational college. A tremor went through me. He grasped my hand and I held on a minute. "That'll fix you up," he went on, "and your father can provide the rest of the funds. This fellowship will pay your tuition."

I stood there and gulped and murmured to myself and then finally stumbled out the words, "But, 'Fessor, I don't want to go there."

"What!" he said incredulously.

"No sir," I said, "I want to go to the University at Chapel Hill."

"That place!" and he looked around at me. "Listen son, if you go there, you're likely to lose your religion." And then he gave me a good long kindly and fatherly lecture. He was a wonderful man, he loved the Bible, he believed it word for word. He believed that this life was a preparation for the next life. Tears were in his eyes. He loved his students and he had a care for me. I knew he did. And I loved him. That was one of the hardest struggles I ever went through in refusing his wonderful offer.

But somehow I stood stout as I could, and finally he realized that I was determined not to go to the college of his choice.

"Why do you want to go to the University?" he insisted dismally.

"Well, sir," I said, "from what I hear about it it sounds good to me. I hear they've got some wonderful teachers up there. One of them I've been reading about.[2] I saw the other day where he was being attacked in the newspapers for some of his modern beliefs."

"What's his name?" he said.

I told him, and he threw up his hands. "Oh, I've heard of that man. He's a controversial figure," and a groan broke from him. "Son, he'll cause you to lose your soul," he said. "I hear he's an infidel." And then he put his arm tighter around me and held me to his side, and he pointed through the door out to a field close by and said, "From the bottom of my heart, I'd rather see you taken out there in your coffin and buried in that ground than to go to the University of North Carolina and run the risk of burning in the fires of hell hereafter." I might say that this wonderful professor later changed his mind. He even invited me back to talk in chapel to his students.

1. Archibald Campbell, Baptist minister and founder of Buies Creek Academy (now Campbell University).

2. Horace Williams, professor of philosophy at the University of North Carolina, Chapel Hill.

I had to look around now and find some way of getting to the University. A fellow can always teach school, I heard someone say. So I did. I was about nineteen then and became the head of a four-teacher school at a nearby crossroads hamlet. My lady assistant who had been teaching fifteen years got forty dollars a month and the music teacher—yes, we had a music teacher even then, I insisted on that—she got twenty-seven dollars a month from her pupils when she could collect it. The primary teacher, a sweet patient-faced young woman, weak and tubercular, got twenty-five. I was paid fifty a month. But try as I could I couldn't save up enough money to get here. One of the reasons was that a foxy insurance agent riding in a yellow Buick car waylaid me in a weak moment and sold me a policy, the premium of which was too much for my saving. So I had to teach another year. My salary was raised to fifty-five dollars a month. I supplemented it a bit by pitching my heart out in the summer on the baseball mound here and there, picking up five dollars and ten, and once I got twenty-five dollars for pitching a game. The price so unnerved me that we were beat nine to one.

*   *   *

## 4.

Well, the Lord—or whatever stands for him—finally had mercy on me and I made it up here. And the struggle was on. But thanks to the generous heart of this great place I was able to stick. The student loan fund saved me along with the devotion of my father.

Some of my expectations were fulfilled in due season. Most of them were not. True, I got a lot of help from my professors, but I got most help, even then, from the Library. And as the days went by a strange thing happened. (Because I love this place so I'll be frank, and I know you'll be patient with me in what I have to say.) I found my teachers long on facts but short on inspiration for living. They were hard-working and clever and dedicated in the classrooms and laboratories and to their subjects but ignorant—now, that's an awful word to say—but ignorant and remiss on the matters of prime concern to me at that time, matters of the human spirit, of the soul, of the building of character in their students, or so it seemed to me. Very rarely, for instance, did I hear any talk about questions of right and wrong, or duty or compulsion, of responsibility, or cooperation among men, or generous attitudes toward different races and nations of mankind. Practically nothing about racial justice or the desperate need of the brotherhood of man in the breaking world—and the world was breaking even then—and the necessity of kindness in that world, yes, of kindness and good will as the prime necessity of the world, as one of the main ingredients in building and preserving a lasting civilization and controlling and containing the surges of hate and animosity that divided so many groups of human beings and continue to divide them today. As I say, I got lots of facts, millions of them. But when these facts finally reached me from the voluble lips or the steering laboratory hands of my teachers, most nearly, always nearly, the life had been wrung out of them and the inspiring power gone from them. They were much like pellets you feed to a dog but not nearly so nutritive.

There were some exceptions — and of course I got a lot more than I thought I did at the time — there were a few exceptions, I say, three or four. I wish I had time to pay my full respects to them. One I remember especially.[3] And what comes to me across the years today from him are the emotion, the infectious spirit of his teaching, the enthusiasm and love for what he was trying to share with us. And in the love he had for his subject I felt his love for me. Love, love. I can still see him as he would look out at his class, his squeaky voice all vibrant and his glasses sparkling with delight, as he read —

> "Our birth is but a sleep and a forgetting,
> The soul that riseth in us, our life's Star,
>    Hath had elsewhere its setting
>    And cometh from afar:
>    Not in entire forgetfulness,
>    And not in utter nakedness,
> But trailing clouds of glory do we come — "

And I would shiver with delight. I still do. I don't remember many of the facts he taught me, but I do still remember him and his enthusiasm.

And I remember another professor.[4] I can still see today that horse-trading craftiness which used to come into the eyes and the face of this man when he was getting ready his deadfall of the grave for some unsuspecting logic student. I can still see him over there in the old Alumni Building, standing up before his class and talking to us about truth as unity in structure difference and law as unity in action difference and praising the Hegelian triad. And often he would really shake us up, stir us up in what he called thinking.

I remember one morning he asked a young serious redheaded girl sitting on the front seat whether she believed in God. It was a shocking question. He was always doing this sort of thing. If I had been close enough to her I would have warned her to watch out, for that sanctimonious look had begun to come over his face. I had already had some experience with that look — a look very

---

3. James Holly Hanford, professor of English (see Green's letter to him later in this volume).

4. Williams.

much like the one that often comes over a deacon's face when he is breaking bread around the communion table.

"Yes sir, Professor," she said, "I do believe in God."

"You believe then that the deity's all-powerful?" he said in his quiet way.

"Yes sir," she answered, "for if he weren't all-powerful he wouldn't be — er — the deity."

"Good," said the Professor. "That's right. You believe he can do anything, then?"

"Yes sir, I do." She was a preacher's daughter and I later married her.

He turned to the window and broke a piece of chalk in his big square hands, and then turned back and in a gentle voice said, "Do you believe God can cook breakfast with a snowball?"

We all sat stunned in a hushed delight. We had never thought of that. Of course if God tried it, the snowball would melt. The young lady turned redder than her red hair with embarrassment.

I remember this professor not so much for his enthusiasm, say, for his subject, though he had quite a lot of that, but the vividness of his fables and his tricks and his sly way of exposing sham and hypocrisy in what he called "the big boys." And by the big boys he meant not only the politicians in the state, nation and world but heads of departments in the university here and especially the science professors. He had a standing quarrel with the scientists as some of you present here today remember. He never tired of poking fun at what he called the analyzing process. "When the scientist analyzes a cat to learn the nature of cat," he said, "the cat winds up dead. Poor cat."

This professor had little or no respect for facts. "Facts," he would say, "too often get in the way of truth."

And so by many of the forward-going teachers here he was considered to be not only a pain in the neck but a hindrance to the development of a good research program in the philosophy department.

This man made an impression on me all right, and an impression on many students. He is still a subject of gossip and conversation in this town. I later became a teacher in his department. And I tried to get him to let's spread out, get some money, get some books and journals for our philosophy students. We had sixty dollars a year then for our department's needs. And most of the time he turned an unspent balance back into the university treasury.

"Why do you want more books and journals?" he asked me.

"Well, Professor," I said. "We need them. You can't have a great university without a great library and you can't have a good department of philosophy without plenty of philosophy books for the students to have access to."

He looked at me and said, "Well, I'll tell you, the people have read so many books now they've got no sense."

He was exaggerating some, but you and I get the point.

### 5.

As I say, I found a lot of discouragement in studying with most of my professors. Their eyes were glued too much on the facts of life, and most of life itself seemed to be passing them by as they worked at their researching. They measured and described, they set down findings, they categorized, catechized, they cut up, they analyzed, they compared and put appraisals upon the process of life not as a miracle of creativeness and growth but as an object as it were to be measured and described under a microscope. And they not only did this to life but to art and literature — which is worse. In place of life and art and literature they thus substituted a method of derivation, giving forth matters of influence and style and types, whether of classic, romantic, realistic, naturalistic, expressionistic, symbolical, allegorical or what not, and on down to as many adjectival examples of labeling as they could dig out of their inkwells or typewriters, being therefore the more solid and scientific in their scholarship, they said.

\* \* \*

When the teachers forget their tokens and labels and signs and hierarchy of pigeon-holing and think of the works, the stories and plays and poems themselves, they find that they are part of the creative process of life and men in life, and as such they can enjoy them, draw from them, be enriched and refreshed through them. Their learned findings of influences and kinds and types only get in the way and are actually a hindrance. They get between the appreciator and the object of his appreciation — that is, a really felt appreciation. And they are deadly for the creative artist. In fact a creative artist can learn only from a preceding work of art or master if he thinks of the painting as painting and the painter or poet as a creative, kindred soul, a fellow technician working at a job, never giving a hang as to what school or movement he might belong to. And what is true of the creative apprentice is just as true if not truer of the student and critic. And if it is true of these why is it not also true for the teachers and schoolmen? For do we not all live by the same bread of life!

Let me continue this personal note a bit.

### 6.

I remember one lonely Sunday on the farm, when I was a boy. From the peddler I mentioned I had got a copy of Shakespeare's *Hamlet*. And with the family gone off to church and the house silent and empty, I read the drama. And as I read, I grew more interested and filled with suspense as to the people and their fate in the story. And emotion became more and more packed up in me. And finally I came to the scene where poor piteous Ophelia enters with brains broken and mind deranged, speaking her little mad and anguished sayings — "there's rue for you, and here's some for me. We may call it herb of grace o' Sundays. O, you must wear your rue with a difference. There's a daisy. I would give you some violets, but they withered all when my father died. They say he made a good end. (Singing.) " 'For bonny sweet Robin is all my joy.' " And the tears gushed from my eyes, my heart opened with a yearning deep and wide —

"O wert thou in the cauld blast,
    On yonder lea, on yonder lea,
My plaidie to the angry airt,
    I'd shelter thee, I'd shelter thee."

That day was a mark in my life. And because of that fresh, wild appreciation, untrammeled and unprepared for by any professional coaching as to influences and types and methods by which the play might have been derived to represent the Elizabethan age or something other than itself — because of that, *Hamlet* has stood solidly by me, a rich storehouse to draw from again and again through the years and has meant more to me than it otherwise could possibly have meant. And Ophelia has continued to live her sweet and piteous life in the chambers of my soul.

\* \* \*

My teachers, caught in a scientific dispensation, found it impossible to accept life as a miracle of creativeness and growth. They were conditioned to believe that anything smacking of a miracle was perforce somehow mystic, medieval, sentimental, vaguely subjective and therefore unsound, not stopping to consider that the process of raising the question even was itself miraculous. It was the old scholasticism back again, the business of practicing the heresies of abstract medieval authority, except in this case the evil of abstraction was intensified. For they made it of a lower scientific down-gazing earthly order, whereas in the old days of the wandering friar and hungry scurvy-bitten monk the gaze, however blinded, was upward and into a beneficent heaven.

I have concentrated somewhat pointedly on literature because I know more about that than, say, science. But I know the same sort of thing applied to our science teachers, to our workers in the laboratories and elsewhere. It is a common failing, I repeat, to look so closely at the facts as ordinary and commonplace phenomena that the wonder, the mystery and the surcharged glory of the facts, their mystic meaning and therefore inspiration, are lost.

*   *   *

7.

Now what has all this to do with the place and purpose of a university in a nuclear age? Everything.

8.

To me, teaching is the noblest of all professions. It is the highest honor and duty that can come to a citizen. And a university professor is at the top. To him more than to any other person in a nation is entrusted the welfare of our young and most vibrant, yes, most gifted people. His is the business of shaping human souls, shaping them toward creative self-fulfillment or not. And he works with them in their most dynamic, formative and dangerous years. Dangerous in that each one is brimful of potentialities — potentialities for success or failure. Compared to a university professor, a millionaire is poor pickings. And of course we professors pick the millionaires whenever we can. The business of the university and its teachers then is the making of men. There can be no greater enterprise than this. And by "men" here I mean free and creative men, men who because they are free and creative are responsible men and have a care and concern for the world. Men of good will then, if you would have it simply so.

And by "world" too I don't mean any special piece of earth or territory marked out with an ancient or modern name and bounded by certain rivers and mountains or other borders and set with its own nationalistic and separate flags, its army and air force, and all bristled up with Atlas missiles and atomic bombs tensioned and ready to blast not only some other nation but its ownself as a nation into annihilation and death. No, I mean mankind — the world of mankind, the human spirit world, the infinite, human world.

And of course in the shaping and building of creative men the university must have complete freedom to so shape and build. All knowledge is its province. All knowledge! There is nothing forbidden to the peering inquiry of its intelligence and the synthesizing power of the mind's summing up. The teacher like the artist must be free to look at the total world and draw his subject matter in from any area he pleases — outside or inside. Nothing is to be forbidden for study and inquiry, I say, by the free intelligence. For thus the intelligence grows strong, firm in itself, becomes a witness to the truth and an implacable opponent of error and evil. Only in face to face opposition to evil and ignorance can virtue and knowledge be strong. Plato puts it right in *The Symposium* to the effect that "Opposites illustrate each other's nature, and in their struggle draw forth the strength of the combatants and display the conqueror as sovereign even on the territories of the rival power." Struggle, that's it, each with the other, face to face and muscle with muscle opposition. For instance, how could a wrestler grow strong if put into the ring to wrestle with his own shadow and no more? And we all know of the famous Jefferson statement which says that — "Truth is the proper and sufficient antagonist to error, and has nothing to fear from the conflict, unless by human interposition disarmed of her natural weapons (which are) free argument and debate — errors ceasing to be dangerous when it is permitted freely to contradict them."

In freedom then and only in freedom can the thoroughly sound and creative man of fine intelligence and with the priceless gift of good will, be produced.

## 9.

Ladies and gentlemen, it is an appalling thing to think that in the short space of some thirty years in this present century — from 1914 to 1945 — more human blood has been senselessly spilled on this globe than in all the years of recorded history before. And we can add the billions of years when there was no history, for primitive man was few then and he had only crude and primitive means for committing killings and murder.

We older ones can remember back some decades when this was to be the century of hope for all — peace on earth and good will for man and booming business everywhere. So we taught our young folks to believe, for so we believed.

Yes, we thought then we were well done with war. Nations of men were no longer concerned with the barbarity of slaughtering one another on the battlefield. Ahead there waited the golden glorious years and days, and all our young people were blessed, thrice blessed in so bright and inviting a future. And we were blessed in them.

Then in 1914 the blow fell. An assassination in Serbia triggered it off. And from that day to now the world has heaved and quaked with the destructiveness of hate and death.

Why, why, we ask ourselves — and we do have to ask ourselves — why has this happened? What has brought man to this bitter state of affairs? What has caused it? Who is guilty? Who?

\* \* \*

Only man himself has done this to man. All psychiatry and Freud aside, man is guilty of this criminality against himself, and there is no other defendant in these lettings of blood. And why has man done this to himself? The answer is that in his journeying through life he has got his values all mixed up, has lost his true perspective, has lost sight of the virtues that denote him man and has substituted the false values of force, of power, of material gain and the like for the true and proper constituents that make human life worth living. Of course he never has had a full and proper devotion to these values. But in these recent decades he has had even less than before. And so with his new technologies his powers for death have been multiplied. And I hasten to add, his powers for life also. But he has not used them for life. Again why?

In this century man, especially western man, has become absorbed in the dramatic adventure of studying matter, of interpreting matter, of finding ways to make it behave to his will, to manipulate it into all sorts of strange and wondrous devices, finally resulting in this incredibly exciting age of what for a better word we call technology. He has invented the great computer, the electronic microscope, he has invented a process of radio astronomy, has created the satellite, discovered atomic power, and is now busy on the verge of discovering the nature of life itself, and someday he will be able to create this life in the laboratory. He is searching out the nature of strange diseases and finding their cure. He is indeed in the full fervor of participating in the inside drama of nature — nature at work in her own will and nature behaving to his superior will.

And yet with all these wonders coming out of the laboratories, coming out of the university trained minds, with all these wonders of communication and transportation, with all these means at hand to eradicate poverty on earth and to conquer most of its physical and terrifying evils, we find this piteous earth convulsed in pain. Thus for all his scientific creativity and partly because of it man has brought more suffering and death and waste into the world in this century than in all other ages combined.

Even at this moment as I talk there hangs over this earth the threat of the total annihilation of the human race. Man the final suicidist! And this power, this nuclear power, which is now compressed in enough bombs to destroy every living thing on the planet, this power cocked for death has in it the potentiality to make this world into a smiling fruitful and beauteous garden. Which will it be? There should be no question. But there is. And in this fact of our uncertain and confused human will is human self-horror enough.

Where is the guilt? Where? Speak up. Is the Pentagon guilty? Yes. Is the Kremlin? Of course. Is the church? Oh, yes. Business and commerce? Yes, yes. All, all of us are guilty.

But isn't it just possible that of all who have failed in their vision and their responsibility for civilization and the happiness of humanity — isn't it possible that we teachers are the most responsible of all? It is a sobering thought. And now that barbarism threatens to engulf the globe, what is our complicity in it?

∗   ∗   ∗

To come straight to one mark—we teachers have fallen into the error of teaching men to deal with matter at the expense of, say, the wisdom of the humanities. There has been too much training in how to manipulate matter and make it behave and too little in the enlargement of the students' minds and hearts so that this control of that matter might be used for the betterment of mankind and not to work mankind woe—too little training for citizenship in one world, the world of man and his spirit and not the world of things. We have placed too much emphasis on teaching skills and not teaching truth. Of course there is at present a rush into practical science which carries its own cooperativeness for universal procedures, but we'll have to watch out on that.

I think we have fallen into the error of letting our students go away from the universities believing in the over-simplified concept that knowledge or rather information makes for power and more positive living. The power complex as we now know to our sorrow is a dangerous thing. To repeat, the student should be taught, should be infected with the conviction and certainty that there are many things the purpose of which is mainly the enrichment and the illumination of the human personality—true wisdom, art, theoretical science, friendship, affectionate relations, and so on—in short a strong feeling for the old virtues of truth, goodness and beauty whatever their various guises and modern dress. And to repeat, the very heart of all of these is good will. If the students are allowed to graduate from a university without having a concern for humanity at large as well as individually, without having any feeling of world responsibility, without good will, then they have missed the most precious blessing of all.

∗   ∗   ∗

4 FEB '00
F-8

# To James Holly Hanford on the Development

# of North Carolina

James Holly Hanford (1882–1969), before taking a position in the English department at Western Reserve University, taught at the University of North Carolina at Chapel Hill (1914–21), where Green took his course in Romantic poetry (focusing on Wordsworth). In "The University in a Nuclear Age" Green remembers Hanford as among the handful of inspiring teachers he had during his student days. Shortly before the present letter, Hanford had written to Green that he was "writing an autobiographical chapter on my experience at Chapel Hill," and that instead of reminiscing he wanted "to try to say what in essence was happening culturally there and why." He asked for Green's help with a series of questions, beginning, "Why did the University and the State take a sudden leap forward in about 1912–18 or did [they]?" (8 December 1946, PG-SHC.)

[Greenwood Road, Chapel Hill, N.C.]
10 January 1947
Dear Dr. Hanford:

I am delighted that you are putting down some of the happenings of your own life, and I know others will be. You have had a rich experience, and your sharing it in published form will enrich many additional lives — thus your teaching goes on and on.

You have asked me some questions I am afraid I can't answer — Why did the University and the state here take a sudden leap forward about 1912–18, by what reason and what agency were certain men such as Dr. Greenlaw, Dr. Branson (and yourself certainly) brought to Chapel Hill, etc., etc.?[1]

Accounting for any phenomenon of culture or of sterility among a people or any section is almost a matter of metaphysics or perhaps meteorology — I

1. Edwin Greenlaw, a historical scholar of the kind Green attacks in "The University in a Nuclear Age," came to the University of North Carolina at Chapel Hill as chairman of the English department in 1914. He hired Hanford along with numerous others in a great rebuilding of the departmental faculty, helped found the University of North Carolina Press, and played a large role in numerous other university developments. Sociologist Eugene C. Branson also came to the University of North Carolina at Chapel Hill in 1914 and pioneered the study of rural economic and social problems.

don't know. What I am going to say below may not make much sense, but if you don't mind I'll ramble on a bit in my inclination and urge to make some reply to the challenging queries you have sent.

Some two or three weeks ago I was talking to the Governor of Virginia.[2] He happens to be interested in a dramatic project which I now have in the making at Williamsburg. During the course of our talk he spoke out with quite some vehemence. "North Carolina is a great state," he said. "If I could only help to wake Virginia up, get her stirring, moving forward the way your state is moving, I would feel I'd done a job of absolute value to my fellow citizens."

"But if North Carolina is on the move now," I replied, "she was long fast asleep while Virginia and South Carolina on either side of her carried the strong bit of leadership far and wide. I need only to start calling the roll — way back — Washington, Jefferson, the Randolphs, the Lees, Richard Bland,[3] the Blairs,[4] the Nelsons,[5] the Pages,[6] the Tylers,[7] the Harrisons[8] and" —

"I know, I know," he said, "but they're all dead. What I'm talking about is the present and especially the future. Look at your University down there — your sociological work under Odum.[9] Your fine University Press. Your dramatic work. Your extension projects. Your great manufacturers — the Haines,[10] Grays,[11] Reynolds, Duke University, your recent movement in good health,

2. Colgate W. Darden Jr., at a meeting about *The Common Glory*, an outdoor historical play by Green that would open in Williamsburg, Virginia, in 1947 (Green diary, 14 December 1946, PG-SHC).

3. Colonial leader and author of the earliest statement against British taxation (*Inquiry into the Rights of the British Colonies* [1766]).

4. James Blair founded the College of William and Mary in 1693 and served as its president until he died in 1743. Francis Preston Blair, a journalist in Richmond, was prominent in national politics from the Jacksonian era until his death in 1876.

5. Influential family during the revolutionary era. Thomas Nelson, member of the Virginia House of Burgesses and the Continental Congress and signer of the Declaration of Independence, commanded the Virginia militia during the American Revolution and became governor in 1781.

6. John Page succeeded Thomas Nelson as governor. Thomas Jefferson Page, a naval explorer in Paraguay prior to the Civil War, served in the Confederate navy.

7. Family of the tenth president.

8. Family of a signer of the Declaration of Independence (Benjamin Harrison), the ninth president (William Henry Harrison), and the twenty-third president (Benjamin Harrison, grandson of William Henry, although born in Ohio).

9. Howard Odum, an influential scholar who came to the University of North Carolina at Chapel Hill in 1920 and, as an outgrowth of his study of rural sociology, founded the Institute for Research in the Social Sciences.

10. That is, Hanes, textile manufacturers in Winston-Salem.

11. Prominent in the R. J. Reynolds Tobacco Company in Winston-Salem.

your schools, your hospitals, your fine race relationship, and the flood of creative writing that is being done at Chapel Hill for instance—think of that. Dozens and dozens of books are coming out of that little village. Almost yearly. Charlottesville where our University is situated is many times as large as Chapel Hill, and yet a book rarely comes from there and when it does it is likely not to have the bite of life's teeth in it"—I'm giving him the figure of speech here. And so on, so on he went. "I could keep calling the roll. You see, I'm talking in the present and looking to the future in reference to your state's accomplishments, and you and I in speaking of Virginia have to do it in the past tense."

Well, anyway, as I told the governor, I can see that Virginia is now beginning to stir, and I prophecy great things for her people.

I believe that about the time you refer to there began to be a gathering of enthusiasm, inspiration, creative scholarship and creative living together in Chapel Hill. To be able to say why is, to repeat, a different matter. It is the custom these days to derive matters by way of historical description—a custom which of course is old and hallowed enough to be just that. Deep down I believe in constant and ever appearing newness, and in any description of causality as well as in the causal process itself, there is always an X either of form or substance which appears fresh[,] new[,] and cannot be accounted for. This X perhaps is essential to and one with the nature of the mind's awareness. Whatever it is, I believe it is, has been and will continue to be. So with this reservation I will continue.

The restless bodies and spirits of the various people who settled this country of ours moved mainly through the medium of ships on water to get here. It happened that Virginia on the north of this Tar Heel commonwealth had deep and easily traveled rivers penetrating up into the heart of the seaboard to the very edge of the Blue Ridge Mountains—such as the Potomac, the York, the James. South Carolina, below us, likewise had the same sort of advantage in the Ashley and the Cooper. So accordingly the tide of moving men and trade entered at two deep seaport places. Norfolk was built and even in the time of the Revolution was a flourishing town of five or six thousand people. Charleston grew up to be a leading metropolis in the colonies. Up the James at the falls, Richmond was built. Halfway between Norfolk and Richmond the cultured little center of Williamsburg grew—here where the early bill of rights and many a document and deed for freedom was made manifest.

Now drawn like a barrier—and it was that—across the eastern seaboard of North Carolina was a stretch of treacherous sandbars and shallow inlets, complicated with the raging and diabolical weather of Cape Hatteras. So a tradition of talent and leadership grew up on either side of us. Virginia and South

Carolina furnished ten important men to the early history of our country to every one North Carolina furnished. And even as late as the Civil War most of our Confederate generals came out of those two states and North Carolina furnished more private soldiers than any other southern state. In fact for generations North Carolina was a sort of hewer of wood and drawer of water commonwealth compared to her swiftly risen aristocratic neighbors north and south. When I was a little boy I heard the old description of Tar Heelia — "A valley of humiliation between two mountains of conceit." I remember with what admiration, awe and twinges of envy I would hear stories of the great plantation houses along the James and Potomac and along the Ashley and Cooper rivers. There were few if any of this sort in North Carolina. My grandfather, John Green, was pretty typical of the yeoman North Carolinian — his grandfather came down out of Virginia in the early 18th century as thousands of others did. In fact North Carolina, I would guess, was settled in great part by indentured servants who had run away, by restless almost criminal young sons, by proguing hunters and now and then a wagon train of religious emigrants — infiltrating, wandering and pouring in overland from either side — and not from the ocean, since the sandbars mentioned shut the door in the face of ships of any size. (I recall now that the failure of the Lost Colony was attributable mainly to the fact that the treachery of the Carolina seacoast made it almost impossible to supply the settlers from ships. And Sir Walter Raleigh himself gave John White and Ananias Dare instructions that they should only come by Roanoke Island, pick up some men who had been left there by Sir Richard Grenville and go up further north and make their settlement on the deep waters of the Chesapeake. They ignored Sir Walter's orders, and so we know that group as the Lost Colony.)

I am being a little emphatic when I say that North Carolina was, up until nearly the end of the 19th century, rather much of a lost colony herself. But things get grown, institutions demand their submissives, and the eager forward spirit gets slowed down by the objects of its own creativity, and finally there comes a day when even the look of Robin Hood himself "turns again homeward." [12]

So did it happen with Virginia and South Carolina. In time a second-hand quality began to pervade their constituency. The fathers were greater than the sons and the grandfathers greater still and so over the meridian mark the process went and life began to get into reverse. (As I say, I am emphasizing a little heavily to brad the point.)

As you see, North Carolina has no such history of pride and attainment to

12. Echo of Alfred Tennyson, "Crossing the Bar," line 8.

look back to. She was a poor white state so long that all of her yearning, her urges, such as they were, were towards the future. So you might expect that if she ever did get started, she would be like a self-made man on the make—she would really go to town with a vengeance. And every inch of accomplishment was a hundred per cent on the plus side and was that much, generally speaking, an advance over his immediately preceding progenitor.

You know something of the story of the Dukes[13]—how old Wash Duke as a bare-footed married man twisted up his home-made tobacco and sold it to the occupying Federal troops around Durham.[14] I don't say that this was the beginning of North Carolina's development, for the seeds of progress, the thistledown from the wings of high-flying ideals were in the air, but I think it illustrates my point. Here was old Wash Duke face to face with the miracle that the superior Yankees wanted something he had. The miracle that his handiwork was good enough for them to pay good money for. So he got busy with that bit of esthetic and economical stimulation. He did some mail order business with these Yankees after they had returned to Ohio, Indiana, Illinois or wherever they went. He got his son Buck working with him at the grinder, chopping up the leaves of tobacco into Duke's Mixture.[15] And so he got started. It wasn't long until he got stallion-proud in his mind and one of his co-workers developed the trademark of Bull Durham, the he creature, the mighty symbol of virility and invigoration.[16] (Of course the phrase "the worm will turn" is a good way to account for the phenomenon of this state's waking up. But that takes care of itself.)

13. Tobacco family in Durham, North Carolina, headed by Washington Duke (1820–1905), then by his youngest son James Buchanan Duke (1856–1925).

14. When Lee surrendered to Grant at Appomattox, Virginia, on 9 April 1865, large Confederate and Union armies were still in the field. Gen. William T. Sherman, with 50,000 troops in Raleigh, was opposed by a Confederate army of 30,000 under Gen. Joseph E. Johnson, forty miles west in Hillsborough, and it was not until 26 April that they arrived at terms of surrender. Their conferences were held midway between Raleigh and Hillsborough, at the Bennett farmhouse near Durham. Following Lee's surrender, Washington Duke, Confederate artilleryman, walked home from New Bern, North Carolina, where he was released, and on his farm north of Durham found nothing to support his family (his wife was dead) but a barn full of tobacco. With the help of his sons he shredded and sacked the tobacco, labeled the sacks "Pro Bono Publico," loaded them in a wagon drawn by two blind mules, and began peddling his ware among the federal troops and others in the area (William K. Boyd, *Story of Durham* [Durham: Duke University Press, 1925], chaps. 3, 5).

15. Later name for Pro Bono Publico.

16. John R. Green (not a close relative of Paul) owned Bull Durham, the most famous and best-selling tobacco in the post–Civil War decades, with its trademark, the picture of a bull. He was a coworker with Duke only in the sense that they were both in the tobacco business. In fact, they were bitter rivals (Boyd, *Story of Durham*, chaps. 4–5).

Washington Duke, his son Buck, began to make good, and the American Tobacco Company came a-borning.[17] Where two men come to accomplishment, you will likely find a third or a fourth or a fifth attracted in that direction even if they have stopped in the bushes to reconnoiter. So we had other men who began to dream the economic dream in textiles, lumber, mines.

Pushing back the enemy on one front emboldens others to attack him in still other places. The stimulation appeared in the field of public education and in politics. The liberation of knowledge was heard of as a fact — but mainly in terms of economic liberation. The more education you have, said the speakers, the more earning power in dollars and cents will be yours. Once started, acceleration was sure. Charles Brantley Aycock stumped the state speaking about the power of books — reading, writing, arithmetic, the Bible, Geography — and down with illiteracy. In the early years of the present century he was our governor[18] and one of our best. He was the "education governor" — perhaps our first, if we exclude Governor Jarvis[19] who was somewhat imbued with the philosophy of learning but lacked the dynamism and selling power of Aycock. There were other men who talked the same language. Walter Hines Page,[20] later ambassador to the Court of St. James, Professor McKiver, at Greensboro,[21] and numerous county superintendents of public instruction took up the chorus of their leaders. We had a movement known as moonlight schools in which the hard effort was made to wipe out illiteracy among the whites, young and old, in North Carolina. (Again a phrase like "the time was ripe" could be invoked to explain a lot of things. But that will take care of itself too.)

The carpetbaggers, poor forlorn and misguided zealots, had been rebuffed finally before the terrible undertaking they found here in the south, and the last of them had long ago gone home.[22] But some of the echoes of their teachings, some of the books they had left behind had done a little bit of leaven-

17. In 1890, when Duke and Sons absorbed four of its rivals in Durham and reorganized under James B. Duke's leadership. In 1898 the American Tobacco Company also acquired Bull Durham from Green's successors (ibid., chap. 5).

18. 1901–5.

19. Thomas J. Jarvis, governor, 1879–85.

20. Journalist in Raleigh in the 1870s, then in New York and Boston (*Atlantic Monthly*, 1895–98), partner in Doubleday, Page publishing company from 1899 to 1913, and Wilson's ambassador to Great Britain, 1913–18.

21. Charles Duncan McIver, who persuaded the legislature to establish the first state college for women in 1891 in Greensboro, over which he presided from 1891 to 1906.

22. Albion Tourgée, best known and most influential of the carpetbaggers, left North Carolina for New York in 1878, after thirteen years in the state.

ing work among the people. Anyway there was the sense of their impress upon us — even as most of us deplored and hated them and their memory. Also the presence of Yankee soldiers up and down the length of the state, drawn from all strata and places of the Union — they too had made some mark upon us. Also, for some reason or another, a few "foreign" teachers from the north, a graduate here and there from Harvard or Yale or Princeton, had happened into the faculties of our state university and colleges. Also I think the rise of Woodrow Wilson, a North Carolinian by residence and friendship, even though Virginia-born, helped the state towards a feeling of pride in his scholarship and the place of education in public life.[23] It may be worth noting that the University of North Carolina was the proud host to him as commencement speaker in 1912.[24]

Whatever currents, connotations, facts, tendencies, were in the air, there were enough for a sensitive man to get their impact. Such a man was Edward Kidder Graham. As president of the University of North Carolina[25] he became a man afire with a zeal for service, for true progress, for scholarship, for enlightenment, in short for true civilization. He, I think, represented the sensitive and feeling fingertips of the state. And not only was he all fingertips, he was also the strong, reaching, grasping, friendly and encouraging hand.

And he was not alone, of course. There were other sensitive young men who could hear the song on the wind with ever so slight a cocking of the ear — men like L. R. Wilson[26] — he especially, Roulhac Hamilton,[27] E. C. Branson (who was sent, called for, and got by these eager men),[28] Edwin Greenlaw, yourself,

23. Born in Staunton, Virginia, Wilson attended Davidson College in North Carolina (1873–74), and his family then resided for a year in Wilmington (1874–75).

24. 1911.

25. From 1913 until his death in 1918.

26. While heading the University of North Carolina at Chapel Hill Library (1902–32), Louis Round Wilson with Edwin Greenlaw established the University of North Carolina Press, becoming its first director (1922–32), and then spearheaded the creation of the School of Library Science and was its first dean (1931–32). In 1932 Wilson went to the University of Chicago to develop a school of library science, then returned to the University of North Carolina at Chapel Hill in 1941.

27. University of North Carolina at Chapel Hill historian (1906–45) and indefatigable collector of unpublished papers and records throughout the southeast, Hamilton founded the Southern Historical Collection (manuscript department of the University of North Carolina at Chapel Hill library), and directed it from 1930 to 1945.

28. In 1913 Branson, from the Georgia State Teachers College in Athens, spoke to a conference in Chapel Hill on the problems of rural life and on his efforts to study and improve rural economic and social conditions. The speech so impressed leaders at Chapel Hill that President Graham, in his zeal to "carry the University to the State," brought Branson to the

Dr. Hanford — one of the best of them all — (I make my bow with thankfulness!), Norman Förster,[29] Marvin Stacy,[30] Addison Hibbard[31] and so on and so on — and not forgetting Frederick H. Koch, one of the most message-carrying of stimulators.[32]

And so as in the active yearning sky, when after a long drought a feel of rain comes in the air, a yeastiness, a gathering of intensity, of mood and sultriness, until finally there is a whiff of a cloudlet and then others and then a combining of these cloudlets into one bigger, blacker, and procreant one, then a flash of lightning, then finally the coming of the enriching, pouring rain — somewhat like this was the gathering of the creative actuality here at Chapel Hill. In terms of weather, the rain is continuing, and the thirsty crops are not satisfied. Even now as I write these words there are some hundred books underway here in Chapel Hill — ranging from volumes of stories through plays, novels to huge humanitarian and sociological tomes. And on other fronts the endeavor is mightily continuing — in dramatic productions, in the University Press, in the extension work, library science, business foundation, medicine, etc., etc.

But alas, I am afraid I glimpse yonder in the distance the breaking of the cloud and a sign of dry weather to return. I hope to God I am mistaken. But our educational leadership seems to me to be weakening here. To change the figure — Watch a flock of birds flying across the land, say they are blackbirds, bluebirds, or robins — whatever they are, they follow and swerve and tend rhythmically after their leader. I have seen flocks of birds mill around in the sky — just milling, energized but in frantic indecision. I hope our faculty flock resembles the first figure and not the last. But as I say, I am apprehensive.

To repeat, you have done your part in helping this "cultural" phenome-

---

University of North Carolina at Chapel Hill as head of the new Department of Rural Social Economics (Louis Round Wilson, *University of North Carolina, 1900–1930: The Making of a Modern University* [Chapel Hill: University of North Carolina Press, 1957], pp. 207, 219).

29. Member of the English department (1914–30), stimulating teacher, and leading Neo-humanist, Förster helped establish the study of American literature with a series of books beginning with *Nature in American Literature* (1923).

30. Originally a professor in the mathematics and engineering department, Stacy was chairman of the faculty (1910–19) and acting president of the university (1918–19) following Graham's death.

31. A member of the English department (1919–30), Hibbard pioneered the study of southern literature and coauthored the influential *Handbook to Literature* (1936) with W. F. Thrall.

32. Koch came to the University of North Carolina at Chapel Hill from the University of North Dakota in 1918 and immediately set about developing the Carolina Playmakers to encourage the writing and production of original plays. It was through Koch and the Playmakers that Green got his start in the theater.

non to be actualized here, and I always look back to the days you used to read Bobby Burns and Wordsworth to us. And I look back with the same sort of thankfulness too to that day when you took me aside on your front porch down on Cobb Terrace and gave me a bawling out for triflingness.

With affectionate greetings,[33]

Among the clippings Harpers sent me about my recent little volume of stories, *Salvation on a String*, was yours. It was very fine and flattering and I thank you.[34]

33. Hanford thanked Green "for the interpretation of the flowering period of Chapel Hill which you so generously wrote out for me" ([1947], PG-SHC) but did not publish an autobiography.

34. "A Master Spins Yarns from Folklore," *Cleveland News*, 5 October 1946.

# Paul Green's Wordbook
## *An Alphabet of Reminiscence*

 4 Feb '00

(From the letter R)

*right down*

Used for emphasis. "It made me right down mad to hear him talk
like that."

*right-hand man*

A dependable person, a trusted one.

*right much*

Very much, used for emphasis. "Aunt Sarah is right much better, I hear."

*right off the bat*

Quickly, at once, unthoughtedly.

*right smart*

Much, a considerable amount. "We had a right smart turnout at the
Legion meeting last night."

*riled (roiled)*

Stirred up, made angry, rubbed the wrong way.

*rinctum-do*

A breakdown, a loud party, a celebration.

*ring-around*

A tetter, a breaking out. There are all sorts of cures for this. One I
remember was to rub the ring-around with the juice of a green walnut hull.

*ring around the moon*

A weather omen. This means that rain is coming soon. We children used to
be told that if there were any stars in the ring, the number of stars would
denote the number of days before the rain or changed weather
would come.

*Ring Around the Rosie*

A children's game. The players form a circle holding one another's hands
as they march around a child, or "It," in the center, singing —

"Ring around the Rosie,
Pocket full of posies
One, two, three — squat!"

The last child to squat or stoop then takes the place of "Rosie" or "It" in
the circle. We used to sometimes sing it —

"Ring around the Rosies
Pocket full of posies,
Green grass, yellow grass,
All fall down."

ringer

A horseshoe that rings or hugs around the pin in the game of horseshoes, also an athletic spy.

ring leader

The principal leader, the boss, usually used derogatively.

ring-tailed

An outlandish person or thing, often as a "ring-tailed snorter." A term of disparagement.

ring-tailed roarer

A brawler, a loud-mouthed braggart.

ring the bell

Hit the mark, succeed well, bring one's purpose to a conclusion.

ringworm

Same as ring-around.

rinky-dinky

Puerile, childish, dull. "My freshman English course at Duke is rinky-dinky, and I'm bored to death."

riot

A whale of a gathering, a turmoiling happy time. "Mrs. Johnson's party was a riot."

rip

A reprobate, usually as "old rip."

a rip

A whore.

rip and tear

To act boisterously. Also a fighting fracas.

rip-off

A cheating procedure. "A lot of this burial insurance sold to Negroes is just a rip-off."

rip-tail snorter

A terrific happening, person or thing. "Zack Broadhuss was a rip-tail snorter." "That storm was a rip-tail snorter."

rise

A flood or freshet. "There's such a rise in the river the flat won't run."
*Rise*, take up thy bed and walk.
The higher the *rise* the greater the fall.

*rise and shine*

To get up in a hurry and move energetically to begin the day's work.

He is not here for He is *risen*.

*a rising*

A boil, a carbuncle.

*ritzy*

Highfalutin, fashionable, putting on airs.

*Do as they do over on the river.*

A sort of living up to the Joneses.

Let us pass over the *river* and rest under the shade of the tree.

A noisy *river* never drowned nobody.

All the *rivers* run into the sea and yet the sea is not full.

*riz*

Rose, past tense of rise.

*roach*

To mound up, as to roach up a grave.

*roaches of the liver*

Cirrhosis of the liver, a drying-up and hardening of that organ, usually attributed to continued overuse of alcohol.

Nello, who shined shoes in the local barbershop and was a long-time friend of mine, was afflicted with this trouble. One day when I went to the shop, he was absent, as he often was. To my inquiry the barber gave quite a voluble and answering discourse.

"What'll it be, Doc?" he first asked, as I stopped by the clothes rack. He gave his barber cloth a few wide popping flaps in the air and held it waiting. I took off my coat, loosened my tie and shirt collar and sat down in the waiting, restful chair.

"A shave and a face massage," I said.

"Right, right as rain," he said. "Make you feel better."

He lowered the chair flat back and spread the cloth over me and began tucking it in and around my neck. I lay looking up at the heavy fluorescent light fixture hanging directly and threateningly above. Heavy, yes! He began stropping his razor.

"A shine too," I said.

"Hey, boy! A shine over here!" he called. He snapped on the lather mixer. I lay relaxed. It whirred. I closed my eyes. Already I felt better. Now he slip-slopped creamy soap foam on my cheeks and chin. He began to rub pressingly.

Outside on the sidewalk the tapping of women's heels went along. I heard it, visualized a bit, and caught the passing mixture of young people's voices —

Easter shoppers, elated, expectant, generous. Christ is risen — the fish are biting!

Now came hot towels and more soap foam. This was good. A bit of more razor-stropping. And then the shaving began. Suddenly a strong hand lifted my foot and put it up on the shine last. I looked out on the incline to speak to Nello as usual, but there sat a stranger, an intense square-cut wide-nostriled young mulatto face, not Nello at all with his wild razor scars and his shifting restless yellow-balled eyes — Nello, friend to me and my shoes these long times gone.

"You've got a new man," I finally said to the barber.

"Yeah, yeah, Doc, we have."

"How's Nello getting along?" I asked.

He shaved on a while and the strong new hands applied polish on my shoes. I was being well looked after, top and bottom. Good.

"Yes," the barber said presently, and I felt him wipe the razor across the swatch of paper-roll across my breast. "His name's Early. Say, Early, fix 'fessor's shoes up right, boy. Fix 'em up." He spoke with good and soul-breezy authority.

He concentrated on his job. The left side of the face now that the right was done, and then the upper lip, carefully — tiny, furtive scrapings and on into the corners of the mouth. Next under the jowls and the chin, and then slip and up under the lower lip. Again the razor was wiped.

"How's Nello getting on now?" I asked, breathing a bit more freely. No answer. "Turn Doctor's pants up, boy, or you'll get that blacking on 'em," the barber said to Early.

"Yessuh," said Early quickly. I felt him fumble about my ankle. Next he was finishing with the paste on this shoe and was polishing away, now and then trying to make his shine cloth pop, but without success. Not the way Nello could do it. Nello could make the train sound of old Ninety-seven coming around the bend — whoo-whoo, he could really play his railroad tune with that cloth.

Then a dampening soft palm-smearing with warm water on my face and a quick second going-over with the razor. Next, three hot towels in succession and the massaging cream — long squeezing palm strokes, half-brutal, half-caressing.

"You been working hard, Doc?" the barber said.

"Oh, so-so."

"Writing more plays?" And again his laugh shattered the air. I wondered some — but not much.

"Well, trying, I guess," I mumbled.

"Soon be time to open up your outdoor dramas again, won't it?"

"Yeah. Time goes by in a hurry."

"Don't it? The older you get the faster it goes. Getting so now seem like I can hear the Sunday papers falling in front of my gate one 'pon top of the other." Again he laughed and I could feel him looking about the barbershop to his fellows with his merry bright blue eyes.

"Yes, and don't the birthdays come fast?"

Rub, rub, rub. "They do." Silence—rub, rub. "Yeh, Nello won't be with us any more," he finally spoke up, quietly, coldly even, without interest, a simple reply to a question remembered.

"Too bad," I said, thinking of the long absences in the past when Nello was away on the chaingang serving time for drunkenness, for fighting. Poor Nello!

"I guess you finally got wore out with him," I said.

The barber pushed down and roiled up the drying cream, cleaning out the dirty and oily pores.

"This is a new kind of cream—really does the work," he said.

"Up—oom—no doubt," I mumbled.

"He was good at shining shoes what time he was sober—Nello, I mean. That's why we kept him on," he said.

"Yeah, he was a good sort of fellow all the same."

"He was and he wasn't. Never could tell what was on his mind. Never talked much."

"Not much," I said. "I noticed that."

And I lay remembering the hard crisp calls of the different barbers in the shop—"Hey, boy, shine 'em up here. Brush here, boy. Make it snappy. Can't wait all day"—these calls and orders of times past. And I could see Nello's flying hands, his quick movements, his extended palm for the coin, the whisk-broom under his arm, his bows, his mask-like scarred face, the yellow-balled eyes—the deep brown pupils that looked at you and didn't look at you— the deep brown pupils smoky and, yes, sightless in their seeing—or what did they see?

"He was mean when he got full of that old wine," said the barber, now brushing away the dirty crumbs of cream from my face.

"Is he back on the roads again?"

"He may be for all I know," and he laughed his shattering laugh once more. "Yeh, if they've got a chaingang in yonder world."

A tremor went through me. "Why? What's happened to Nello?"

The easing hot towel again now and then another.

"Too hot?"

"Noo-unh."

"Just right?"

"Uhm—yes."

The towel was lifted now, and next began the slow, long, seductive rubbing, not rough now, not at all, but soothing, sweet, almost like a woman's tender loving. But something—a worry. Nello—my bruised and lost and wordless friend. Nello.

"You ain't been in lately," the barber queried and announced half-accusingly.

"No, I've been staying in sort of close at home."

"Working at your plays?"

"Some."

"You hadn't heard 'bout Nello? He conked out—croaked, I mean."

"What?"

"Yeh, up and died last week."

"Good gracious!" I half sat up as if that would help, then lay back again.

"Had it coming to him, I reckon," the barber said.

"How you mean?"

"That old wine and stuff. Runs 'em crazy, burns up their liver. Want some witch hazel, 'Fessor?"

"Yes, oh yes. Anything."

"Mighty good for the tender face. And you're sort of tender down around your Adam's apple."

Next the stinging cool and scented lotion. "Been scraping yourself kind of close down there, ain't you?"

"Yeah, but Nello—"

"Gone."

"Goodness! He was a young fellow."

"Brush here, boy," called another barber down the line. Early laid my foot up finished and sprang away. Now came the cool dry final towel, smelling of the heat of the laundry, like the sheets my mother used to dry on chairs before the wood fire on rainy days long ago.

"It was roaches of the liver got him," said my barber. "He was plumb et up with it. Didn't know it either. Worked right up to the last. He come in here to work a-Wednesday morning and he was dead Thursday, the next day. Some of the fellows said to him, 'Nello, you're moving mighty slow today'—that was Wednesday—'Nello, make it snappy,' we would tell him. And old Nello would mumble something 'bout not feeling so good. 'Reckon I ort to see a doctor,' he said long about quitting time."

"That old wine," said Joe, the barber at the right.

"Roaches of the liver—yeh. My granddaddy went like that. The doctor said his liver was about the size of a trabball[1] and hard as a hickory nut."

"Yeh," said my barber, "it'll kill you—booze will. Powder, 'Fessor?"

"No—yes, powder, a little."

Then the dab, dab, pat, pat of the end-folded towel. Sweet stuff. Mennen's.

The barber slammed his foot on the chair pedal and swung me up sitting. His hands wriggled and dug into my scalp. "Your hair's mighty dry, Doc. Some lanolin? Make you feel better."

"All right."

"Good for the scalp. Seems Nello got home and went to bed Wednesday. Then the doctor come—Doctor Abernathy it was. He examined him and saw he was already half-dead. 'I got to get you to Memorial Hospital,' he said. And he left him. Sure puts a shine on your hair, this sheep's grease does."

"Did they get him to the hospital?"

"Well, yes—the next day—Thursday."

And all night Nello lying in his ragged bed, looking at what, thinking of what? He never would talk much. Now the barbers are stropping their razors, winking and jibing—Been with that old wine again, eh, Nello? Ninety days again. Now the bark of the convict boss,—Lift up that pick—heigh you—swing on it—roll that Georgia buggy, boy—tell the news—make your time—make it sweet and low.

"The next day Doc come, as I say," said the barber. "Thursday morning. They go in to wake Nello and no waking." Again I felt the brush, brush, the comb, comb, and brush, brush again. "Your hair is standing up in a sort of cowlick here, 'Fessor, where you been sleeping on it. I'll get it down in a minute. He was already in a coma—lying there, his sister said, scarcely breathing at all. They started with him in the ambulance. Yeah, in a stooper he was and he was dead when they got to the ambulance entrance at the hospital. Well, there you are, Doc."

The cloth was unpinned, a bit of air-hosing inside my collar followed, and I stepped from the chair. I tied my tie, and Early helped me on with my coat and brushed me industriously off. I paid my barber and I gave Early a little extra.

"Feel better, Doc?" said the barber as he crashed the cash register open.

"Yeah, better!"—I almost shouted the words, then I softened them down as I saw his eyes flare. "You've fixed me up fine."

1. "A homemade ball, out of ravelled old stockings. We used to wind the string around a center wad until we had a ball about the size of a small apple. . . . So far as I can find out, the term came from the ancient English game of trapball or trapbat" (*Paul Green's Wordbook*).

"Come again, 'Fessor."

"Yeah. How long did Nello work here for you folks?" I asked.

"Oh, ten, fifteen years maybe — off and on," said the barber. "And all the time that old wine, that old booze business. We were mighty patient with Nello."

"I see," I said.

And going out, I let the door slam hard, I didn't mean to let it slam maybe. It just did.

And as I walked on I could hear my barber saying to his fellows, in my mind I could hear it. "What's the matter with 'Fessor? Seem like he went off kinder mad or sump'n — let the door slam like that."

"Can't tell about these writing fellows," said Joe the nearby barber. "Next!" my barber called.

The *road* to hell is paved with good intentions.

You won't travel no good *road* if you cross a crooked stile to get to it.

It is a long *road* that has no turning.

The shortest *road* to the penny, longest *road* to the dime.

*road cart*

A two-wheeled light gig.

*road hog*

A driver who hogs the road and has no care for others' rights.

*road itch*

Wanderlust.

*Roanoke*

Indian wampum or shells used for money, therefore the name "Roanoke Island."

*roasting ears (roas'n ears)*

The milky ears of corn just before they harden into ripeness, a special garden delicacy.

*Robbers*

A game. One or two children (robbers) hide along the path where the other children (travelers) have to pass. After the robber or robbers have hidden, the travelers come walking along saying —

"No robbers out today,

No robbers out today.

We are singing on our way

For there's no robbers out today."

Suddenly the robber or robbers rush out and try to catch the rest. Those who are caught become robbers in their turn and try to catch others.

*all around Robin Hood's barn*

This saying means to go a long ways around to get to the main point, like going around the elbow to get to your thumb.

A *robin's song* is not pretty to the worm.

*rock*

A solid, reliable person.

To cover with rocks or crushed stone. "We've got one more mile of road to rock, and then we're finished."

*St. Peter's Rock*

The Catholic church.

*rock bottom*

The basic essential, the lowest price or place, the limit.

*rocker*

Common sense, sanity. "He's off his rocker."

*Rocking* an empty cradle will bring a new baby to fill it.

It is bad luck to rock an empty *rocking* chair.

*rocking chair man*

An easy-going person, an indolent person.

*rocking chair woman*

A spoiled, lazy, good-for-nothing female.

*"Rock of Ages"*

A favorite old hymn that has comforted countless thousands in the Valley with its enduring symbol of strength.

> "Rock of Ages, cleft for me,
> Let me hide myself in Thee.
> Let the water and the blood
> From Thy wounded side which flowed
> Be of sin the double cure,
> Save from wrath and make me pure."

> "While I draw this fleeting breath,
> When my eyestrings break in death,
> When I rise to worlds unknown
> And behold thee on Thy throne,
> Rock of Ages, cleft for me,
> Let me hide myself in Thee."

*rocks*

Money, coins.

*rock-skimming*

A rock-throwing-on-water contest. We boys also called this rock-skeeting. We'd take flat stones and throw them one at a time with all our might along the surface of the creek or pond. Sometimes one would be able to make his rock go skimming with four or five bounces and be declared the winner.

*rocky*

Rough, hard going. "How is it with you, Joe?" "Rocky, son, rocky."

*Rocky Mountain canary*

A jackass.

*rod*

Gun, a pistol, also the penis.

Spare the *rod* and spoil the child.

Thy *rod* and thy staff they comfort me.

*roguish*

Wandering, obstreperous, undomesticated. "I've got a roguish cow, and no matter how high the lot fence is, she can sail over it, so I'll just have to put a yoke and tongue on her."

*roke*

Past tense of rake.

# Textual Notes

ASL   Avery, Laurence G., ed. *A Southern Life: Letters of Paul Green, 1916–1981.* Chapel Hill: University of North Carolina Press, 1994.
DOS   *Dog on the Sun.* Chapel Hill: University of North Carolina Press, 1949.
DW    *Drama and the Weather.* New York: Samuel French, Inc., 1958.
FPS   Gassner, John, ed. *Paul Green, Five Plays of the South.* New York: Hill and Wang, 1963.
LC    *The Lost Colony: A Symphonic Drama of Man's Faith and Work* (Four Hundredth Anniversary Edition). Privately printed, 1980.
PGW   Wynn, Rhoda H., ed. *Paul Green's Wordbook: An Alphabet of Reminiscence.* Chapel Hill: Paul Green Foundation with Appalachian Consortium Press, 1990. 2 vols.
SOS   *Salvation on a String and Other Tales of the South.* New York: Harper & Brothers, 1946.
UNA   "The University in a Nuclear Age." Chapel Hill: The University of North Carolina, [1964].
WF    *Wide Fields.* New York: Robert M. McBride, 1928.

## PLAYS

*In Abraham's Bosom*: text, FPS. First presented by the Provincetown Players at the Greenwich Village Theatre, New York City, 30 December 1926. Published in *The Field God and In Abraham's Bosom* (1927) and *Out of the South: The Life of a People in Dramatic Form* (1939). Revisions tend to soften dialect.

*Hymn to the Rising Sun*: text, FPS. First presented by the *Let Freedom Ring* Actors' Troupe (Federal Theatre Project) at the Civic Repertory Theatre, New York City, 12 January 1936. Published separately (1936) and in *Out of the South* (1939). Revisions alter character names and some other details. Also published as a story, "Roll On, John," in SOS.

*The Lost Colony*: text, LC. First presented by the Roanoke Island Historical Association at the Waterside Amphitheatre, Manteo, North Carolina, 4 July 1937. Published separately (1937, 1946, and 1954 by the University of North Carolina Press) and in *Out of the South* (1939). Extensively revised. "This edition of the drama is the author's definitive version and is to be the master guide for all productions. P. G." (LC, p. iii).

Music and lyrics used in the play are given in the backmatter of LC (pp. 104–41) and in the 1946 edition. See also *The Lost Colony Song-Book* (New York: Fischer, 1938).

## STORIES

"The Cornshucking": text, WF. Published in SOS and *Home to My Valley* (1970).
  Revised to first-person narrator. Revisions not incorporated in this volume.
"Salvation on a String": text, SOS.
"Saturday Night": text, SOS. Also published as a play in *Out of the South* (1939).
"Bernie and the Britches": text, DOS. Published in *Home to My Valley* (1970).
  Revisions, shortening the story, are not incorporated in this volume.
"The Ghost in the Tree": text, DOS.
"Fine Wagon": text, SOS. Published in *Land of Nod* (1976). Revisions, softening
  dialect, are not incorporated in this volume. Also published as a play in *Wings for
  to Fly (Three Plays of Negro Life)* (1959).

## LETTERS

Texts, ASL. Notes adapted for this volume.

## ESSAYS

"Drama and the Weather": text, DW. Published in *The Hawthorn Tree* (1943).
"The University in a Nuclear Age": text, UNA.

## *WORDBOOK* EXCERPT

Text: PGW, vol. 2.

# Paul Green's Works

## ONE-ACT PLAYS

*The Lord's Will and Other Carolina Plays*. New York: Holt, 1925.
*Lonesome Road: Six Plays for the Negro Theatre*. New York: McBride, 1926.
*In the Valley and Other Carolina Plays*. New York: Samuel French, 1928.
*Wings for to Fly: Three Plays of Negro Life*. New York: Samuel French, 1959.

## PLAYS

*The Field God and In Abraham's Bosom*. New York: McBride, 1927.
*The House of Connelly and Other Plays*. New York: Samuel French, 1931.
*Roll Sweet Chariot: A Symphonic Play of the Negro People*. New York: Samuel French, 1935.
*Shroud My Body Down*. Iowa City: Clio Press, 1935.
*Johnny Johnson: The Biography of a Common Man*. New York: Samuel French, 1937.
*The Lost Colony: An Outdoor Play in Two Acts*. Chapel Hill: University of North Carolina Press, 1937.
*Out of the South: The Life of a People in Dramatic Form*. New York: Harper and Brothers, 1939.
*The Enchanted Maze: The Story of a Modern Student in Dramatic Form*. New York: Samuel French, 1940.
*The Highland Call*. Chapel Hill: University of North Carolina Press, 1941.
*Native Son: The Biography of a Young American* (with Richard Wright). New York: Harper and Brothers, 1941.
*The Common Glory: A Symphonic Drama of American History*. Chapel Hill: University of North Carolina Press, 1948.
*Ibsen's Peer Gynt: American Version*. New York: Samuel French, 1951.
*Wilderness Road: A Parable for Modern Times*. New York: Samuel French, 1956.
*The Founders: A Symphonic Outdoor Drama*. New York: Samuel French, 1957.
*The Confederacy: A Symphonic Drama Based on the Life of General Robert E. Lee*. New York: Samuel French, 1959.
*The Stephen Foster Story: A Symphonic Drama Based on the Life and Music of the Composer*. New York: Samuel French, 1960.
John Gassner, ed. *Five Plays of the South*. New York: Hill and Wang, 1963.

*Cross and Sword: A Symphonic Drama of the Spanish Settlement of Florida.* New York: Samuel French, 1966.

*Texas: A Symphonic Outdoor Drama of American Life.* New York: Samuel French, 1967.

*The Honeycomb.* New York: Samuel French, 1972.

*Trumpet in the Land: A Symphonic Drama of Peace and Brotherhood.* New York: Samuel French, 1972.

*The Lone Star: A Symphonic Drama of the Texas Struggle for Independence.* New York: Samuel French, 1986.


## SHORT STORIES

*Wide Fields.* New York: McBride, 1928.

*Salvation on a String and Other Tales of the South.* New York: Harper and Brothers, 1946.

*Dog on the Sun.* Chapel Hill: University of North Carolina Press, 1949.

*Home to My Valley.* Chapel Hill: University of North Carolina Press, 1970.

*The Land of Nod and Other Stories.* Chapel Hill: University of North Carolina Press, 1976.


## NOVELS

*The Laughing Pioneer.* New York: McBride, 1932.

*This Body the Earth.* New York: Harper and Brothers, 1935.


## ESSAYS

*The Hawthorn Tree: Some Papers and Letters on Life and Theatre.* Chapel Hill: University of North Carolina Press, 1943.

*Forever Growing: Some Notes on a Credo for Teachers.* Chapel Hill: University of North Carolina Press, 1945.

*Dramatic Heritage.* New York: Samuel French, 1953.

*Drama and the Weather: Some Notes and Papers on Life and the Theatre.* New York: Samuel French, 1958.

*Plough and Furrow: Some Essays and Papers on Life and the Theatre.* New York: Samuel French, 1963.

*Trifles of Thought* (poems). Greenville, S.C.: Privately printed, 1918.

*Paul Green's Wordbook: An Alphabet of Reminiscence*. Chapel Hill: Paul Green
  Foundation with Appalachian Consortium Press, 1990.

Roper, John Herbert, ed. *Paul Green's War Songs: A Southern Poet's History of the Great
  War, 1917–1920*. Rocky Mount: North Carolina Wesleyan College Press, 1993.

Avery, Laurence G., ed. *A Southern Life: Letters of Paul Green, 1916–1981*. Chapel Hill:
  University of North Carolina Press, 1994.